PrimaryVoices K-6

PREMIER ISSUE • APRIL 1993

ASKING QUESTIONS/ MAKING MEANING

Inquiry-Based Instruction

NATIONAL COUNCIL OF TEACHERS OF ENGLISH

CONTENTS

Primary Voices K–6 is published four times a year in August, November, January, and April by the National Council of Teachers of English, 1111 W. Kenyon Road, Urbana, Illinois 61801-1096. Annual subscription is $15. Single copy, $5.00 (member price $3.75). NCTE membership is $40 annually for individuals, of which $26 is for a subscription to *Language Arts, English Journal,* or *College English,* and $47 (plus $3 shipping and handling fee) for institutions, of which $31 is for a subscription to *Language Arts, English Journal,* or *College English*; $5 of each is for *The Council Chronicle.* Add $3 per year for Canadian and all other international postage. Remittances should be made payable to NCTE by check, money order, or bank draft in United States currency.

Communications regarding orders, subscriptions, single copies, change of address, and permission to reprint should be addressed to *Primary Voices K–6,* NCTE, 1111 W. Kenyon Road, Urbana, Illinois 61801-1096. POSTMASTER: Send address changes to *Primary Voices K–6,* NCTE, 1111 W. Kenyon Road, Urbana, Illinois 61801-1096.

It is the policy of NCTE in its journals and other publications to provide a forum for the open discussion of ideas concerning the content and the teaching of English and language arts. Publicity accorded to any particular point of view does not imply endorsement by the Executive Committee, the Board of Directors, or the membership at large, except in announcements of policy, where such endorsement is clearly specified.

Copyright 1993 by the National Council of Teachers of English. Printed in the United States of America. ISSN 1068-073X

 Printed on recycled paper

A MESSAGE FROM THE EDITORS

A few months ago, or so it seems, the three of us were having conversations about what the volume you have in your hands might look like. What would be in it? Who would it be for? Who would put it together? How often? Why?

And now this volume is going to press and three other volumes (the volumes for year one) are in process. Amazing stuff, publishing.

The process we went through was exciting, challenging, invigorating, and exhausting. We are glad to be done; we would do it all again. We came into this project for different reasons, with different backgrounds, with different perspectives. We send this first volume to printing with a sense of having formed a community along the way. It feels good to have formed that community, to have made those connections, to have worked alongside each other on *Primary Voices K–6*. We share a sense of pride in this document; it evidences our work and effort and time and thought.

Once all four volumes for the first year are completed, our community will officially disband. Already we live in different places: Kathy is in Goshen, IN; Karen in Urbana, IL; Diane in Honolulu, HI. However, our sense of having been a community will continue and, by that time, we also will have become a part of an even larger community: the multiple communities who take responsibility for *Primary Voices K–6*. Beginning next year, each issue of *Primary Voices K–6* will be envisioned, developed, and edited by yet another community. Soon we will have communities of communities: each group having been responsible for one or more issues of *Primary Voices K–6*. We hope you will read the call for issue proposals and become one of those communities.

To put together this volume, we first thought about what really mattered to us at this time in our teaching careers and which of those topics might overlap with challenges we thought other teachers might also be facing. We picked "Inquiry" and asked Jerry Harste to write about the ideas behind inquiry-based instruction. Then we asked Joby Copenhaver, Mary Glover, and Chris Boyd to write about their classrooms so that we could "see" how the idea of inquiry-based instruction gets played out in actual classroom experiences. We asked for floor plans so we could better envision these classrooms and we asked for "Lingering Questions" because we really wanted to be able to hear them talk not only about what they had done (which was in their article) but about where they might be going next.

Across all the pieces, our intent was not to offer solutions, but, first, to consider possibilities and, second, to try and start conversations. For those reasons, the bibliography contains a number of sources that we felt widen the range of possibilities and inform the conversation. In our reflection section, we chose to focus on assessment. Assessment is often a tension that accompanies new ideas and we thought it best to figure out what we thought about it now rather than as a subsequent response to our own "Yes, buts . . ."

We hope this issue proves useful, that it does indeed offer possibilities, start, and inform conversations, and that your community will take on the challenge of editing an issue and so become heard in the national conversation. We know teachers are that kind of competent. We think it's a good idea to let others know that too.

With best wishes,
Kathy, Diane & Karen

Kathy Meyer Reimer

Diane Stephens

Karen Smith

INQUIRY
INSTRU

(handwritten note:) Language learning is = "a process of sense-making"

Jerome C. Harste

Indiana University

"The trouble began," to quote the children's book Winnie the Witch (Thomas, 1987), when traditional beliefs about language learning and about what young children know about reading and writing prior to going to school began to be seriously challenged by current educational research. This research demonstrated that children do not go through a developmental sequence in their attempt to learn language (Donaldson, 1978; Harste, Woodward & Burke, 1984). It also established that the young mind is capable of learning lots of things. Some five year olds, for example, know as much, if not more, about stories as do some sixth graders. The key to understanding language learning is experience—not age, stage, or Piaget.

This early-language research also challenged traditional curricular anchors. One of these anchors, the belief that there is an inherent order in the way language is learned and that this order can be used as a basis to sequence instruction, undergirds the skills-based approach to the teaching of reading and the language arts. Another anchor, the belief that there is an inherent order in mental development and that this order can be used to plan appropriate instruction, is the foundation of the developmental perspective on curriculum.

The new research provided a third alternative—that in response to this research, curriculum be anchored in meaning, in the underlying processes in language use and learning. From this perspective, language learning is seen as a process of sense making. Aspects of this process include making meaning, sharing meaning, extending meaning, evaluating meaning, savoring meaning, and generating new meaning. Because one cannot evaluate meaning prior to making meaning, the focus is on keeping things "whole," as in Whole Language. Instructional activities highlight key subprocesses but never in isolation of other subprocesses and never outside the very real context of language use.

I'm going to argue, however, that neither theory nor curriculum ever sleep, that despite the instructional progress that this new theory has brought, it hasn't gone far enough, and that the agenda ahead should be conversations about better places to anchor curriculum. These conversations need to be about the nature of knowledge and the role of language and other sign systems in knowing: they need to be about learning and the role in the learning process.

(handwritten note:) Key to Lang. Learning!

Curriculum as Inquiry

One source of curriculum has always been the disciplines—science, mathematics, social studies, literature, art, anthropology, music, etc. Unfortunately, we have reified the disciplines in curriculum largely because we have used them as a starting point. And, if this weren't bad enough, we then have taken reification a step further by calling for "integrated approaches to curriculum" without questioning why we used them as a starting point in the first place.

Inquiry is an alternative way to organize curriculum. When we use inquiry as an organizational device for developing curriculum, the disciplines are not ignored. In fact, the inquiry questions that children ask cut across all disciplines. Instead of the disciplines becoming the masters of curriculum, however, they become servants to curriculum.

When inquiry topics arise (whether from student or teacher interest, a compelling context, state mandates, or the adopted paper curriculum) the disciplines do what it is they are good at, namely, provide perspective.

In the past, teachers worried about setting objectives. The problem with this approach to planning was that it fixed what could be learned. If inquiry is truly inquiry, it must be open. No one can predetermine the outcomes. This is really the difference between "discovery learning" as a curricular model and inquiry.

Sources of Knowledge

There are three sources of knowledge that need to be addressed in planning an inquiry curriculum. These are the disciplines, the sign systems, and personal knowing—the relationship that learners in the classroom have to the topic under discussion.

The Disciplines. What the disciplines offer an inquiry curriculum is perspective and possibility. In planning an inquiry curriculum the teacher needs to use the disciplines as a lens on the topic under investigation. My advice is to rotate the topic through the disciplines. For example, what would an anthropologist want us to learn (what principles, generalizations, or conclusions would they want drawn) from a study of war? What would a psychologist want us to learn? What would a biologist want us to learn? What generalizations would a historian want us to walk away with? What would a philosopher want us to learn? A sociolinguist? And the list goes on. These don't become objectives so much as possible directions that students might pursue given their particular interests and inquiry questions.

Disciplines are not static bodies of knowledge so much as ways of thinking. Knowledge is socially constituted. What we know changes. Because new knowledge these days, more often than not, is created interdisciplinarily—just think about the advances in our own discipline of language offered by a socio-psycholinguistic perspective—an inquiry curriculum is a natural site for knowledge generation. The inquiry itself, not the disciplines, organizes what is open to be learned. Disciplined conversations and conversations among and between disciplines become resources for the kind of lives we wish to live and futures we wish to envision. Inquiry assumes an openness to new learning.

The Sign Systems. Sign systems (e.g., language, music, math, art) are the ways

If inquiry is truly inquiry, it must be open.

Knowledge as relationship? (handwritten note)

that we as h...
They allow u...
communicat... ...
record and crea... ... we think
it is or as w... ...k it might be.
Language, of course, is a key sign system, and the recent history of language education has furthered our understanding of the role that language plays in learning.

What we have not done so well is to look at other sign systems, like music, art, dance, math, and more. Like the disciplines, the sign systems offer perspective; movement across and between sign systems offers new insights and new knowledge. Semiotically this process is called transmediation (Eco, 1976). Transmediation is the taking of what you

> **From the standpoint of planning an inquiry curriculum we must, as teachers, find out in what ways the children relate to the topic under discussion.**

know in one system and recasting it onto another. Seeing something familiar in a new way is often a process of gaining new insight. It is the same process that undergirds metaphor and, even more generically, making connections. In the study of "war" mentioned earlier, the teacher might consider what aspects of war get picked up in song that do not get captured in books, what contributions art makes to our understanding of war, what war looks like from a mathematician's perspective or a dancer's perspective, and so on.

Personal Knowing. What we know is very much a function of the company we keep (Wells, 1986). Knowledge only gives the illusion of residing in books,

people, and disciplines. In reality, knowledge is a relationship that resides between and among people in particular times and contexts. That is why creating a classroom of inquirers is so important. They not only feed off one another, but create and recreate each other.

Technology has proven that knowledge can be transmitted. But as any inquiring teacher knows, to say that knowledge is transmitted is not to say it is learned. It takes two to Tango and two to learn. Which conveniently brings me to a discussion of the third source of knowledge, personal knowing. _Scaffolding_ (handwritten note)

What learners currently know—regardless of how little or how much—is the only starting point from which they can learn. This understanding is what is missing in a skills curriculum. It assumes that kids know things they don't (and don't know things they do) and, since it provides no other access point than the one outlined on the worksheet, children fail to make the necessary connections to learn.

"But the kids I work with don't have language," one teacher said to me. "But the kids I work with don't have experience," another said. The problem here is not that the kids don't have language and experience, it is that the language and experience that the kids did have was not acceptable to these teachers as beginning points for instruction.

From the standpoint of planning an inquiry curriculum we must, as teachers, find out in what ways the children relate to the topic under discussion. In the Indianapolis Public Schools and Lilly Exchange Teacher Project (Harste & Burke, 1991) we simply put up big sheets of butcher paper and wrote the word "war" in the middle. We then asked kids to "jot down everything that they currently knew about war and what they wanted to learn." Tommy's grandfather had been killed in Viet Nam. Jimmy's dad was a Viet Nam vet who had lots of problems. This kind of information, coupled with what teachers already know, helps them decide which invitations to make to particular children in their particular classroom.

Jocelyn Mokulchua teaches gifted and talented children in Hawaii. For some reason the gifted and talented "curriculum" calls for the study of rain forests in fourth grade. After planning, that is, rotating the topic through the disciplines, exploring what dimensions of the topic get captured in other sign systems like song, dance, etc., and after having studied how the children in her room related to the topic, Jocelyn decided to start with "chocolate," as this was a point of common knowledge and connection for the children she was teaching. To this end, she set up several invitations around food that drew the children into the topic and supported them in finding their own inquiry questions about the rain forest.

How we conceive curriculum affects the roles we play as well as the criteria we use to judge our own as well as our students' learning and inquiry. Curriculum as conversations between disciplines, sign systems, and personalized knowing provides the teacher with a frame for planning an inquiry curriculum. This frame alerts teachers to curricular possibilities of a specific topic and provides them a process vehicle for readying themselves for handling an emerging curriculum.

From this perspective, a curriculum is not a course to be run. Rather, curriculum is a meaning-making potential where knowledge is created, acted upon, and recreated at the point of experience. It provides opportunities for both teachers and students to experience themselves as learners, engaged together in inquiry in order to create, critique, and transcend their present realities.

Bibliography

Donaldson, M. (1978). *Children's minds*. New York: Norton.

Eco, U. (1976). *A theory of semiotics*. Bloomington, IN: Indiana University Press.

Harste, J.C., Woodward, V.A., & Burke, C.L. (1984). *Language stories & literacy lessons*. Portsmouth, NH: Heinemann.

Harste, J.C., & Burke, C.L. (Eds.). (1991). *Curriculum as inquiry: Help for the inner-city reading teacher* (1990–91 Report of the Lilly/IPS Teacher Exchange Project). Indianapolis, IN: Office of Professional Development, Indianapolis Public Schools.

Thomas, V. (1987). *Winnie the witch*. Illus. by Korky Paul. New York: Kane-Miller.

Wells, G. (1986). *The Meaning makers: Children learning language and using language to learn*. Portsmouth, NH: Heinemann.

INSTANCES OF INQUIRY

Joby Copenhaver

Assistant Professor of Education, SUNY, Geneseo

Rise Paynter and I came to know each other when the preservice teachers in my reading methods class were placed in her fifth-grade classroom for their field experience. At the time of our first encounter, we learned that we shared questions about collaborative research, and that Rise had concerns about how to support inquiry in her classroom.

As a result of our mutual questions and concerns, we decided to devote last fall to learning how and what questions are generated and pursued in a classroom of fifth graders where inquiry is supported, and most especially, how to engender questions from a group of 29 ten and eleven year olds that would personally involve and intrigue each of them. I hope to share with you some of the strategies we developed in the course of this effort and give some examples of the dialogue that ensued.

A Place for Wonderful Questions

Two people cannot have a dialogue with each other if only one of them is asking the questions. Yet the mandated curriculum is loaded with someone else's voice asking all of the questions and demanding all of the answers. In order to provide us some respite from that voice, we put our heads together with Carolyn Burke and invented the Explorers Club. Explorers Club met three times a week during the last hour of the day. This was to be a time for children to generate and pursue their own questions without

regard to any curricular constraints. They could work alone or in groups. Rise and I helped them as much as we could, but they had the major responsibility for finding resources and data.

The kids had a week to come up with questions. They preserved them in their Wonderful Questions Journals, which we made by folding and stapling eight half-sheets of 8 1/2" x 11" paper so that everyone would have a booklet with "Question:" and "Why is this important to me?" reproduced on each page (Figure 1). To help the kids generate questions that might sustain their inquiry for several weeks, we used a variation of Carolyn Burke's "Save the Last Word for Me" strategy. Every night for a week, kids dreamt up and jotted down their questions— along with their personally important reason for asking them—into their Wonderful Questions Journals. The next day, each student chose one question to read to the group. That student would then stop and listen while the rest of us speculated as to why we thought it was powerful. The author was given the last word when he or she revealed why the question was personally important. As Franny said, "This helped me because

Wonderful Questions
Question:
Why is this important to me?

Figure 1

I was able to spot a good question that could keep me going for at least a week."

It wasn't necessary for the questions to be brilliantly articulate at first; it can take a long time to formulate a question when you don't have the answer. As I look back on it now, it's surprising that the students' initial questions for Explorers Club were so clear. Here are some examples:

Josh asked, "How did outer space come? I've heard one scientist say there was a big blast, and another has said that everything was once gas. I'd like to get as many theories as I can and talk to some scientists. Then decide for myself."

Kristen wanted to know, "Why don't we have tails? I'm interested because most mammals have tails. I know we're mammals and we have a tail bone, but it doesn't stick out. It only goes about three quarters of the way down our backs."

Jennifer wondered, "Who was the first person with AIDS? I want to know where it started and how he got it. My mom tells me when I'm a teenager a lot of things can happen, and you can catch AIDS. I don't want to. I think it was some kind of a plant that started it and somebody caught it."

Carolyn Burke has said, "Learning is social inquiry. We must be intent on investigating personally powerful questions in collaboration with colleagues who share a topic of interest with us." As the kids heard each other's wonderful questions, they got further ideas about how they might gain from other perspectives of their own inquiry.

Jennifer's question about AIDS attracted Sandi, who said, "I think Ryan White was the first person who got AIDS, and I'd like to know what is the most common age to get it. I don't want to get sick and I don't want my friends to either." So the two girls worked together. They got information from the AIDS clinic; they interviewed a nurse; they took notes from a TV special on AIDS; they went to the school and public libraries.

Kristen, Franny, and Heather sat together and talked about each other's research even though their individual questions were unrelated. They would collaborate by selecting and transforming each other's data for their own use. For instance, when Heather, whose initiating question was related to dog diseases, saw Kristen's diagrams of mammal skeletons with and without tails, she decided to share her insight that dogs and humans are more similar than different by displaying a photocopy of a dog and a human skeleton side by side. Kristen, on the other hand, decided she would publish her findings in a book called *If People Had Tails*. She asked Franny and Heather to respond to her ideas and help her with the illustrations. Franny did most of her research at home with her parents, but she still needed partners to demonstrate an ancient numbers game she found in the course of her question on the origin of numbers ("Were numbers invented or discovered?"). She asked Heather and Franny to help her teach the game to the whole class.

Eli had a question about how planets were formed, and Steve wanted to

As the kids heard each other's wonderful questions, they got further ideas about how they might gain from other perspectives of their own inquiry.

know more about the force that kept planets on course. They teamed up with Josh on his questions about the universe.

Gathering Data in the Library

In August, before school began, Rise and I helped ourselves to the empty textbook crates by the "Up for Grabs!" sign in the teachers' room. We scrubbed off the publishers' labels so that the sturdy blue and yellow plastic containers would be just right for holding text sets for Explorers Club. We knew that when inquiring people get together with two or more texts related to their topic or question, the possibilities for exploring expand. So on the Tuesday in September when the class went to the library with their Explorers' Club questions, we were pleased to see that we had enough crates for every topic. The kids who had similar questions, like Josh, Eli, and Steve, had so many books that they needed two crates. Kristen and Franny each had their own text set because their questions weren't particularly related to anyone else's.

That first day in the library the kids spent their time browsing and assembling books, tapes, and computer printouts into the crates they'd labeled with their topic name. Since the library rule was that there could be no more than two books per child, and unlimited books for the teacher, Rise signed out all of the books in her name. The text sets were kept on the counter by the classroom door so that they'd be accessible when they were needed. As time went on, people brought books, photographs, newspaper clippings, magazine articles, and other artifacts from home or the public library and put them into the crates for the researchers to use. It wasn't unusual for people to bring in information for topics other than their own. Elisabeth, whose own question was about spiders, brought in her Isaac Asimov's *Library of the Universe* book for the boys studying space. Eli, in turn, loaned Elisabeth a *Natural Science* magazine that featured spiders. He shared his dad's copies of *Beyond Einstein* and Carl Sagan's *Planets* with his colleagues in the space group. During uninterrupted reading and writing time, it was also common to see kids sitting on the floor around their text set and sharing their books with each other. When someone is genuinely interested in a topic, others want to know what it is that intrigues.

Rise and I were struck by the diversity, the complexity, and the honesty of the questions. Kids asked questions we had no ready answers for, and while we teachers may have been occasionally overwhelmed by the complexity of some questions, the students themselves were always willing to collaborate in their exploration of those complex questions.

Public Celebration

Once the students understood it was okay to invent their own research, and that a written report was not required, they came up with some novel strategies for sharing their work with the rest of the

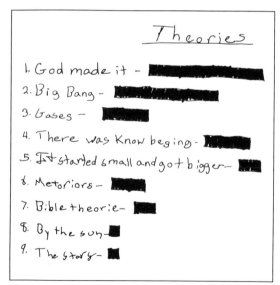

Figure 2

class. The space group put all their work together on a bulletin board covered with black butcher paper. Josh asked his class members and his parents, as well as a physicist and an astronomer, how each thought the universe began. He displayed his bar graph of the results next to Steve's chalk drawing of the solar system (Figure 2). The boys included photocopies of articles they thought were significant and diagrams of their conjectures of the origins of the earth. Eli added a crayon drawing of how the universe might have looked when it was nothing but gases. Josh later wrote in his journal, "I wish I could have a half a year during school to gather information and then have a big wall and a day or two to show it all to my class."

Other class members used a variety of approaches. Sandi and Jennifer did a skit of two teenage girls talking about AIDS. Kristen read her book after she shared some facts about animal tails (Figure 3). Matt gave his information on a video. Garrett shared what he knew about taxes with overheads and then involved the class in a tax information game.

People would have much worse fights.

Figure 3

Evaluating with Three Plusses and a Wish

Each member of the audience responded to the presentations with plusses and a wish (Figure 4).

Here are some responses to Garrett's extensive work on taxes. Garrett was interested in taxes because, as he explained, his parents were always talking about having to pay so much:

Three Plusses and a Wish
Name of Researcher
_____
Your Name
_____
Topic
_____
+
+
+
WISH

Figure 4

Jessica's big plus to Garrett was, "I like the way you chose a complicated topic instead of an easy one. I don't think taxes are easy to explain." But still, she added, "I wish you'd explained more of the stuff that's hard to understand." Franny gave Garrett a plus for "involving the audience in a tax information contest." She also commented, "You showed lots of pictures that helped me understand taxes." Her wish: ". . . that he had more time to share what he had learned because it was so interesting."

Marco gave Garrett plusses because, he said, "I learned a lot. Like, I didn't know Alaska pays the most taxes in the world." Marco wished that he himself knew more about taxes. Eli gave Garrett a plus for admitting that he didn't know answers to questions people asked. He wished there had been more details about the feudal system.

Garrett used the same form for a self-evaluation. He gave himself three plusses:

1. It was a hard topic to find things out, but I managed to find out a lot of information on this topic.

2. I think I answered their questions in a good way.

3. I think it was a good idea making a chart that you can understand.

The common knowledge that was being generated in the classroom community as people explored their questions was made formal through presentations of the research in progress. In responding to others and hearing others' responses, the presenters shifted stances and took a more critical look at their own formal presentations. We noticed that these efforts at evaluating themselves and others lead to their use of more effective strategies for sharing their research the next time around.

As they completed their first Explorers Club Inquiry, we all reflected on our experiences (Figure 5). Here are some of the surprises people had:

Kristen: "One thing that surprised me was that Mrs. Paynter and Mrs. Copenhaver even let us do this [pick our own questions]. Another thing that surprised me was learning how interested you could get in one question. The reason I say this is because usually when I have a question, I ask one person, but this time I got a lot of different opinions."

Elisabeth: "I was surprised that people had found facts about their topic that I did not know about. Like with cats, I didn't know that Manx cats have less bones in their ears. I learned a lot more too."

Josh: "I was the most surprised over how much information I got and how long I could have kept going. I want to keep on doing this research on my question in my free time and on my own. I'm going to buy a booklet to keep all of my research in so when I stop I can find my place a different time. I still want to ask an astronomer and a scientist how they think the universe began. I read a book written by a scientist who said the most logical theory is the BIG BANG theory. I like the BIG BANG theory and most of the people in my family do too."

> *Elisabeth said: "I was surprised that people had found facts about their topic that I did not know about."*

> **Explorers Club Reflections**
>
> Looking back at your involvement in Explorers Club
>
> + What surprised you?
>
> + How was this different from your social studies topic research?
>
> + What would you do differently next time?

Figure 5

When the students were asked to reflect upon their learning, they were thinking about not only what they had learned, but how they learned it. They were true explorers; the journey they took was as interesting as where they'd been and where they were going.

First Quarter Evaluation

The imminent arrival of the first report card marking and parent conference week motivated us to come up with two interrelated strategies for including parents' and kids' voices in the conversation: Learner's Evaluation and Parents' Evaluation.

Learner's Evaluation

Rise and I valued the kids as collaborators for two reasons: 1. We needed their responses to our ideas and invitations as we worked them through to formal presentation; 2. If we were intent on supporting inquiry in the classroom, we could not do it without the kids' collaboration. We created this Learner's Evaluation (Figure 6) to assure that the kids' voices were heard in the parent conferences. The children were invited to attend.

For John, the best learning experiences so far this year were: Explorers Club, Science Focus Studies, and math in general. John gave the following explanations of what he liked and why:

Explorers Club: "... because I like finding out about things I want to find out about, not

> **Learner's Evaluation**
>
> 1. What were three of the best learning experiences you've had so far this school year?
>   Why were they powerful?
> 2. What was the least effective? Why?
> 3. How have we helped you learn
>   a. at school?
>   b. at home?
> 4. How can we help you more
>   a. at school?
>   b. at home?

Figure 6

things I *have* to find out about." Science: ". . . because we are able to choose who we want to work with." Math: "Because we are learning in neat ways." The least effective was Reflections: "... because," he said, "my hand hurts when I write."

Parents' Evaluations

On a table in the hall outside of her classroom, Rise placed a spiral bound class book containing all the children's self-evaluations for the parents and children to look through as they waited for their fifteen-minute school conference. She also invited them to use the Parents' Evaluation form we had designed (Figure 7) so that they could respond in plusses and wishes to their child's learning experience. Here are some typical evaluations from parents.

> **Parents' Evaluation**
>
> 1. Three plusses and a wish about my child's learning experience this school year.
>
>   +
>
>   +
>
>   +
>
>   WISH:
>
> 2. Any stories or insights about learning at home or at school.

Figure 7

Matthew's parents' evaluation:

PLUSSES

+ learning by incorporating topics of interest to Matthew.

+ Matthew likes to read for the first time.

WISH

That Matthew would be always blessed with this kind of positive reinforcement throughout his school year.

STORIES

Matthew wrote down some questions about baseball and called his grandmother to interview her about what she knew. She's quite an expert and was thrilled that he took notes on what she had to say.

Jennifer's mom's evaluation:

PLUSSES

+ She really loves doing all the "research."

+ She seems to really enjoy learning experiences this year, especially writing stories.

+ She's reading many more books on her own this year.

STORIES

We had a lot of fun with her family story about the time her brother fell in the lake with all his clothes on while we were watching fireworks at Jennifer's great aunt's house. Her great aunt got involved in remembering what happened.

Zac's mom's evaluation:

PLUSSES

+ My son has gained a lot of self-confidence this year. He was able to show that he knew a lot about something.

+ He has made many new friends this year (possibly due to Explorers Club).

+ He was interested in finding out about his subject in his free time.

+ He found that learning was fun!

WISH

I wish that these positive aspects of his learning experience would continue into the sixth grade and then middle school.

An Invitation to New Conversations

When Rise and I look back on the development and success of Explorers Club, we are both struck by the breadth and the quality of the questions that the children asked, as well as by the depth and quantity of knowledge created. The students pursued questions that we would have given up on. They collaborated and made connections we could never have imagined. They revamped games that go back to Pythagoras and invented new games to celebrate what they knew. In

In one month, we saw kids shift perspectives from that of an astrophysicist to one of a poet and then across to that of a veterinarian and on to one of an illustrator.

one month, we saw kids shift perspectives from that of an astrophysicist to one of a poet and then across to that of a veterinarian and on to one of an illustrator. And we saw them as explorers, sitting on the edge of their chairs in fascination as one of their collaborators talked about—of all things—taxes!

We encourage you to begin an Explorers Club by inviting your students to pursue their own personally important questions. Rise and I guarantee that you will hear conversations in your classroom far different from any you have heard before.

I am deeply indebted to Carolyn Burke for her many insights. She invented the Explores Club as well as, directly and indirectly, all of the strategies for supporting inquirers in my research.

Resources

Barnes, D. (1975). *From communication to curriculum*. London: Pelican.

Burke, C. (1992). *Personal communication*. Bloomington, IN: Indiana University Press.

Calkins, L.M., & Harwayne, S. (1991). *Living between the lines*. Portsmouth, NH: Heinemann.

Dyson, A. H. (1991). Why little girls like rainbows: Understanding literacy. *Research in the Teaching of English, 91*, 214–220.

Harste, J., Short, K. & Burke, C. (1988). *Creating classrooms for authors*. Portsmouth, NH: Heinemann.

Hartshorne, C., Weiss, P., & Burks, A. (Eds.). *Collected papers of Charles Sanders Peirce* (6 vols., 1931–58). Cambridge: Harvard University Press.

Houser, N. (1987). Toward a Peircean semiotic theory of learning. *The American Journal of Semiotics, 5* (2).

Siegel, M. (1989). *Critical thinking: A semiotic perspective*. Bloomington, IN: ERIC Clearinghouse on Reading and Communication Skills.

Tchudi, S. (1990). *Travels across the curriculum: Models for interdisciplinary learning*. Toronto: Scholastic TAB.

Watson, D.J., Burke, C.L., & Harste, J.C. (1989). *Whole language: Inquiring voices*. New York: Scholastic.

Wells, G. (1986). *The meaning makers: Children learning language and using language to learn*. Portsmouth, N.H.: Heinemann.

Classroom Floor Plan

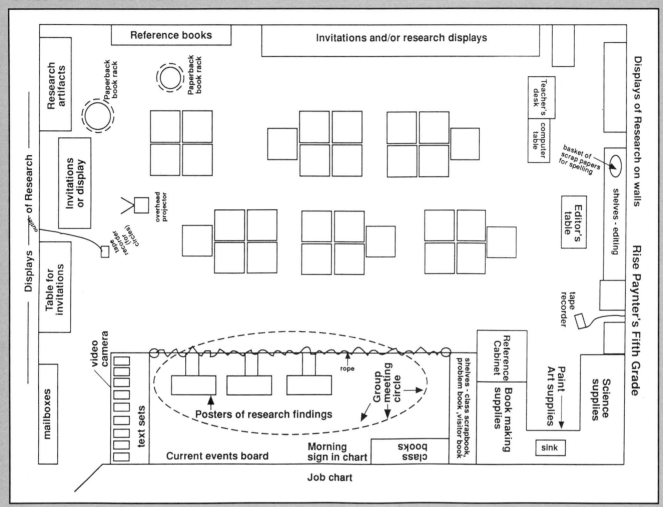

Lingering Questions

1. What happens when the child's question isn't interesting any more?

2. How do you help students present what they know in relevant and interesting ways?

3. Who works with whom and when and why?

4. How can the teacher be an inquirer? If we don't "tell" any more, how do we show what we know?

5. How do we help students learn to respond to their collaborators?

6. What if kids are so transfixed with their research they don't stop to write notes?

Daily Schedule

Monday	Tuesday	Wednesday	Thursday	Friday
8:50 - 9:05 Attendance, jobs, lunch, check schedule				
9:05 - 9:45 **Uninterrupted reading/writing/sharing**				
9:45 - 10:30 **Invitations and Strategy Instruction**				
•Literature Circles •Invitations in math social and physical science and humanities	•Writers Guild •Invitations to math social and physical science and humanities	•Literature Circles •Invitations in math social and physical science and humanities	•Math Engagements	•Literature Response Activities (i.e. Reader's Theater. Sketch to Stretch. letters to authors...)
10:30 - 11:05 **Demonstrations** Inquiry Strategies Math Math Language Strategies Language Strategies				
11:10-12:00 ART	11:10-11:35 P.E. **Current Events**	11:10-12:00 MUSIC	11:10-12:00 P.E.	11:10-11:45 ART 11:40-12:05 MUSIC
12:00 - 12:20 **What's On Your Mind?** (Large group sharing)				
12:20 - 1:00 **Lunch/Recess**				
1:00 - 1:20 **Language** 1:20 - 1:50 Stories	1:00 - 1:30 **Library** 1:30 - 1:50 Stories	1:00 - 2:00 **Math and Science Engagements**	1:00 - 1:20 Stumpers 1:20 - 1:50 Stories	1:00 - 2:00 **Math and Science Engagements**
1:50 - 2:00 LOCKERS			1:50 - 2:00 LOCKERS	
2:00 - 3:00 **Focused Studies:** Science, Social Stdies or **Explorer's Club**	2:00 - 3:00 **Focused Studies:** Science, Social Studies or **Explorer's Club**	2:00 - 2:30 Stories 2:30 - 2:45 REFLECTIONS	2:00 - 3:00 **Focused Studies:** Science, Social Studies or **Explorer's Club**	2:00 - 2:30 Stories 2:30 - 2:45 REFLECTIONS
3:00 - 3:15 REFLECTIONS		2:45 - 3:10 **Recess**	3:00 - 3:15 REFLECTIONS	2:45 - 3:10 **Recess**

A Bag of Hair: American First-Graders Experience Japan

When I think about our class study of Japan, the thing I remember most is all the hair. On the floor, under the tables, inserted in research folders amid crumpled papers, sticking out of clay sculptures, adhering wildly to the heads of child-versions of Japanese dolls, clinging tenaciously to exhausted glue bottles—hair was everywhere!

I recall the day Maureen proudly walked into the room with her Ziploc bag of the precious stuff. She announced that she had made her mom give herself a haircut so we could have some for our projects. Somewhere along the way, one of the children had discovered that Japanese doll-makers use real human hair for their dolls. Maureen took this bit of information to heart. The hair from her little Ziploc bag flew about freely, literally permeating our classroom environment. And so did Japanese culture.

The children chose the study of Japan from a list of 20 or 30 other possibilities they had generated. Some of their other choices included: volcanoes, space, electricity, China, Egypt, and the ocean. We got off to a slow start but gained momentum as we went along. In the beginning, I had the children work in groups of four to create a web of potential ideas for the study. I wanted to see what they already knew about Japanese culture. Following this exercise, we came together as a group and made a class web. This enabled us to focus on the specifics of our study (Figure 1).

In the meantime, I began reading *The Big Wave* (Buck, 1947). It was the first long book I had read with this group of first-graders. I was surprised by the depth of their response to this wonderful story of Kino and Jiya, two Japanese boys who develop a greater understanding of life and death when a tidal wave hits their village. The class eagerly chose to explore the story further through dance. This experience continued weekly throughout the course of our study, eventually culminating in a dance performance.

We read every Japanese folktale we could get our hands on, quickly drawing parallels among other previously studied folktales. Through the folktales we learned of Japanese animals, Japanese humor, and Japanese ways of living. We began to learn how the Japanese think and gained insight into their value system. Our reading of folktales and other books continued throughout the study. As we read together, we reflected on the similarities and differences between our own culture and that of the Japanese. We made an effort to look at contemporary Japanese life as well as the more exotic historical aspects.

From the class web generated earlier, we made a list of possible topics for small group research:

- Japanese food
- statues
- Japanese clothing
- festivals and celebrations
- dolls

- Japanese boats
- animals in Japan
- houses
- volcanoes
- cherry trees

Mary Kenner Glover

Director, second grade teacher, Awakening Seed School, Tempe, Arizona

Reprinted by permission of Mary Kenner Glover and the Association for Childhood Education International, 11501 Georgia Avenue, Suite 315, Wheaton, MD. Copyright © 1990 by the Association.

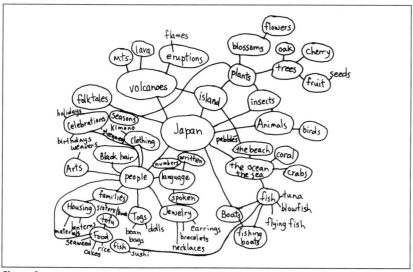

Figure 1

Figure 2 *(translation)*

Dear Toshiko,

We are in Mary(s) class. Our whole class is studying Japan. Me and Jennifer is doing a separate thing on volcanoes and we need some information on Mount Fuji. Will you please send us some information to us?

Love,

Tara and Jennifer K.

P.S. Mary told us that you lived by Mount Fuji. That is why we wrote.

Awakening Seed School
1130 W. 23rd Street
Tempe, Arizona 85282

Dear toshiko we are In Mary class. are howl Class Is stoping. Japan Me and Jennifer Is Doing a saprat Thing on volcanos And we need some anofrmashan on montan foDJgy woll you ples sanb us some anofrmashan to us

Love tara And
Jennifer K.

P.S. That Mary Tolo us You Lavd By mtan foDJgy That Is whay we rowT

Awakening Seed School

1130 W. 23rd street Tepe Az 85282

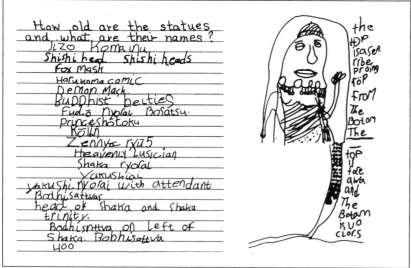

Figure 3

How old are the statues and what are their names?
JiZo Komainu
Shishi head Shishi heads
Fox mask
Harukoma comic
Demon Mack
Buddhist beities
Fudō Nyorai Bosatsu.
Prince shotoku
Koun
Zennyo ryus
Heavenly Lusician
Shaka ryorai
Yakushiai
Yakushi Nyorai with attendant
Bodhisattvas
head of shaka and shaka
trinity.
Bodhisnttva on Left of
Shaka. Bobhisattva
Hoo

the top isaser ribe proing top from The Botom The top Is tre awa and The Botom Is UO clors.

The children paired up into teams, choosing the topics of most interest to them and then listing questions about their topics. The questions were compiled into a research folder, one question to a page. We made a group chart that listed different ways to obtain information. We talked about how you can interview people, write letters, watch films, take field trips and visit museums, in addition to getting information from books. A few of the teams wrote letters to individuals. Jessica wrote to her aunt living in Japan to inquire about Japanese houses. Tara and Jennifer, suddenly interested in Mt. Fuji as a result of their study of volcanoes, wrote a letter to a former student teacher who grew up near Mt. Fuji (Figure 2). They were thrilled when pictures and letters arrived two weeks later!

As the children acquired their information, they recorded it on the appropriate page. Emily and Caitlin's work on Japanese statues demonstrates this process. In addition to written information, they included drawings in their accumulation of data (Figure 3). The gathering of information was actually the most challenging part of the process. Because most of the materials were written for older readers, much of the content had to be read to the children. We did most of this in class and asked parents to help out at home as well. The children also learned how to use an index and collected much of their information from the illustrations and photographs.

Once the information was gathered, I asked the children to put their notes away and just write what they remembered about their topic. After their initial shock at my request and a few arguments about how to begin, they managed to get their information on paper. In reference to her partner Tara, Jennifer typically expressed their difficulties, "First she was crying and then I got her brain

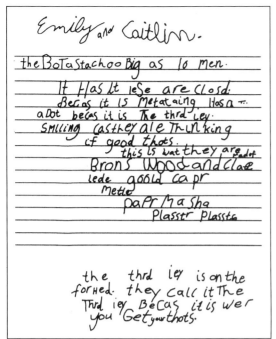

Figure 4 *(translation)*

The Buddha statue [is] as big as 10 men. It has its eyes closed because it is meditating. [It] has a dot because it is the third eye. [It is] smiling because they are thinking of good thoughts. This is what they are made of: bronze, wood, clay, lead, gold, copper, metal, paper mache, plaster, plastic. The third eye is on the forehead. They call it the third eye because it is where you get your thoughts.

moving!" Once the writing occurred, most of the children were surprised at how much they actually knew. Charlie and J.J. exclaimed, "We never could find out so much [about boats] but we were surprised we wrote so much!" Other teams, while not surprised at their writing but nevertheless pleased with themselves, said, "We were not surprised. We did a great job of writing. We started out arguing but we got it together!" Emily and Caitlin's draft was typical of the writing produced at this stage (Figure 4).

As the teams completed their drafts, I sat with them and we entered their text on the computer. In some cases I typed their writing verbatim, while in others the children verbally filled in information they realized was missing. For example, Ben and Brian wrote a rather lengthy piece about Japanese food. They knew what they were trying to say, but in the process of writing down their information they had confused some of the ideas.

They were able to verbally sort out the meaning of their piece as my fingers on the keyboard committed their clarified thoughts to print. Still others used this opportunity to revise the ordering of their information to make their text clearer. We worked as a team to bring order and focus to their reports. When everyone was satisfied with the content, the reports were printed and illustrated. Jessie and Mia's illustrated report exemplifies the children's final work (Figure 5).

As this process was taking place, other events occurred in the classroom. Two Japanese students visited us one Friday morning to demonstrate origami, Japanese calligraphy, and the Japanese tea ceremony. Our room slowly took on an oriental decor as colorful windsocks, paper cranes, and illustrations of *The Big Wave* appeared. Two other books, *Sadako and the Thousand Paper Cranes* (Coerr, 1977) and *Faithful Elephants* (Tsuchiya, 1988), led us to ponder the horrors of war as we learned more about the U.S. dropping the atomic bomb on Japan. The children were astounded when they discovered it was *their* country that had

They were able to verbally sort out the meaning of their piece as my fingers on the keyboard committed their clarified thoughts to print.

Figure 5

dropped the bomb. Through the discussions that followed, we all came to realize that regardless of cultural and philosophical differences, as human beings we all share the same feelings, concerns, and vulnerabilities.

Once the written reports were nearing completion, the projects began. Each team wrote up a project plan and taped it to the side of a cardboard box (Figure 6) in which the partners were to put all of the materials necessary to complete their projects. The projects varied. Included were clay sculptures, collages, dioramas, a miniature Japanese house, drawings, cardboard and cloth replicas of Japanese dolls, and a stuffed dragon. This is where Maureen's bag of hair made its debut. As the projects developed, becoming more elaborate with each passing day, the hair found its way to the heads of any available Japanese figure, no matter what shape or form. East had truly met West.

This magnificent bonding of two cultures needed a culminating event to bring it to closure, so we mutually decided to hold a Japanese festival to celebrate our learning. We planned "The First-Grade Festival: A Japanese Experience." The event included a dance performance of *The Big Wave*, mounds of unforgettable Japanese cuisine, and an array of intriguing project displays complete with guidebooks. Parents, a few special guests, and the entire student body were invited for this memorable occasion. The children captured the essence of *The Big Wave* as they whirled about with blue streamers, held the shape of the tidal wave while farmers and fishermen were leveled to the ground, and quietly dragged each other across the floor to depict the corpses being carried out to sea in the storm's aftermath. Just as the food prepared by Kino's mother brought Jiya back to life, the feast waiting elegantly in our room brought the crowd of guests alive. Trays of sushi, rice balls, tiny chick-

Parent guests eventually left, but the steady stream of children from throughout the school didn't cease until several hours later.

Figure 6

en wings, bean paste pancakes, almond pinecones and Japanese noodles were devoured by all. Wooden chopsticks challenged many a nimble-fingered person. In the end, fingers ruled as the primary utensil. Once the eating ritual was well established, the children began taking their guests around the room to view the displays. Their written reports had been compiled into guidebooks for others to read. The children proudly shared their knowledge of Japan with anyone who cared to listen.

Parent guests eventually left, but the steady stream of children from throughout the school didn't cease until several hours later. Finally, when the last rice ball was eaten and the few remaining questions were answered, our festival came to an end. Much later, after the children had gone, I discovered small bits of rice left here and there by chefs and connoisseurs alike. Further wielding of the broom and dustpan swept up the inevitable—a few more of those marvelous hairs. In the end, I was left to ponder these small bits of discarded protein and their significance to our study of Japan. I decided that they were the connecting link between our culture and one that was unfamiliar. Maureen's bag of hair made Japan come alive for her, just as the real human hair used by Japanese doll-makers gave life to their dolls. When Maureen brought the plastic bag of her mother's hair, it was her way of saying, "I understand." Once again I was reminded that children need the security of the familiar in order to grasp the unknown. Who could have guessed that such insight would be contained in a small plastic bag of human hair?

References

Buck, P.S. (1947). *The big wave*. New York: Curtis.

Coerr, E. (1977). *Sadako and the thousand paper cranes*. New York: Dell.

Tsuchiya, Y. (1988). *Faithful elephants: A true story of animals, people, and war*. Boston: Houghton Mifflin.

Resources

Friedman, I.R. (1984). *How my parents learned to eat*. Boston: Houghton Mifflin.

Gamberg, R. et al., with G. Edwards. (1988). *Learning and loving it: Theme studies in the classroom*. Portsmouth, NH: Heinemann.

Katz, L.G., & Chard, S.C. (1989). *Engaging children's minds: The project approach*. Norwood, NJ: Ablex.

Laurin, A. (1981). *Perfect crane*. New York: Harper & Row.

McDermott, G. (1978). *The stonecutter*. New York: Penguin.

Mosel, A. (1972). *The funny little woman*. New York: E.P. Dutton.

Sakade, F. (Ed.). (1958). *Little one inch and other Japanese children's favorite stories*. Rutland, VT: Charles E. Tuttle.

Yagawa, S. (1979). *The crane wife*. New York: Mulberry.

Yashima, T. (1955). *Crow boy*. New York: Penguin.

Yasudea, T. (1956). *Old tales of Japan*. Rutland, VT: Charles E. Tuttle.

Classroom Floor Plan

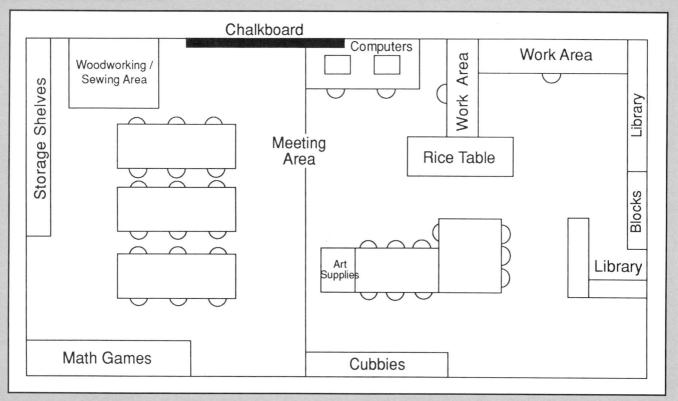

Daily Schedule

9:00   Opening Circle, Daily News, Singing, Poetry Sharing

9:30   Mini-lesson, Writing Workshop, Author Sharing

10:45 RECESS

11:00 Read Aloud (usually a chapter book)

11:30 Individual Reading, Small Group Literature Study

12:00 LUNCH/RECESS

1:00   Math/Computer

2:00   Content Study Work, Music, Japanese, Science

3:00   Dismissal

Friday's schedule is different. We have Buddy Reading with the 3-year-old class, then they go to P.E. and return to the classroom to do Journals. From about 11:00 through the afternoon (except 45 minutes for Creative Movement after lunch), they do self-selected projects, including: sewing, woodworking, blockbuilding, drawing, reading, writing, clay, computer, and art.*

*A great deal of art is included in the curriculum. It appears as children illustrate books they have written and is also a major part of the projects they do, either related to a content study (e.g. making a skeleton out of clay for our human body study) or as a self-selected project. Art is also chosen as a way to respond to a specific event, such as a trip to the art museum.

Lingering Questions

■ How can I better assist those children who have not yet learned to read at the level required for many of the books we use in our studies?

■ How can I guide and organize the research time so that children are more focused in their work and there is less fooling around?

■ How can I improve my record-keeping and evaluation methods for the children's content study work?

■ How can I incorporate more science into my curriculum?

■ What are the best ways to set up the environment so that the children can construct their own meaning with the content they encounter?

■ How can I improve my teaching methods to meet the needs of children at such varying levels of development?

■ What are some successful ways other teachers have helped children struggling with abstract concepts?

■ How can I find time to write and reflect about what is happening in my classroom every day, making changes based on those reflections?

CREATING CURRICULUM FROM CHILDREN'S LIVES

Chris Boyd

Kindergarten teacher, Roadrunner School, Washington School District, Phoenix, Arizona

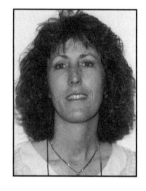

I once asked my kindergartners how they thought of questions to ask during our writing discussions. After a few puzzled looks the following comments came forth:

Michael: They tell us their writing.

John: And then—pop—they come in your brain.

Michael: Like they tell you and your idea goes pop.

John: Your brain comes popping.

Part of the reason they were initially confused by my question was that five year olds don't consciously try to "come up with" questions. Question-asking for these children is wanting to know—it's a part of daily living, listening, learning, and figuring out. Their questions come from the very source of their beings and their senses of wonderment. Their inquiry takes the form of restating or describing mental images of what they are trying to learn. I believe this comes from learners taking ownership of their learning within a community that demands listening and participation.

Establishing Expectations

On the first day of kindergarten, I begin establishing expectations with what I call "cocktail party conversation." The children sit down as they come in and make small talk with the other children. It sounds easy, unless you have worked with kindergartners entering school for the first time. It is similar to getting acquainted with adults in an elevator; at first it is very quiet. I ask the children what they talk about with each other, and no one knows. I then speculate, "I'll bet it's hard to decide what to say when you have so much in your brain." Then I share with the class what I talked about with my own student "cocktail party" partner (brushing my teeth!). Soon the ideas begin to flow.

At the beginning of each day, as I circulate among the small groups of children, I listen and wonder aloud about their comments. Sometimes I ask one of them to tell the class about their conversation. When Megan talked about her new shoes, I wondered aloud if they were the ones she was wearing. When she said no, I asked if she were going to bring them to school. She wasn't sure but we did all get to see her blisters. As the weeks went by, parents in the classroom wondered what happened to the quiet class I started with.

I truly believe my interest in the things children come to school thinking and talking about gives them power inside the classroom that extends to their lives beyond it. My questions help me understand them and their stories. Their answers make the students more aware of each other and more interested in their own stories. As stories are explored, listening becomes necessary, distractions become unwelcome, and storytellers command attention. As they become confident with sharing their lives, they look more deeply at them and begin to question each other. Questions grow from a need to understand, to clarify, to discover.

When children begin writing down their stories, the questions often change from requesting information concerning a specific story to asking how to get their ideas on paper and then how to read them again. For instance, Cellena asked for help with how to sound out words:

Cellena: When everybody's talking I can't do my letters.

Valerie: What do you mean?

Heidi: Do you mean you can't concentrate?

Cellena: (Nods her head, "Yes.")

Alicia: Why don't you think of the letters in your head?

Zachariah: Do the letters in your mind.

A demonstration followed (a very quiet demonstration). Another time, while Michael was working with the class on how to figure out letters from specific sounds, he discovered that he heard more sounds than there are letters in the alphabet. "I need more letters!" Michael had gained enough confidence to question even the tools he was using.

During this conversational time of day, my role becomes that of a recording secretary. My pad of paper makes it much easier for me to stay out of the center of conversation by keeping me busy and preventing eye contact with the students. If conversations drift, I read aloud the sections that indicate where the conversation had been heading, or mention directions or patterns that had become apparent in my notes. The children also do this on their own. As Kate cautioned during one extended conversation that lost its focus, "I think we're heading down the wrong river."

The students hold frequent debates about whether to allow more than one person to talk at one time—some students find it intolerably rude. I mention that it is hard for me to take notes during these "chorus" conversations. "One at a time" becomes a recurring phrase during discussions. Kim decided to sit by herself as she wrote, with a sign that said, "Get your face out of my place," to see if it helped her concentrate. Michael tried writing fast and slow to see which one worked better. The whole class decided to have a "silent time" so no one could goof around or ask other children to help them during the last few minutes of their personal writing time. Of course, working things out in the beginning is difficult and the children sometimes call on me to help.

In the following discussion, the children were helping Matthew learn how to write something. Matthew wanted answers, but the class was distracted and wasn't responding very well.

Matthew: People don't listen to me. They just keep talkin' louder and louder.

Michael: Sometimes people don't listen to anyone.

Shaun: Matthew, you need to let people know your problems and your ideas. This problem is harder to solve.

Jason: What do you mean?

Tommy: The more problems you have, the harder they are to solve.

Matthew: Everybody should be quiet and let the teacher talk for a darn change.

I ask the children what they talk about with each other, and no one knows.

Research and Resources

Frequently, more information is needed, so research is in order. It is interesting to see how inquiry pushes the students' desire to know. As the content of investigations deepens, the students' need to know grows, and their confidence to question and test expands. Questions become tools for both the asker and the asked. For example, during writers' workshop, the group told Eric that he should watch his baby sister to see if she did anything more than look at the ceiling, sleep, eat, and burp.

This type of discussion and study holds true for other areas as well. While observing bubbles form and pop during water experiments, questions began to surface and from those questions, theories arose about how bubbles are made, how they disappear, and where they go when they "come out." When bubbles became part of a discussion of erosion—a more challenging concept—I began to ask the questions:

Ben: The roots go through the land like when you put your hand down through the water in the bathtub and you come up through the bubbles on top. Like the roots come up on the land and they kind of pop the land like the bubbles pop.

Teacher: How does the land pop?

Ben: It pops like a volcano bursts open. There's big pieces of land kind of like the rocks by the roots.

Teacher: But bubbles have air and they disappear. How does that work?

Ben: The bubbles have air inside and it's pushing the bubble and that's how it pops. Like they even pop without you doing anything.

Teacher: How is that like the land?

Ben: The land has dirt and it's pushing up like the air in the bubble and it bursts the bubble.

The pursuit of learning is focused on finding out, not just wondering.

By this time of the year, the children have learned to listen to each other well, so a child can try out new understandings with the class and expect to be questioned, supported, or corrected. Although the children are involved in many discussions, verbalizing and arguing are not sufficient unto themselves. Data sources are crucial. To move beyond our current knowledge, science observations and discussions require second looks, relocating pictures and information in books and magazines, and studying primary sources and student notes again and again. How else do you settle an argument over whether water sticks together when it pours or not? Knowing, then, becomes powerful as the discussion is substantiated by information.

During these discussions, the primary data source, whether it be a handwritten story, a piece of literature, turtles, bubbles, the William Tell Overture, or Picasso's *Three Musicians*, assumes power and centers the discussion. The pursuit of learning is focused on finding out, not just wondering. In the beginning, the children's questions are often repeated from one discussion to the next as they try to participate but do not quite know how—it is merely the expectation of answers that brings forth questions. The quest for answers then begins to take many forms. An object may be re-examined, a story reread, a fight re-enacted, an overture replayed, a painting re-viewed as knowledge is being researched. During a study of skeletal structures, students may feel each other's bones and look closely at dinner's leftover chicken bones. Observing a small group literature study discussion may entail watching children flip back and forth in their books, backing up their own opinions, and evaluating the observations of others. Personal writing interactions may involve several readings of each story to verify information, needs, and changes. An up-to-date map and globe are central to new social studies information. Should the children note a similarity between Bach and Mozart, there are fugues to be listened to and books to be read.

Children often theorize and risk their own hypotheses. For them, an hypothesis is a question, a flexible statement wanting an answer. These theories challenge the class and the student to look in new ways at what they are learning. New theories are discussed and defended, and disregarded easily when proven wrong or replaced by others. Inquiry becomes a pattern of theory and testing. The children naturally make guesses about how the world works. Every question they ask seems to have an answer ready. Sometimes we formalize this process by recording our hypotheses on paper. In the beginning of an observation, we sometimes use a form that says, "What will happen?" at the top and "What happened?" on the bottom. The children talk and guess together, but they usually work individually as they write down their final hypothesis. These papers then help them look at our subject of study in a new way.

Their initial hypothesis doesn't seem to limit their observation or learning. On the contrary, it seems to expand it and makes them more aware of their study by focusing their thoughts on the subject. For instance, one day a parent brought a four-foot lizard to class. Before we went outside to observe the reptile, I asked the children to write down what they thought a four-foot lizard would do or look like. My class came outside, took one look at the giant and threw their papers up against the wall so they could write. It looked like a police line up. Twenty-five kindergartners lined up against the wall with a four-foot lizard pacing back and forth behind them. They continued to observe and write. Each time someone noticed something new, he

or she would scream it out and everyone would start writing. (I'm sure the lizard had theories of her own on that.) After the more obvious facts were noted, the children began to invent tests to observe. One little girl volunteered to let the lizard walk on her. She sat down on the grass and as the lizard walked across her legs she shouted what it felt like for the note-takers to record.

Of course, the note-taking did not happen just because of our classroom's hand-out "hypothesis form." It happened because of our classroom stance that important things are written down and saved. Note-taking is part of our thinking process. Several years ago I suddenly realized how wonderful kindergartners were at taking notes. They naturally write just the important words. "L F S," means, "the lizard's feet feel scratchy when she walks on your legs." It takes sixth graders a long time to learn to take quick notes using key words.

Content of Study

Our classroom subjects emerge from the lives and curiosity of children. The importance of a study is determined by the questions it generates. Is there a need to know? Are the questions genuine? As a result, our studies aren't monumental, but they are consequential. They aren't necessarily exciting, but they are absorbing. For example, a study of France was deemed important during the Olympics. How else were we to understand what the announcers were saying during the ice dancing competition if we didn't learn French? And I was so glad that we had studied Vivaldi (during a previous study which included Italy and the Ninja Turtles, of course) when the children came leaping into the room with excitement because they heard one of Vivaldi's works being

One little girl volunteered to let the lizard walk on her. She sat down on the grass and as the lizard walked across her legs she shouted what it felt like for the note-takers to record.

played during one of the ice dances. The children then wanted to know who wrote the other songs. Puddles on the playground inspire wonderful investigations of bubbles, ripples, and surface tension. Writing leads us into uncovering other questions and connections concerning the process of writing. The woman with an

Inquiry in my classroom is a way of life.

attitude in "The Magic Fish" made us ponder many things about life as well as how an author reveals character.

Several years ago, Carole Edelsky and I were working on a research project in my classroom. One of the questions we asked the children was, "What do we study in this class?" The children answered with things like bones, water, space, animals, temperature, etc. We then asked them why we didn't study the ABCs. They just stared. I repeated our question. They answered, rather patronizingly, "Letters are something you use to study, not something you study about."

The Learner

As inquiry expands, knowledge and insight are gained. As knowledge and insight are gained, inquiry expands. Early in the year, many of the questions about a story a child may be writing are generated by a desire to add information. Later in the year, students spend their time helping each other clarify, reorder, reword, rethink, and polish their work rather than just adding to it. Much the same thing happens in small group litera-

ture studies. The questions change as the students' knowledge and priorities change. A typical question in September may be, "What page did you like?" In contrast, April's questions will range from character comparisons and ponderings, to connections to other literature. Confidence and competence envelop the students as they gain respect for themselves as researchers and knowers. Intense study is possible because students become confident in their ability to discover, to think, and to ask again. They learn that finding answers and solving problems give them a sense of power and control over their lives.

And they also discover that the community is powerful because none of us is as powerful or as smart as the group. It is powerful because risks can be taken, thought can be challenged, and problems can be observed and recognized together. It is powerful because we recognize that some of our questions are the same, that some of us have trouble with those questions, and that each of us knows things the others do not. One student may know a lot about baseball, but another knows a lot about rocks.

Inquiry in my classroom is a way of life. The students take control of their learning by taking responsibility, questioning, theorizing, prioritizing, respecting, and connecting what they learn. This does not happen in a specific period during the day or through exciting units of study. It grows as learners develop confidence, competence, and community.

Classroom Floor Plan

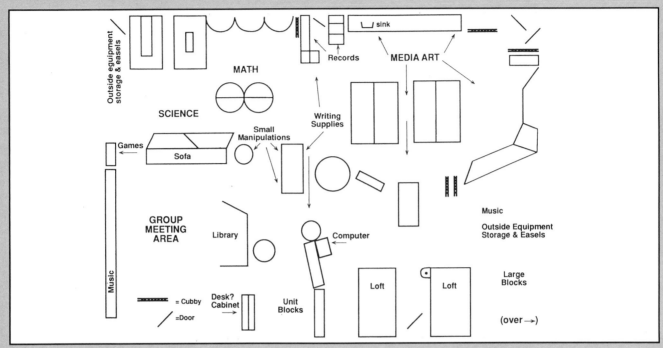

Daily Schedule

(All times are approximate and never adhered to en masse.)

8:00 - 8:50 a.m.   Personal Writing and Discussion Time. (School really starts at 8:15 a.m., but my students come at 8:00 a.m. to have more time to write.)

Between writing and discussion the children take attendance. They count in different languages and discuss social and geographical information about each country at this time. (It takes about 5 minutes.)

8:50-9:00 a.m.   Recess (stretching out and outside play).

9:00- 9:10 a.m.   Cool down and Music Appreciation.

9:10-9:30 a.m.   Content Discussion (research, information given, experimentation, charting knowledge, etc.).

9:30-10:15 a.m.   Choice activities and jobs. (Jobs - content related requirements. Activities - however the children choose to spend their time; reading, writing, building, lego-ing, housekeeping, puzzling, creating, investigating, etc.)

10:15-10:45a.m. Dismissal (on a good day).

It's hard to nail down times with subjects because each area of the day has literature, writing, science, music, art, etc., all jumbled up in it.

(The afternoon schedule is a repeat variation on the morning time theme.)

Lingering Questions

The children seem to theorize* more than question. Is that actually what is happening?

Does theorizing or question asking occur more often when...

the subject is well-known?

the subject is unfamiliar?

*By theorizing, I mean trying to explain a phenomenon rather than asking about it.

Kathy Meyer Reimer

Diane Stephens

Karen Smith

As editors of this issue of *Primary Voices K–6*, one of the most exciting tasks we faced was selecting the exemplary classrooms featured in this issue. We wanted good classrooms. We shared an implicit sense of what "good" meant and had many good classrooms from which to choose. We eventually chose the three you have just read about and were delighted when Joby, Mary, and Chris agreed to write about those classrooms. Shortly after we had their articles in hand, we began to talk about the classrooms, and, in so doing, found ourselves making explicit our shared (and formerly implicit) ideas about what makes a "good" inquiry-based classroom.

To date, we have identified four critical and necessary components of what we consider good inquiry-based classrooms: values, focus, opportunities, and assessment. These elements, which we have sketched in Figure 1, are evident in all of the classrooms talked about in this volume (as well as in many classrooms across the country). To illustrate these components, we talk about just one classroom, Mary Glover's, simply because it seemed easier to consistently refer to one setting, rather than jumping across several.

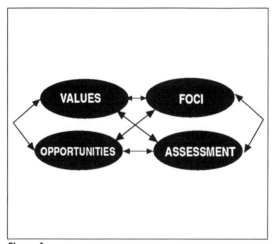

Figure 1

Values. Values are those beliefs and ideas that teachers and students render important and that guide and inform the classroom broadly, across all events and time frames.

In reading about Mary Glover's classroom, we made hypotheses about the values that might be influencing her as teacher. First, it seems to us that Mary views learning as a socially constructed phenomenon that requires interactions with other people, in both large and small groups. She understands that classrooms are about conversation and that everyone in the classroom, including the teacher, should have a voice in those conversations. She consistently welcomes students' ideas about the content to be studied, the topics to be explored, and the meaning that is created. While no one voice in Mary's classroom is privileged, Mary does use her experiences and knowledge about Japanese culture to inform the conversation and to help move students toward conceptual understandings. For example, Mary notes that by reading books about Japanese culture, she and the children "began to learn how the Japanese think and gained insight into their value system."

Second, Mary understands that she must provide time, space, and multiple resources in order for these learning endeavors to be generative and productive: time to explore and shape ideas; space to create, explore, and express ideas; and multiple resources to enrich experiences and provide diverse perspectives.

Third, Mary views teaching as a process of action and reflection and makes curricular decisions based on individual and group needs and experiences as well as on the conceptual understandings that she has identified as important to a topic of inquiry. Her flexible working arrangements, working in small groups for one project and with the total group for another, demonstrate that she bases her decisions on what she knows about the nature of the task to be accomplished, the context of the situation, and the students' needs.

Fourth, Mary exhibits patience in the learning process. She takes time to help children become skillful at processes and procedures. For Mary, reading and writing are ways for the children to gather, explore, create, and express meaning; these ways take time and are not skills which should be quickly learned and then practiced in isolation.

Fifth, Mary understands that there are multiple ways of knowing and expressing ourselves and the world (e.g., story, dance, art, and drama) and she sees these as essential to the creation of multiple perspectives and deeper understandings. In addition, she wants children to use their new knowledge, and she provides many opportunities for the children to make public the knowledge they have created. These opportunities make it possible for the children to learn from and with each other.

Focus. We believe that, in any academic endeavor, teachers have both explicit and implicit ideas about where the endeavor is headed and about what the potential for learning will be along the way. We refer to these ideas as *foci*. We believe that these focii are flexible, ever-changing, and generative. At the same time, we believe that they guide learning experiences and center interactions around a particular topic. Some focii are long-term, informing curriculum over extended periods of time; others seem to be more closely tied to specific events.

Based on Mary's description, we hypothesized that during the unit on Japan, Mary focused on helping the children think beyond the actual experiences and come to some conceptual under-

standings about Japanese culture. In her article, we "saw" her helping students draw parallels among folktales in order to learn about Japanese animals, Japanese humor, and Japanese ways of living. From this, she helped them move to understandings about how Japanese think and to insights about the Japanese value system.

When Mary read to the class and discussed stories about WW II, in particular the dropping of the atomic bomb on Hiroshima, she and the children together pondered the horrors of war. When the children came to the realization that it was their country that was responsible for dropping the atomic bomb, Mary helped them to realize that regardless of cultural and philosophical differences, all human beings share the same feelings, concerns, and vulnerabilities. Throughout the unit, Mary deliberately focused on the conceptual understandings of culture so that the children could move from the particulars of the Japanese culture (animals, humor, calligraphy, etc.) to the more global understanding that there are similarities and differences across cultures and that ways of thinking and value systems are not universals, but functions of culture.

Opportunity. One of the illusions that we, as educators, have long held is that if we teach "it," "it" will be learned, or if we create the context, "it" will happen. Recently, we have tried to face the fact behind the illusion: that all we can do is provide children with rich opportunities to learn—opportunities made rich by the conceptual framework of the teacher as well as by the teacher's skill in helping children successfully negotiate and express meaning.

Mary provided several such opportunities. Some of these opportunities focused on content:

When the children came to the realization that it was their country that was responsible for dropping the atomic bomb, Mary helped them to realize that…all human beings share the same feelings, concerns, and vulnerabilities.

Just as important, we would argue that it is the collaborative nature of good inquiry-based classrooms, the continual, reflexive dialogue, which ensures that voices of teachers and children are, as indeed they should be, the primary voices in the curricular conversation.

She helped children identify, focus, and organize information by creating webs of what they already knew and what they wanted to know, and making lists of questions they wanted to explore.

She provided an opportunity to experience a piece of Japanese life by helping them connect between their lives and the story worlds of *The Big Wave* and various Japanese folktales.

She made possible new insights and the creation of new meanings by providing opportunities for the children to talk with or write to people who had directly experienced Japanese culture. She and the children also visited museums, watched films, and read books.

Mary and the children made connections between cultures and within cultures by discussing stories, folktales, and the information they were generating from their inquiries.

Other opportunities focused on helping children organize materials and learn particular skills:

Mary helped the children gather and organize information by providing notebooks and folders for keeping track of new information and by providing crates for artifacts.

Mary helped the students to fine-tune their research skills: she helped them learn how to generate and keep track of questions, conduct interviews, write letters and invitations, use an index, and take notes.

She assisted them as they planned and carried out a Japanese festival, and she helped them to prepare and present a project that exhibited insights and understandings about Japanese culture.

Assessment. Assessment is an integral part of good teaching. Every day, we think about what is happening now, what is going to be happening next, what that child said, how best to respond. These assessments are informed by our values and our focii as well as by the opportunities we provide children. In turn, as we tried to show in Figure 1, each is informed by the other. Neither is first, nor last; all co-occur and are built into each and every instructional moment.

In order to help maintain a generative relationship among these components, many teachers have developed systematic ways to focus and organize their observations and reflections. Mary, for example, might have developed an observation form (see Figure 2). Similarly, she and the students might have gathered documents and artifacts to chronicle their work. These items might have included:

- lists of books that each child read and those that were read to each child

- the web each child created as a part of a small group and a copy of the web that the large group created

- each child's work folder, showing the questions the child asked and the information that was gathered along the way

- the guidebooks that the child produced with a partner

- pictures of projects as well as pictures taken during the Japanese festival

- anecdotal notes

The observation form and the documentation combined with students' self-assessments would detail the breadth and depth of children's learning and in turn inform the teacher's continuing assessments.

In the opening article, Jerry Harste argues that neither theory nor curriculum ever sleep. We agree. And we would argue that the transactive nature of inquiry-based classrooms, the generative relationship among values, focii, opportunity, and assessment, contributes to our ever-evolving understanding of the teaching/learning process. Just as important, we would argue that it is the collaborative nature of good inquiry-based classrooms, the continual, reflexive dialogue, which ensures that voices of teachers and children are, as indeed they should be, the primary voices in the curricular conversation.

Observation Form for Inquiry

CONCEPTS: COMMENTS:

CONCEPTS	COMMENTS
Draws parallels between Japanese and other cultures	
Draws parallels between Japanese culture, past and present	
Understands that values systems are functions of a culture	

PROCESSES: COMMENTS:

PROCESSES	COMMENTS
Formulates interesting questions	
Generates appropriate methods for answering questions (e.g. writing letters, visiting museums, reading books)	
Spends time reading, writing, constructing, observing, reflecting etc.	
Talks to others to make sense of data	
Explains, shows, helps others to make sense of their data	
Asks good questions	
Plans, organizes and carries through on tasks	

ATTITUDE: COMMENTS:

ATTITUDE	COMMENTS
Is willing to be challenged	
Is productive and involved during work periods	
Expresses enjoyment as a result of hard work and achievement	
Contributes to group work	
Displays sensitivity and respect for others	

PRODUCT: COMMENTS:

PRODUCT	COMMENTS
Is well developed and organized	
Is visually pleasing	
Shows detail	
Effectively communicates what the student has learned	

PRESENTATION: COMMENTS:

PRESENTATION	COMMENTS
Articulates and/or demonstrates ideas clearly	
Is well informed	
Handles questions with authority and control	
Gives good examples	

Figure 2

Bibliography

Altwerger, B., & Flores, B. (1991). The theme cycle: An overview. In K. Goodman, L. Bird, & Y. Goodman (Eds.), *The whole language catalog* (p. 295). New York: Macmillan-McGraw Hill.

Atwell, N. (1989). *Coming to know: Writing to learn in the intermediate grades.* Portsmouth, NH: Heinemann.

Bird, L. B. (1991). Supporting real research. In K. Goodman, L. Bird, & Y. Goodman (Eds.), *The whole language catalog* (pp. 296–297). New York: Macmillan-McGraw Hill.

Duckworth, E. (1987). *The having of wonderful ideas and other essays on teaching learning.* New York: Teachers College Press.

Edelsky, C., Altwerger, B., & Flores, B. (1990). *Whole language: What's the difference?* Portsmouth, NH: Heinemann.

Fine, E. S. (1989). Collaborative writing: Key to unlocking the silences of children. *Language Arts, 66,* 501–508.

Gamberg, R., et al. with G. Edwards. (1988). *Learning and loving it: Theme studies in the classroom.* Portsmouth, NH: Heinemann.

Glover, M. (1992). *Charlie's ticket to literacy.* Richmond Hill, Ont.: Scholastic Canada.

Goodman, Y. (1991). Education as inquiry [Videotape]. In J. C. Harste & E. Jurewicz (Eds.), *Visions of literacy* [Videotape series]. Portsmouth, NH: Heinemann.

Goswami, D., & Stillman, P. R. (Eds.). (1987). *Reclaiming the classroom: Teacher research as an agency for change.* Upper Montclair, NJ: Boynton Cook.

Kamii, C., & Joseph, L. (1989). *Young children continue to reinvent arithmetic, 2nd grade: Implications of Piaget's theory.* New York: Teachers College Press.

Katz, L. G., & Chard, S. C. (1989). *Engaging children's minds: The project approach.* Norwood, NJ: Ablex.

McGuffee, M. (1991). Hands-on science. In K. Goodman, L. Bird, & Y. Goodman (Eds.), *The whole language catalog* (pp. 317–318). New York: Macmillan-McGraw Hill.

Meek, A. (1991). On thinking about teaching: A conversation with Eleanor Duckworth. *Educational Leadership, 48,* 30–34.

Short, K. G., & Burke, C. L. (1992). *Creating curriculum.* Portsmouth, NH: Heinemann.

Watson, D. J., Burke, C. L., & Harste, J. C. (1989). *Whole language: Inquiring voices.* New York: Scholastic.

Wells, G., & Chang-Wells, G. L. (1992). Constructing knowledge together: Classrooms as centers of inquiry and literacy. Portsmouth, NH: Heinemann.

Wigginton, E. (1986). *Sometimes a shining moment: The foxfire experience.* Garden City, NY: Anchor Press/Doubleday.

PrimaryVoices K-6

Volume 1 Number 1 • AUGUST 1993

Making Meaning through Writing

Writing to Learn

NATIONAL COUNCIL OF TEACHERS OF ENGLISH

CONTENTS

Primary Voices K–6 is published four times a year in January, April, August, and November by the National Council of Teachers of English, 1111 W. Kenyon Road, Urbana, Illinois 61801-1096. Annual subscription is $15. Single copy, $5.00 (member price $3.75). Add $3 per year for Canadian and all other international postage. Remittances should be made payable to NCTE by check, money order, or bank draft in United States currency.

Communications regarding orders, subscriptions, single copies, change of address, and permission to reprint should be addressed to *Primary Voices K–6*, NCTE, 1111 W. Kenyon Road, Urbana, Illinois 61801-1096. POSTMASTER: Send address changes to *Primary Voices K–6*, NCTE, 1111 W. Kenyon Road, Urbana, Illinois 61801-1096. Application to mail at second-class postage rates is pending at Urbana, Illinois.

It is the policy of NCTE in its journals and other publications to provide a forum for the open discussion of ideas concerning the content and the teaching of English and language arts. Publicity accorded to any particular point of view does not imply endorsement by the Executive Committee, the Board of Directors, or the membership at large, except in announcements of policy, where such endorsement is clearly specified.

 Printed on recycled paper

A MESSAGE FROM THE EDITORS

For the past year, the three of us have worked in cooperation with many of you developing *Primary Voices K–6*. We started by creating a publication for educators whose main interest is kindergarten through grade three. We soon found that many of you wanted us to expand this range to include grades four, five, and six—so we did. We also received requests for a journal that would be made up primarily of teachers' voices—thus, the format and the title. We agreed when you insisted that we keep the publication short and keep its creation community-based. The proposal submission guidelines for *Primary Voices K–6* state that a single issue cannot exceed 44 pages. And after this issue, each will be written and edited by a literacy community and will focus on an important literacy concept this community is exploring.

One of our goals for *Primary Voices K–6* is to generate conversations around the country about important educational concepts, issues, and concerns. In order to support this goal, each article will include a section entitled *Lingering Questions*. These questions are meant to reveal the unanswered concerns of the issue's contributors. We think these lingering questions make a case for teaching as inquiry, and they open up topics for discussion among educators who may be asking the same questions.

Each of this issue's authors offers new insights and generates interesting questions about writing to learn. Donald Graves's article helps us think about what constitutes topic choice. He argues that it is no longer enough to simply ask children to select topics that are quick decisions of the moment. Instead, teachers must show students how to connect honest struggles and issues with the chance to choose their topics. The teachers who do this best, Graves contends, are those who have taken time to examine their own literacy, and who demonstrate to children how they use writing to confront issues in their own lives.

In the dual role of parent volunteer and teacher researcher, Marsha Winship describes in detail a first-grade classroom's first attempt to write informational books. Marsha captures the complexity of the process while providing a structure that maps out a process that many teachers will find helpful.

Susan Stires provides insights into how students in her classroom use writing to learn all day long. Unlike many classrooms where writing is relegated to a block of time called language arts, Susan's students use writing throughout the day for a variety of reasons: They write in logs in order to construct and reflect on critical concepts; they write to entertain others; and, they write to bring order to their worlds. In each case, they write for an authentic purpose.

Tom Tracy reminds us that moving away from a teacher-centered and textbook-driven language arts program is a complex process that has both ups and downs. Tom's stream-of-consciousness piece gives us a glimpse into some of the day-to-day struggles one teacher encounters as he tries to create a safe place for his students to struggle with and discover the power of using written language in purposeful and meaningful ways.

Colleen Buddy shows us what is meant by reflection in action. She is challenged by a student's imagination. Instead of denying her student his imagination as a means to order and make sense of his world, she finds ways of supporting it. Colleen Buddy has taken an important first step in helping us understand the importance of making room for children's passions and imaginations in our classrooms, and we applaud her contribution.

We hope this issue offers new insight and generates questions for you. We also hope that your literacy community will take on the challenge of editing an issue of *Primary Voices K–6* and so become heard in the national conversation.

Sincerely,
Kathy, Diane, & Karen

Kathy Meyer Reimer

Diane Stephens

Karen Smith

CHILDREN CAN WRITE AUTHENTICALLY IF WE HELP THEM

Donald H. Graves

Professor Emeritus, University of New Hampshire

"My son was killed when he missed a turn in the fog and hit a tree head-on," the man seated next to me explained on our Delta flight to Atlanta, Georgia.

"That's terrible," I replied. The sizeable man sat immobile and open-faced, reading a Marine journal about the Tet Offensive in Vietnam. "So your son was killed in Georgia?"

"Nope, happened in Boothbay Harbor, Maine. Can't seem to cry now, and I couldn't cry after 'Nam. I'll pick up a van and my father in Valdosta, then drive back to Maine."

"Boothbay Harbor, Maine? Did your son ever have a teacher named Nancie Atwell?"

"Did he ever! He wasn't doing anything until he got her. She wrote this book you know, *In the Middle*, and my son has three things in it."

We continued to discuss his son, B. J. Sherman, and B. J.'s writing of "A New Beginning," (Atwell, 1987, p. 235) in which he tells about leaving his mother to live with his father. Later I called Nancie to tell her of my meeting with Mr. Sherman. After discussing B. J.'s tragic death, we, too turned to "A New Beginning." "Yes," Nancie said, "In that piece of writing, I learned that B. J. was struggling with moving from his mother's to his father's home. He couldn't write it as personal narrative; I recommended that he write it as fiction. Somehow I was able to help him realize that writing was a way to make sense of things. Once he tied into that he just kept writing and writing; he even wrote in other classes, and sometimes that got him into trouble."

In the past, I argued that you can't ask children to write on topics they know nothing about, that children learn to write when they are well informed on a subject and have a passion for the truth of things. Further, I insisted that children need to have a sense of ownership about their writing, to feel in control of their subjects, not to write in response to topics I give them. I said all this to counter decades of teaching that required children to write about the teacher's pet topics which had little to do with engaging the child. However, I've come to understand that choice is meaningless unless we show our students how to connect choice with honest struggles and issues. Unless we as teachers demonstrate how we make this connection, children will remain prisoners of Saturday morning television with its high-speed chases and toy industry promotions. Currently, I see too many children mired in inane personal narrative accounts, characterless fiction, and poetry with little investment by the author.

Fostering the Authentic Voice

Mr. Sherman and I had a substantive conversation about his son's death and Vietnam. In the midst of our conversation, I realized that another piece of writing might fit into our discussion. I opened my briefcase, pulled out *Build a*

Literate Classroom (1991), turned to page 139, and passed him a piece by Sean, a struggling student in Linda Rief's classroom:

My Dad in the Vietnam War*

This story is really hard for me to write. It's about my Dad who was in the Vietnam War. All the terrible things that happened. How he lost really good friends. Or about one day when my dad was in a Bar. And some kid rolled alive grenade in. It lucky didnot esplode. Or how he would be walking down the street and a Religious monk who had drenched himself with gasoline, would light a match and burn himself to death just because he was protesting. This year at my Dads birthday, my sister and her friend bought my Dad a book on the Vietnam war. My Dad didn't want to talk about it because he had to many bad feelings. Someday when my Dad can talk about it. I hope he talks to me.

Mr. Sherman wept and I wept with him. Sean's text may stumble a bit, but his voice is authentic. Writing that tells the truth connects people; Mr. Sherman and I were bound together by the writing of his son and a young man far away in Durham, New Hampshire.

When teachers have authentic voices, their students have them, too. Both Linda Rief and Nancie Atwell have strong literate teaching voices, and their students write authentically. Pat McLure, first-grade teacher at Mastway School in Lee, New Hampshire, has a quiet but authentic voice. Don't mistake loud, apparently confident voices as necessarily authentic. Pat's economy of language follows careful observation of her classroom (Newkirk and McLure, 1992). She seizes on the truth of situations and, with a single, quiet, honest question, affects an entire room of children. When her class goes through the process of hatching chicks each spring, she quietly wonders aloud, "Hmmm, I wonder why this chick weighs so much more than that one over there?" Children know she asks questions only because she doesn't know the answers to them.

Playwright Neil Simon (1992) struggles with the anatomy of writing comedy in *Broadway Bound* through two characters:

Stan keeps asking Eugene for the essential ingredients in comedy, and when Eugene can't answer, Stan says, "Conflict!" When he asks for another key ingredient, and Eugene can only come up with, "More conflict?" Stan says, "The key word is 'wants.' In every comedy, even drama, somebody has to want something and want it bad. When somebody tries to stop him—that's conflict."

Indeed the key word is "wants." B. J. *wanted* to understand the meaning of moving from his mother's home to his father's. Sean *wanted* to understand why his father couldn't speak about Vietnam. Their teachers helped them to realize that writing holds the key to understanding. B. J. and Sean were writing to satisfy their own curiosities; they kept on writing until the text satisfied their *want* in dealing with the conflict around them.

Another student, Jeff, much younger than the ones above, dealt with conflict of a different sort. He *wanted* to understand writer's block. Jeff wrote:

> When teachers have authentic voices, their students have them, too.

* Reprinted by permission of Donald H. Graves: *Build a Literate Classroom* (Heinemann, a division of Reed Publishing (USA) Inc., Portsmouth, NH, 1991).

Four Ways of Curing Writer's Block*

I am talking about what authors fear most—writer's block. But don't worry, I have invented cures. But first, let's get to know the disease and the symptoms. If you can't think and you can't write, it's a pure case of writer's block. You feel fed up and wishing you were in Disney World. You can get writer's block with fiction or non-fiction. Let's hear the cures.

Cure #1 - Forehead pressure. This cure is quite simple. All you need is a pencil. You put the eraser part on your forehead and the point on your desk. Then push, the pressure will make you think.

Cure #2 - Brain storm. If you have an X girl friend or boy friend, you know what I'm talking about. How you hate their guts. Believe me, I know what I'm talking about; I've got one myself. Think of ways of killing them. That should give you ideas.

Cure #3 - Alf tips. If you have seen the show Alf, you know this cure. Clothes pins in the hair. Nice pressure to make you think.

Cure #4 - Food poisoning. This cure makes you write or you upchuck. This is what you would use: tuna fish and jelly sandwich. Mayonnaise on pancakes or pizza with chocolate sauce and even brownies with tartar sauce. *Caution:* Be near a bucket—side effects do happen!!!

If these cures do not work, you are hopeless as a writer. Your disease put you to the end of your writing career. Maybe you should go to Disney World after all.

Here, Jeff has taken the common conflict of struggling with writing and composed a spoof about the problem.

Writing to Understand

Children today boil with just as many *wants* as their older brothers and sisters. Every day, they face divorce, insult, separation, moving away, loneliness, and the craving for "things." How well I recall a fiction workshop I did in an elementary classroom in West Des Moines, Iowa, a few years ago. We were to compose fiction together as a class. As a starter, I asked students to choose three situations; then we'd vote and choose one we'd like to use. They suggested: "lost on an island all alone," "kidnapped" (both rather typical selections), and "Mother and Father in an argument; there's going to be a divorce." The vote was unanimous: the divorce. The class orally composed one of the most sophisticated and authentic pieces about human want and conflict I have ever experienced.

Human angst isn't the only criterion for examining *want* in young children. Roger was a seven-year-old perfectionist. He had a vision for his piece and wouldn't settle for anything less. He composed a piece about constructing a puppet booth in six stages. His teacher said to me, "Don, would you please speak with Roger about publishing his piece? It is really good, but he seems to be reluctant to publish it. I sense he wants to. See what the trouble is." I approached Roger and was surprised by his answer: "Well, this may be good, but you see I haven't used the directions yet to actually build the booth. When I actually build it, I'll probably have to make some changes. It's not time yet to publish it."

As teachers, our job is to help children tap into their wants and also help them realize that writing can be a solution. Until we begin to help our children connect with themselves, the choices they make will be based on quick decisions of the moment. The best thing we can do, it seems to me, is to begin with our own literacy. Children need to hang around a teacher who is asking bigger questions of herself than she is asking of them. They take their cue for learning from the teacher's own literate life. It will be no surprise to teachers when we say children observe them constantly. When a teacher wears a new pair of earrings, parks a new used car in the school lot, or walks in with a new briefcase, within minutes the class is buzzing about the changes in her life.

* Reprinted by permission of the Jeff Rohr family.

"Today I'm writing about our old family dog. She is sick right now and I'm wondering what we'll do if she gets any sicker," the teacher announces to her second-grade class. "First, I'll show in my writing how she walks because that's what I see that reminds me how old and sick she is. I'm writing this because I need to think about her. Writing to show how she walks is hard for me." The children hear their teacher's struggle to tell the truth in her writing. They also learn something about how a writer approaches the subject. In this case, the teacher is writing about the dog for herself; this is the real issue she needs to understand. If the piece is written only for the benefit of the children, it will be hard to tell the truth, to find out what she really wants to learn.

A teacher who shows what she is trying to learn through writing isn't afraid to ask children what they are trying to learn through their own writing. "What do you *want* to say? Why do you think it is important to say that? What will you be working on to make this a better piece of writing?" Truth seekers have a way of helping others to get at the truth; they question children just as they question themselves.

The teacher's questions invite risk taking. As a writer herself, she knows when a child takes a risk. She knows that a *want* piece will contain emotion, and that emotion usually contains some degree of risk. Children sense that the teacher who writes provides a much wider safety net to support the risk taking that goes with exploration. "My teacher has been there," a child senses.

Knowing Your Own Literacy

If you haven't found that writing is a means to learn anew about the exciting world we live in, then finding the time is especially difficult. I find that writing ten minutes a day, showing the details of the world I live in, makes a big difference in the quality of both my writing and living. (See *Discover Your Own Literacy* 1989). Writing and asking questions of what you see can set a whole new tone of literacy for you and your children.

Our children live in a world so invasive they can scarcely see and feel beyond the stimulus of the moment. Stimuli caress them, then slap them in the face. There is a world of people who calculate how to make children want what they sell. Most of their selling is deceptive, like that of Stromboli in *Pinocchio*. We and the children are told what we want in the plastic, commercial

> A teacher who shows what she is trying to learn through writing isn't afraid to ask children what they are trying to learn through their own writing.

world that advertisers call real, and then are subtly cultivated until we are convinced that we have made our own decisions. We lose touch with the land and ourselves. We hunger for touch and weep in the boredom of our wants.

Virtually all children in our classrooms *want* to understand the complicated world in which they live. Some of the pieces they write resemble noisy arcades in which they mindlessly punch out words to fill a page. Indeed, they are exercising the choices we've given them. Like B. J. and Sean, they need to meet teachers who ask tough questions of themselves and then show their children how to reach beyond Saturday morning cartoons.

Bibliography

Atwell, N. (1987). *In the middle: Writing, reading, and learning with adolescents.* Upper Montclair, NJ: Boynton/Cook.

Graves, D.H. (1990). *Discover your own literacy.* Portsmouth, NH: Heinemann.

Graves, D.H. (1991). *Build a literate classroom.* Portsmouth, NH: Heinemann.

Newkirk, T., with McLure, P. (1992). *Listening in: Children talk about books (and other things).* Portsmouth, NH: Heinemann.

Simon, N. (1992). The art of the theatre X. *Paris Review, 125,* 167–213.

WRITING INFORMATIONAL BOOKS IN A FIRST-GRADE CLASSROOM

The children in Mrs. Koerber's first grade classroom are on a new adventure, writing their first informational book. Mrs. Koerber intends to build on and extend her students' knowledge by asking them to write on a topic of interest. My role, as a teacher researcher and parent volunteer in the classroom, is to capture and record the process.

Setting the Stage

Today the children are going to the library to find, gather, and read more information on a topic they have chosen. Before going to the library, Mrs. Koerber has the children listen to two second-grade students who have come to share an informational book they have written. The first graders listen carefully as one second grader reads about a lizard. When they finish sharing, the first graders ask questions:

Liz: Where did you get your information on the lizard?

Rebecca: Well, a man named Tom came to our classroom. He brought several animals with him. I listened to what he said about the lizard. Then I wrote what I remembered in my journal. I also drew a picture of the lizard.

Liz: You said the lizard has three eyes. Where is the third eye?

Rebecca: On the top of its head.

Two important things are happening in this first- and second-grade exchange: The second graders are receiving support and praise from the first graders, and the first graders are learning how to collect information and write on a topic.

By the time the first graders begin their first research venture, they are well prepared. They have seen models of student researchers and they have had time in their own classroom to rehearse for such a major undertaking. They come to the project with skills and knowledge acquired through seven months of writing workshop where they were given opportunities to listen and respond to each other's work.

During these workshops, Mrs. Koerber's demonstrations help the children learn how to respond. When a child shares a story with the group, Mrs. Koerber doesn't sit in the back of the circle and ask "teacher questions"; rather, she responds honestly to the content of the writing: "The beginning of your story brought me right into your piece. I can't wait to hear more!" "When you read the part about setting up the tent, I could see it happening." "The expression in your voice tells me you were very happy."

When listening, she sits next to the child, makes eye contact and gives a gentle pat on the shoulder. Mrs. Koerber's questions and compliments teach her students how to support each other as writers and readers. Learners know they need support for their efforts. If they do not get enough encouragement, they may be afraid to try something new. If they don't venture into the unknown, they won't grow, change, learn.

Marsha Winship

Literacy Consultant K–5, Brunswick, Maine

Choosing a Topic/Getting Started

Mrs. Koerber has made a decision to let the students pursue their own interests. She begins by asking the children to make a list of three topics they know about, are interested in, and want to know more about. Lauren, one of the students, lists doctors, cats, and dogs. She later chooses "cats" as her topic. She explains how she came to her decision.

Well, I had doctors, cats, and dogs on my list. I looked at some books that Ms. Menendez (the librarian) had out and then I decided to do either doctors or cats. I like dogs but I don't have one so it might be hard to write about, but I do have a cat. I want to be a doctor someday but my birthday is coming up and I really think I'm going to get a kitten. And since I already have a grown up cat, I think I know a lot about cats and would know more to write about. Plus I need to get ready for that kitten. So I could read about how to take care of kittens.

After the students decided on a topic, Mrs. Koerber asks them to pick one other classmate to work with who has chosen the same topic of interest. Lauren explains that she and Nick decided to work together because they had both listed cats, and they were already friends.

Lauren is able to share her decision-making process for choosing a topic and a classmate to work with, thus establishing herself as a reader and a writer. Lauren has learned to do this by herself because Mrs. Koerber has provided time to talk about "topic search" with the group. And talking is something writers do. When she talks with the students who volunteer to share their topics, she sets into motion "patterns of response" students can anticipate all year long (Atwell, 1987, p. 82). All of the children probably won't pick up on this the first time, but through continued modeling of response all of the children will begin to understand and make sense of their options and her expectations.

Learning + Journals = Learnals

Sam gave us the equation, L. + J. = Learnals, in a spontaneous burst of creativity. "We were laughing and then Mrs. Koerber said we should vote on the name. So we did and everyone voted for Learnals. We were cheering!" Each group of students working together uses their Learnal to record initial information that might later be written down in their informational book. The Learnal is a simple way to keep track of new information.

But how do the partners decide what information will be recorded in their Learnal? How do they use them?

Chris: We wanted to write things we wanted to learn about or teach to people.

Lauren: Yes, we got books we needed and read for facts about things.

Chris: I picked stuff that would be interesting to kids.

And who actually writes the information in the Learnal?

Lauren: Well, the first time I was so busy reading to Nick that he did all the writing. Next time he can read to me and I will write.

Chris: Seth and I did it another way. We both read. Then we took turns writing our stuff in the Learnal. We read what we wrote to each other.

I pressed partners Sam and Elizabeth to explain how they decide exactly what to put in the Learnal.

Sam: You look at books, read the pages, talk about what you read with your partner. Then you decide what's important out of the stuff you remember.

Elizabeth: Yes, Sam's dad is a doctor.

Sam: Well, actually he's a physician. He takes care of big people.

Elizabeth: Okay, Sam. But he asked his dad what it's like to be a doctor.

The writing these children are doing leads them to read many informational books. They read to find out something. Whether they want to know about snakes or different types of cats, they read to learn. Writing and sharing with an audience further clarifies their understanding of the chosen topic.

Gathering Information

The students begin researching their topic by using resources from the library, the classroom, and from their homes. Mrs. Koerber explains what she did to help the children begin:

I asked the children to brainstorm questions on their topic that they wanted to either answer or find out about. We spent a few days on this process because these questions would guide their research. I encouraged them to come up with at least five questions. The children wrote the questions in the front of their Learnal so they could easily refer to them. The questions helped them when they chose books on their topic and took notes in their Learnals.

Ms. Menendez, the school librarian, helps students locate books on their chosen topic in the library. Earlier in the week, she had read several informational books and showed the children where these books were located. Mrs. Koerber gathered books for the children to use from the classroom library and the town library, organizing and displaying them in the room. Even the parents were involved. Many children went home asking their parents to help them find information. One mother shared this:

I've never seen my daughter so excited about school! She came home and asked me to look up medicine in the encyclopedia. I read a lot of information to her. Then we had to find a copy machine so she could take the "really good stuff" with her to school. The next day my daughter took her important information to school with her in a manila folder.

First Day of Research

The children are sitting together with their partner(s), their Learnals, and their pencils. Also in the room are the principal, a speech therapist, a Chapter I teacher, two parent volunteers, and a "Grandma" volunteer. These adults had responded to Mrs. Koerber's call for support. Each adult works specifically with two groups of children. Mrs. Koerber instructs her students to spend their time in the library reading to each other and writing key words. She reminds them to use their own words, and to share important information with their partner as they write in their Learnal.

Eager young researchers walk down the hall and up the stairs to the library. The partners are ready to begin recording in their Learnals. The small groups sit at round tables with piles of books to look at and read. Adults are reading to students, students are reading to each other, students are reading to the adults, and some are reading independently.

Mrs. Coates, a school volunteer, reads from *The Remarkable Chameleon* by Lilo Hess. Every few paragraphs, the girls stop her so they can record the information they want in their Learnal. Mrs. Coates prompts them to question, to look at pictures, and to pick out interesting facts. And the hum of learning goes on and on.

These children are learning where to find information: in books, magazines, newspapers, interviews, other students' books, and reference materials. Their questions are helping them to focus on the information and look at specific details they want. They come to a writing conference for the same reason they turn to informational books—to learn from the author, or in this case, a classmate (Hansen, 1987, p. 145). They have taken control of their learning because

These children...have taken control of their learning because they have chosen their own purposes for reading.

they have chosen their own purposes for reading.

At the end of the first day, Mrs. Koerber has the opportunity to reflect on her observations of the children in the library.

I've been thinking about what to do next. The children were so excited to begin learning about their topic today. But as I watched them in the library, I noticed some were overwhelmed with the number of books they had. We (the librarian and I) wanted to provide them with plenty of information but it may have been too much. Even with their guiding questions some children felt they had to get information from all of the books just because they were there. And yet some children enjoyed having many books. I noticed a couple of children beginning to copy from the books. I want them to read to get information, share with their partner, and then write it in their own words. Now that they've actually started they will be able to talk about what has happened so far. Tomorrow I will have the class gather and share with each other "Things That Worked" and "Problems So Far" and I will record what they say on chart paper. We will recognize the successes and help each other with the problems. This is new to me and the children so we will learn together.

The next day, children are working in the classroom. They are at desks, on the floor, at tables, and in the hall outside the classroom. There is a buzz of talk as they read, write, and share with each other. Nick and Lauren have their Learnal in front of them and are reading from two different sources. Lauren is reading a book and Nick is reading a magazine.

Another pair is working on information about planets. Lindsay is writing in the Learnal and Garrett is reading to himself.

Interviewer: Will you read to me what you have so far?
Lindsay: Sure.
Garrett: We just have to find out how many moons each planet has. This says Uranus has 17 moons but that's wrong. I know it has at least 26. I read it at home.

Interviewer: When was this book written? (Garrett checks dates in all the books.)
Garrett: This one is newer. Should I use it first?
Interviewer: Good idea. The information will be more up to date.
Lindsay: Oh, look at this. The asteroids separate the outer planets from the inner planets.

Garrett and Lindsay discuss a picture illustrating this.

When children write about information they have chosen, they are learning, as these two show us. Children read content books and choose to write about the parts they find particularly interesting. A child may not highlight the same points that we would, but that is also true of adults when two or more of us read a book. Different people find value in different parts of what they are learning. We try to foster this in our students (Hansen, 1987, p. 149).

Group Share

The group gathers on the carpet at the end of writing time. Several groups share the information they have gathered today.

Mrs. K.: (to Garrett & Lindsay) Last time you were overwhelmed because you had too much information. (She looks at the class.) They had so much information they didn't know what to do. How did it go today?
Garrett: It went great! We wrote down some questions that we wanted to know about. And we are just looking for the answers to those questions.
Lindsay: We want to know how many planets there are. What are their names? What they look like. If planets have moons. We want to put them in order and make illustrations.
Garrett: Uranus looks like a blue marble but with rings. Neptune is very cold. It has ice on the surface.

These children are being shown how to choose a subject, take notes, conference and share along the way, and enjoy the process of learning.

As Garrett and Lindsay share their written work from their Learnal, the other children listen and if their interest is piqued, they ask questions. The two writers enjoy the interest their audience shows. They know more than what they wrote about, so they can answer many questions. The sharing time sets the tone for learning, because everyone in the classroom is learning about something. Every time a group shares, they teach a science minilesson to the entire classroom. They share their information, share the books they are reading, often introducing new books to their classmates which may be read by some of them at a later date. They "go public" with their writing problems and offer solutions to each other: What to do when you don't know where to start? What to do with too much information?

At the end of the group share, Mrs. Koerber asks the children to rate themselves from one to five, five being the highest, by holding up the number of fingers in the air. Most of the children hold up a hand showing five fingers. Then Mrs. Koerber invites the children to share successful strategies they used. The children offer aspects of teamwork, such as taking turns, providing for quiet time, and acting as mutual resources for information and vocabulary.

The group share ends on a positive note. These children are being shown how to choose a subject, take notes, conference and share along the way, and enjoy the process of learning. Many, if not most, people go a lifetime and never find out that writing nonfiction reports can become a part of their lives. Yet those people who can acquire this tool early will never lose either the joy in learning or the power to learn (Graves, 1989, p. 104).

Writing the Report

After they gather information and record it in their Learnals, the children must organize it. They make decisions about which facts to include or exclude in their final piece. Garrett and Lindsay explain how they make these decisions.

Interviewer:	How did you two decide what information to include in your final piece?
Garrett:	We circled the stuff (in the Learnal) we wanted to share and crossed out the stuff we didn't want.
Interviewer:	How did you decide what to cross out?
Lindsay:	We picked things people already knew, or things that were boring, or things people might not really understand.
Interviewer:	Then what did you do with the circled information?
Garrett:	We put the circled stuff in order on another piece of paper. We put the parts together that went together.
Lindsay:	Mrs. Guest [a parent volunteer] helped us with the table of contents.
Interviewer:	Did you rewrite all your sentences, or did you cut and paste them on another sheet of paper?
Garrett:	We wrote it all. Next time I would cut and paste.
Interviewer:	Then what?
Lindsay:	Mrs. Guest typed the information on the computer as we read it to her from our piece of paper. Then she helped us glue the pieces in our published book. Now we just have to do the pictures.

Diana and Alison take turns reading pages from their completed informational book entitled *Chameleons*. A discussion in group share follows:

Lauren:	What is the table of contents?
Diana:	It tells what the pages are about.

> **Mrs. Koerber...chose to search for a new way to grow and took her students with her.**

Lauren: Like chapters?

Mrs. K.: It is similar to chapters.

The girls continue reading their book, but Diana realizes they have copied an unfamiliar word.

Diana: What are traits? (The two girls look at each other and then shrug shoulders)

Alison & Diana: Uh-oh.

Mrs. K.: Specific traits are how they look or what makes them a chameleon. You learned you didn't put that in your own words. Why is it so important to use your own words?

Alison: Well, we couldn't really explain this. And we have to be able to tell about what we put in our book.

In this session, the children discuss the importance of understanding the information they may include in a report and rewriting information in one's own words. Mrs. Koerber uses this sharing time as an opportunity for her students to question the writers and discuss the content of the report. As the children research their topics, they often choose a more difficult text than they might choose in their regular classroom work. This may be due to the high interest of the self-selected topic. These children have been set up to be successful. They have been immersed in print about their topic. They have been involved in reading, rereading, retelling information in their own words, therefore clarifying information, writing, and sharing daily with an adult, another peer, or in group share. Mrs. Koerber has created and allowed a spiraling of planning, discovery, discus-

sion, sharing as they learn, and feedback from adults and peers to take place during the entire process.

The children in this first grade class are reading a variety of material, responding to each other, learning about the interests of others, and stretching and adding to their knowledge about themselves as readers and writers. Mrs. Koerber has tried something new this year. She is already an excellent teacher but she chose to search for a new way to grow and took her students with her. When we become aware of new options, we read professional material, share with colleagues, take a deep breath, and leap! Mrs. Koerber is a learner. And when our students see a learner in action, they learn how to learn.

Bibliography

Atwell, N. (1987). *In the middle: Writing, reading, and learning with adolescents.* Upper Montclair, NJ: Boynton/Cook.

Calkins, L.M. (1986). *The art of teaching writing.* Portsmouth, NH: Heinemann.

Freeman, E. (1991). Informational books: Models for student report writing. *Language Arts, 68:* 470–473.

Graves, D. (1989). *Investigate nonfiction.* Portsmouth, NH: Heinemann.

Hansen, J. (1987). *When writers read.* Portsmouth, NH: Heinemann.

Hansen, J. (1992). The language of challenge: Readers and writers speak their minds. *Language Arts, 69:* 100–105.

Hess, M. L. (1991). Understanding nonfiction: Purpose, classification, response. *Language Arts, 68:* 228–232.

Hints that Affect Successful Reporting by Children

In *Investigate Nonfiction* (1989, p. 100), Donald Graves suggests some broader questions for teachers to ask themselves relating to room conditions and practices that affect successful reporting by children.

Room responsibilities

How well do students accept broad room responsibilities? How self-sufficient are they? For example, in Mrs. Koerber's room the children are expected to be aware of their responsibility to self and classmates and to decide and rate themselves on how well they do.

Reading/writing process

Students should be well versed in working daily with books and writing. Both the reading and writing process should be familiar to them. In this first grade classroom, reading and writing workshop are a daily occurrence; that's the "way it is" so children can easily transfer a "new" task into an already predictable structure.

Time

Writing reports is a daily activity requiring a good block of time. If you consider the importance of being able to use all the language processes in putting literacy to work, the time children take for their reports will come into proper focus. An entire language arts block is a good use of time (60 to 90 minutes maximum). Mrs. Koerber is committed to large blocks of time for learning.

Grouping practices

If children have been grouped homogeneously, then a sense of community and responsibility are affected. Some children are "in" and others "out," thus affecting children's sense of self-sufficiency and their ability to function independently. Children in this classroom work together in many different ways and with many different partners. Mrs. Koerber has an incredible understanding of the importance of having children work in cooperative groups.

Writing Workshop Schedule

10:30–45 SETTLING IN
1. Children get writing folders and needed writing materials.
2. Children pick a spot in the classroom to write.

10:45 MINILESSON
1. The class comes together for a five to ten minute mini-lesson.

10:55 CLASS CHECK IN
1. Each child states what writing project is being worked on.
2. Children tell if they have a note on the **I Need Help** board.
3. Children tell if they are ready for a conference or need to publish.
4. The teacher assigns children to work with parents.

11:00– WRITING TIME
11:30
1. Children write sloppy copies, conference, or publish writing projects.
2. The teacher works with children and takes notes stating what the writer has done well and what goals need to be set for the next writing project.

11:30 CLASS SHARE
1. Children pick classmates to share a writing project.
2. Classmates give the writer compliments or ask questions about the writing project.

11:40 CLOSING UP
1. Children rate the writing time, telling what went well and what they need to do to become a better writer.

Lingering Questions

1. How can I involve the children in developing and presenting minilessons based on the many skills I see them using in their writing?

2. What can I do to help the children focus more on particular successes and/or problems they are encountering in their writing?

3. So much is taking place during writing workshop and it is difficult to capture it all. How can I work with and begin to train parent volunteers who are willing to write anecdotals as they work with the students? This would help to broaden parents' knowledge about the process and aid in understanding and evaluating children's writing behaviors, content, and conventions being used.

WRITING ALL DAY

Susan Stires

First-grade teacher,
The Center for
Teaching and
Learning,
Edgecomb, Maine

On a warm spring afternoon nearly eight years ago, I was with one of my students and his sister. We were walking on a path in the woods behind their house, headed for the shore of the river that bordered on the property. Joe and Marcy were intent on showing me the "windbegin." And I was curious. From the time Joe entered my primary level resource room in kindergarten to now, five years hence, he had been keen on learning about the world around him. Together we had explored his chosen topics from sea urchins to comets. On this day, I knew there was a phenomenon that he had named, developed theories about, apprenticed his sister to, and would eventually write about. A few minutes later, I experienced it: an on-shore breeze where there were breaks in the vegetation.

Joe was my student for reading and writing, and I worked with him both in the resource room and in his classroom. We didn't often have opportunities to go beyond the classroom walls, but Joe did a lot of exploring during his after school hours. At writing time, he would do further research and write about the real world topics that grabbed his attention. From Joe I learned how important it was to use writing to learn.

When I became a classroom teacher again, I was able to promote writing to learn throughout the day and on a scale larger than with a small group of students. Today, in my primary classroom, my "special" students are integrated into the class along with everyone else. My students use writing time to pursue their many scientific, historical, literary, and personal interests. Some of their chosen topics come from what is personally compelling; other self-selected topics grow out of the larger curriculum.

Reading and Social Studies

Students naturally write about reading as they play out their reading experiences with story structure, characters, literary language, plot, and genre. Recently, we have had an explosion of tall tales, which resulted from a study of them as a kind of folktale. Experimentation with fiction influenced by reading is perennially popular, as students often adopt or invent characters. Amy adopted Amelia Bedelia for her story about taking violin lessons, and on one page of the story plays with the word "bow." Amelia Bedelia experiences her usual language troubles.

During reading time, students write to me about the books that they are reading, and I in turn write back in the form of letters. I base this on Nancie Atwell's work, as described in *In the Middle* (1987). I respond to what the students are doing and encourage them to do more. Much of what appears in the letters is a result of minilessons or conferences; these entries show that the student has learned or is in the process of learning about a particular aspect of reading. Since I cannot have as many face-to-face conferences with my students as I would like, this weekly exchange of letters allows for additional conference time.

In one of her letters, Emily expressed her sadness about *The Littlest Reindeer*, her frustration in understanding *Will's Quill*, and her desire to read *The Lily Cupboard*, which I had recommended to her. Tristan called *And to Think that I Saw It on Mulberry Street* a "round book"; he was identifying the circle story structure that we had often discussed. Maya compared two versions of *Goldilocks and the Three Bears*, one by Jan Brett and the other by James Marshall. She concluded that the Brett version was "nicer and calmer" (Figure 1). She also asked about my favorite folktale or fairy tale and told me hers was *The Seal Mother*.

Katherine enumerated the personal connections she made with the same book by telling me what parts of the book reminded her of, including how the bear family's walk reminded her of walks her family took to the river near their home. Students also make many literary connections. David identified the problem in the story *The Blue-Nosed Witch* as a grouchy character, touching on characters as we had been doing in whole class minilessons.

In our school, The Center for Teaching and Learning, the faculty selects two overarching themes per year, and then we study various topics that fit under those themes. All of the students study the topics together, and this ensures a continuous conversation among the students and teachers throughout the school. In the three years that we have existed as a school, our themes have been communities and

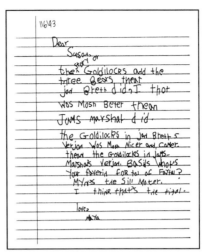

Figure 1 (translation)

Dear Susan,

The story of <u>Goldilocks and the Three Bears</u> that Jan Brett did, I thought was much better than James Marshall did. The Goldilocks in Jan Brett's version was much nicer and calmer than the Goldilocks in James Marshall's version. Besides what's your favorite folktale or fairy tale. Mine is <u>The Seal Mother</u>. I think that's the title.

Love,

Maya

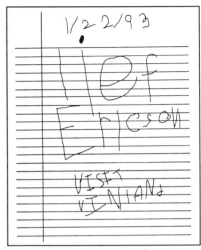

Figure 2 (translation)
Lief Erikson Visit[s] Vinland

changes, structures and systems, and energy and exploration. The students keep folders, learning logs, or journals on the various topics to record, reflect, or respond. Quite often the teachers provide prompts, but the students, accustomed to journals, also use them spontaneously.

Both student initiated and teacher initiated uses occurred during our study of the Vikings. After learning about the evidence of the Vikings' presence in North America, the students experimented with a runic alphabet to leave runic inscriptions of their own. In order to establish the contribution of Leif Erikson in their minds, I asked the students to write a headline about it, as if that media existed in 1000 A.D. Kyle's headline shows how he processed the information (Figure 2).

At times, students even change the course of history as Greg did in his *The Grny of Clambs* (Figure 3). We had been

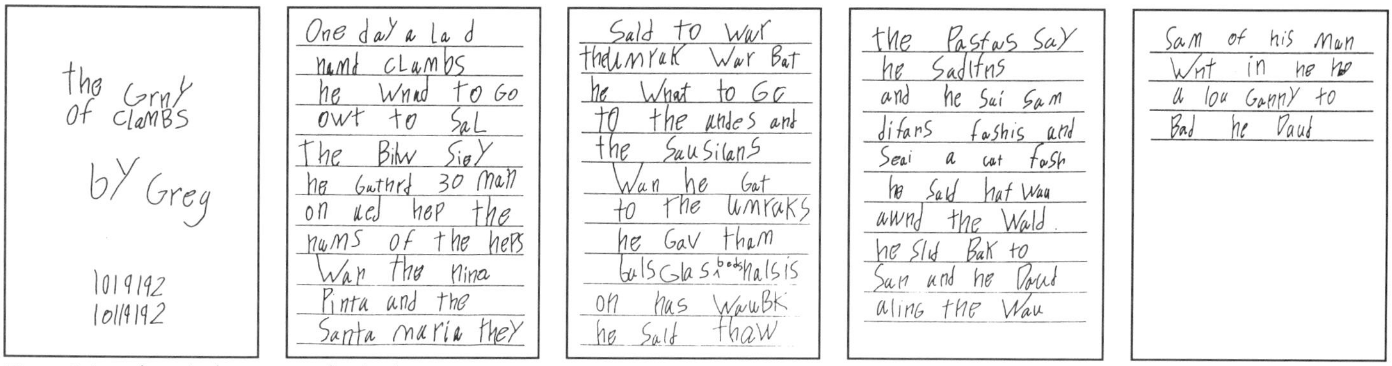

the Grny
of ClaMBS
by Greg

10 9 92
10 9 92

One day a lad
namd clambs
he wnnd to Go
owt to Sal
The Bilw sioy
he Guthrd 30 man
on ues hep the
nums of the hebs
Wan the nina
Pinta and the
Santa maria they

Sald to war
thelmrak War Bat
he What to Go
to the andes and
the Sausilans
Wan he Gat
to the umraks
he Gav tham
bels Glass bods nalsis
on has WawBk
he Sald thaw

the Pastas say
he Sadltns
and he Sai Sam
difans foshis and
Seni a cat fosh
he Sald haf Waa
awnd the Wald
he Sld Bak to
San and he Daud
aling the Wau

Sam of his man
Wnt in he he
a lou Ganny to
Bad he Daud

Figure 3 *(translation) The Journey of Columbus*

One day a lad named Columbus he wanted to go out to sail. The people say he gathered thirty men on each ship. The names of the ships were the Nina, Pinta, and the Santa Maria. They sailed to where the America(s) were but he wanted to go to the Indies and the Spice Islands. When he got to the Americas he gave them (Tainos) bells, glass beads, and necklaces. On his way back he sailed through the Pacific Sea. He sailed fast and he saw different fishes and saw a catfish. He sailed halfway around the world. He sailed back to shore and died along the way. Some of his men went and he had a long journey. Too bad he died.

studying about Columbus because of the quincentennary, and had read about his early life and work, his support by the Spanish monarchs, and his subsequent encounter with the Tainos in North America. We had left Columbus for awhile to learn about Tainos when Greg wrote his book, where he imagined an ending for Columbus which is reminiscent of Magellan, an explorer yet unknown to Greg.

Much of what the students learn comes from excellent student magazines, like *Cobblestones*, as well as the many fine nonfiction and fiction books for children. Often I read these books aloud, as I did with *Morning Girl* and *Marco Polo: His Notebook*. After I finished reading the Marco Polo book over a span of four days of reading and talking, I asked the students to make a diary entry from some period of Marco Polo's journey to China, as if they were the great traveler. Anne wrote about both the beginning and end of the trip; David selected Polo's arrival in China and his meeting with the Khan, as well as some initial impressions; Alex remembered Marco Polo's governorship and travels to other parts of the East.

Planning is an important step in learning and in the process of organizing information. Sometimes students use mapping or webbing as several students did in a small cross-age group study of the native people of the Southwestern United States. At another time, when our class planned to build a model city, students used lists with and without illustrations. Catherine began her list with bridges, skyscrapers, and statues to characterize the city she envisioned. Previously, when we studied our own communities—small and rural towns—students first wrote from the standpoint of their personal knowledge, and then proceeded to interview their parents, neighbors, and town officials to find out more about their towns. Finally, the members of each of the thirteen communities orally reported about their town to the rest of the school.

Science and Mathematics

Writing is so naturally a part of science; observation begs recording and speculation. Prediction is crucial. When setting up an experiment on seed germination, Corrine first wrote down what she expected to see based on the shape of the seeds. By the end of the following week she drew and described the process that she had observed (Figures 4a and b). Ellen Doris's very simple observation sheet has proved highly useful for recording science experiments. Tristan first used it as a kindergartner observing frogs' eggs (Figure 5).

In our recent study of electricity, the students kept a journal. After discussions, experimentations, and demonstrations with static electricity, they wrote about their experiences both in and outside of school. Some students narrated individual encounters with static discharges; others recorded experiments; still others defined electricity and drew and wrote about the static electricity machine that I borrowed from a local high school.

During a technology study that included the building of model cars, boats, and houses made from wooden stock they measured and constructed, students kept logs of what they did on a given day—at least in part. Greg developed the style of an on-the-spot reporter (his description) when it was his day to write in the log. The students worked in pairs and shared responsibilities, i.e. alternating writing and clean-up. The logs were places to identify problems, as well as to solve them.

All of this writing is first draft writing. Sometimes content area writing becomes a product. In the case of the cross-aged group who studied the nervous system last year, the writing became reports to the rest of the school, presented and videotaped before a live audience. Likewise, my class's water energy time line of posters and written reports on rivers, mills, steam engines, hydroelectric plants, tides, and geothermal energy were presented and hung on display to celebrate and share with our learning community, not unlike a scientific conference.

The writing that my students have done in math is mainly with data collection and problem solving. Students enjoy collecting data from one another on questions that interest them, such as bedtimes, number of pets, popularity of

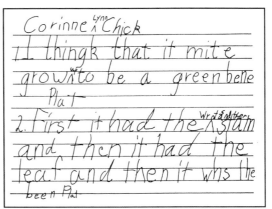

Figure 4a (translation)

1. I think that it might grow up to be a green bean plant.
2. First it had the roots and the stem and then it had the leaf and then it was the bean plant.

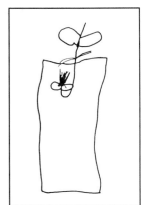

Figure 4b

school pets, and favorite sports, authors, and ice cream flavors. The surveys that the students conduct depend on what matters to them, and they enjoy sharing the results. They write their question and tally the results according to charts I demonstrate and their own inventions.

Telling math stories is often spontaneous. One day I wore mouse earrings to school, and Kate, a great animal lover, noticed them at the beginning of math class. She then said, "I found a nest of five baby mice, but three of them died right away, and, even though we fed them with an eye dropper, the other two died a couple of days later." I recorded her story in words, and then we translated it into number sentences with the correct student-identified operation, subtraction. I abandoned my previous plans for the class, as the students launched into the telling of a plethora of mouse tales, using both addition and subtraction, as well as fact and fiction. I asked the students how we could remember the tales, and they rushed for the papers and pencils to author their story problems.

Figure 5 (translation)

Some are round and some are curved.

I wonder about how they got out.

Later, they shared a selected problem for the class to solve. Like many others, Krystin left out the question. She learned that it was essential when presenting the problem to others to solve.

At other times, I set up the possibility for story problems either as part of the math class or as integrated with what we are studying in reading, science, or social studies. When we studied money, we set up a store and a bank. On three successive days, the students had opportunities to role play clerks and cashiers, customers, and bankers. Following the role plays, they wrote at least one math story for each of the three roles they played. They learned how to count and record money, how to carry and borrow, how to give change, and how to estimate. They used a real cash register, retrieved from the dumpster of a local restaurant, and real money. All in all, they had a wonderful time.

Shared and Collaborative Writing

Shared writing is common in our class, as the whole group assists me in capturing what we have learned or are learning every day. Perhaps its most satisfying use is when we "make reading" for our weekly school newsletter under the subtitle "Highlights of the Week, Susan's Group." Students recall the events of the week, and I write them on a chart. The chart is then published in combination with the highlights from the other classes. Parents report that their children often read the highlights to them at the dinner table on Friday evening.

Collaborative writing is always enjoyable because it is usually integrated with another subject and because everyone contributes to the project. We have produced numerous class books on particular topics we have studied or on an author or genre. The most enjoyable of our collaborations has been the book we are writing this year about Lily, our class rabbit. Each day, on a rotating basis, one child is in charge of the calendar, passing out folders, and observing and writing about Lily, a large palomino rabbit who lives in the play place of our school. Lily is wonderfully soft and usually friendly, unless she doesn't want to return to her cage after her daily romp during our oral sharing time. On such occasions, she growls or leaps about wildly. This, of course, makes for good copy in *Lily's Journal*, as do her investigations into the dress up clothes and blocks. Some of the students' entries include:

10/23/92 Lily weighs five pounds, and she doesn't like to be held very much. Anne

10/26/92 Lily stretches out like a school bus. Peter

10/29/92 Lily likes lots of doors (cupboard) because Lily scratches them and drums them. She wiggles her nose very funny. Greg

The class collaborated to write rules to be posted by Lily's cage. They each brainstormed rules they thought were sensible, and from their lists we gleaned what they considered the best ones. They were especially concerned that no one chase Lily or poke objects into her cage, and their poster communicated their concerns.

Figure 6 (translation)

Dear Susan,

I hope you had a good weekend. I did. About the computer, I thought they [students on the computers] were going to do "Mouse Practice." It seems like they are doing typewriter [keyboarding program].

Love,

Greg

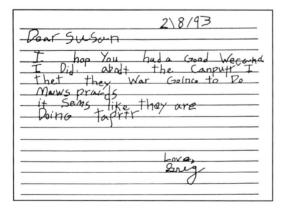

Although I have no specific category for one last kind of writing, it is too important to be overlooked. It is "keeping in touch" writing. Its vital function is for students to communicate with me, their peers, and members of the school community, their sense of how things are going socially or organizationally. We exist in a social brew that affects learning. Having the opportunity to write allows students to determine what they are affecting, how things are affecting them or simply to know what to anticipate (Figure 6). Our school postal system exists to support and legitimize this type of writing.

Why Write to Learn?

Toby Fulwiler once defined writing as visual thinking. When I first heard that, I was struck with the power of those two words. As thinking, writing is clearly a tool for learning because it allows the learner to see his or her thoughts and evaluate them. Since it is visual, it leaves marks like tracks in the snow, identifying the creator and pointing their direction. However, writing is more permanent since it can be preserved to tell the story of the writer's growth. It is a record etched out that allows for review and reflection by the learner and the teacher. Finally, it becomes an artifact to study and celebrate, as its creator moves on as a learner.

In my class writing is an all day affair; it is not confined to the writing workshop. Writing is there to support learning in all its modes and subjects.

Bibliography

Atwell, N. (1987). *In the middle: Writing, reading, and learning with adolescents.* Upper Montclair, NJ: Boynton/Cook.

Brett, J. (1987). *Goldilocks and the three bears.* New York: Dodd, Mead & Co.

Cobblestone: The History Magazine for Young People. Peterborough, NH: Cobblestone Publishing.

Cohen, M. (1985). *Starring the first grade.* New York: Dell.

DeWitt, J. (1946). *The littlest reindeer.* Chicago: Watertower Books.

Dorris, M. (1992). *Morning girl.* New York: Hyperion.

Embry, M. (1984). *The blue-nosed witch.* New York: A Bantam Skylark Book.

Freeman, D. (1977). *Will's quill.* New York: Puffin Books.

Gerstein, M. (1986). *The seal mother.* New York: Dial Books for Young Readers.

Marshall, J. (1988). *Goldilocks and the three bears.* New York: Dial Books for Young Readers.

Oppenheimer, S. L. (1992). *The lily cupboard.* New York: HarperCollins.

Potter, Beatrix. (1973). *The tale of Peter Rabbit.* New York: Dover Publications.

Seuss, Dr. (1937). *And to think that I saw it on Mulberry Street.* New York: The Vanguard Press.

Where to Begin

I have learned about writing from my students, past and present, as I researched my teaching and their learning. That is one of two primary sources of my knowledge. The other has been the wealth of research that has been published in the last fifteen years. (See the Bibliography at the end of this volume.) From Nancy Martin and her colleagues and from Toby Fulwiler, I first became familiar with the research that supported what I was experiencing with my students in the early eighties. In 1985, I took a course with Mary Ellen Giacobbe at the University of New Hampshire, where we looked at both reading process and writing to learn.

Two years later, Nancie Atwell conducted a writing to learn project in three Maine schools for intermediate level classroom teachers. Although I did not participate in the project, I followed it closely since I taught in one of the schools and was Nancie's colleague. The project resulted in the book *Coming to Know*, a valuable resource for elementary teachers. Since then, I have read and studied numerous books that have helped me to think about what is possible for my students. I believe this is the best investment that a classroom teacher can make. For greater stimulation, I suggest finding a couple of colleagues who would be interested in studying together.

In addition to *Coming to Know*, I recommend that a study group or single teacher also read Giacobbe's article "Learning to Write and Writing to Learn in the Elementary School" and Pappas's *An Integrated Language Perspective in the Elementary School: Theory into Action*. In order to understand what is possible with poetry and writing to learn, especially with young children, Georgia Heard's book *For the Good of the Earth and Sun* is essential.

For further reading, I would suggest Toby Fulwiler's *The Journal Book*, Donald Graves's *Investigate Nonfiction*, and Jack Wilde's chapter "The Written Report: Old Wine in New Bottles" from Newkirk and Atwell's *Understanding Writing*. And for anyone who has not read Nancie Atwell's *In the Middle*, her writing about reading through letters is a model to be followed. Finally, Nancy Martin's *Writing and Learning Across the Curriculum 11–16* is a foundation book.

Specific readings in science that I have enjoyed and found to be helpful are Ellen Doris's *Doing What Scientists Do* and Barbara Bagge-Rynerson's "'This Fish Is So Strange To Me': The Use of the Science Journal." The most recent exploration for me has been writing in math, and David Whitin's *Living and Learning Mathematics* has been especially useful in helping me with data collecting and basic problem solving. Penny Skinner's *What's Your Problem: Posing and Solving Mathematical Problems* has advanced my thinking in the uses of story problems for learning addition and subtraction.

These have been some of the books that have been useful to me, ones that I recommend to you because they are filled with practice grounded in explicit theory. By actively observing my students, I can make sense of the ideas and try them out. Teacher research and study are essential to my practice and, I trust, to the practice of other teachers who continue to be learners.

Daily Schedule

8:30	Morning Meeting
8:45	Reading Workshop
10:00	Snack/Recess
10:20	Math/Science
11:15	Oral Share/Social Studies
12:00	Lunch/Recess
1:00	Read Aloud
1:30	Writing Workshop/Computers
2:30	Afternoon Meeting

Art and Music specialists provide instruction on alternating Monday mornings; otherwise art and music are integrated into the curriculum. Physical education and movement are taught on alternating Wednesdays.

Lingering Questions

1. How can young children use writing to learn more efficiently so that the writing does not dominate the other science, reading, social studies, or math activities?

2. Am I providing a balance between prompted and unprompted writing?

3. How much writing should remain first draft, and how much should be brought through to a product?

4. How can we share what we have written more efficiently and systematically?

5. How can I incorporate different forms of writing in reading and math?

6. Am I really getting at speculation and hypothesis making through writing?

7. How can I make better use of computers for writing to learn?

8. What different kinds of writing do mathematicians and historians engage in and how can I incorporate those in my class?

REFLECTIONS FROM A SPEEDING ROLLER COASTER

Kyle begins to read at Share Time, and early on we know that this is an intimate sharing. He writes of the tragic death of his grandmother, who died in an automobile accident in which he was also involved. We are silent at the end. No one knows what to say. All I can think to do is to tell him how sorry I am for all the pain he has been in.

A week later, a classmate who sits next to Kyle writes of the tragic loss of a much-loved cousin. It seems that Kyle's sharing gave Esteban permission to tell a story that he hadn't yet told. Esteban never shared his writing publicly in Share Time.

Kyle returned to Share Time often during the year with that story as he worked it out. One time a student giggled after a reading. The giggle was unrelated; nonetheless, it was poorly timed and created an unsafe moment. Kyle stood up and left the room. My eyes met Esteban's and we both knew he was the one to go be with Kyle. He stood up to go find Kyle.

Three-fourths of the way through the year, Kyle wrote another story about his grandmother—the kind of story that we would want for a young boy to write about his grandmother—a grandmother who fixed breakfast on the weekends, went to church on Sundays, and yelled the loudest at baseball games. "Now she is gone. Everyone misses the way she could make you laugh at games. We miss her cooking, but the thing everyone misses is her love. Now before I go to bed I say goodnight, Sayha."

It is moments like these that remind me of the importance and power of writing with children, of giving children the real chance to write. I watch in my classroom as young people discover the power of using written language in purposeful and meaningful ways. They stir the deep-down pot of themselves: They relive and dream as they capture yesterday's basketball game but then make themselves the slam dunker who saves the game in the last 5—4—3—2—1 seconds of the game. They are heroes fighting off aliens or mad-dog villains in the dusty western towns. They try to make sense of the cousin and the grandmother who were never grieved. They express the love for a mother and father that they have never quite been able to express in words: "Mom and Dad, you're special to me because you take me places. You listen to me when I have a problem. But I don't tell you because it makes me feel weird. But most of all, I love you" (Albert).

When I was asked to write this article, I felt excited and privileged. Then, as the deadline loomed, I panicked. What am I going to say, especially now at a time when I do not feel particularly satisfied about my "writing program"? Even though I know that scenarios like Kyle's are very real, I am not necessarily always in touch with them, nor are they always happening that way. The roller coaster of writing with kids in a classroom sometimes swings downhill. It's like that, you know. Sometimes you are up at the peak enjoying the breathtaking view; at other

Tom Tracy

Fifth- and sixth-grade teacher, Machan School Phoenix, Arizona

times you are screaming headlong into the low spots, forgetting that it has to turn and swoop back up.

Right now, the roller coaster is rattling through the low spots. I suppose I start here because that is just the way it is with this writing thing that we do with kids. I share with you a recent entry from my own notebook:

For the umpteenth millionth time, I quit this crazy stuff. There are too many kids and not enough of me. And they are all over the place. Everywhere. I have no idea what they are doing. It's like throwing open the starting gate and everybody goes in all directions and never again will they be at the same place. I look out there or walk around in it and I am overwhelmed. Are they just taking me for a ride? Do I trust them? Will they come around? What about Eric? Will he ever write? Does he have to?

Sound familiar? I cannot count how many times I have said, "That's it. I quit! I will never do this again," only to have it evolve from that point.

I soothe myself by remembering to trust. Trust this whole process. There is nothing simple about thirty-three young people and one adult writing together. It is a ride filled with excitement and chaos. I forget this sometimes, forget that it takes being able to dwell in the chaos. How else can it be if you are going to really set people free to write what's there for them to write and not get in the way? Writing is as alive as the human beings who do it. Put a bunch of them together and it is teeming with humanity. There are no formulas that will work. There are no certain ways to do this. I have tried many of them to prove this to myself. I am so thankful for the current thinkers and pioneers like Murray, Graves, Atwell, Calkins. They are my heroes, but I have to adapt my style to fit the young people I am working with. And I have to constantly change my own style because it is always ready to get

stuck somewhere. I have felt the heat of passion when writing is really alive in our room, and I have felt the dampness of stagnation when I have gotten stuck in a mechanized writing process. Hot. Cold. And somewhere in between.

So, that is one thing I want to say. Trust. As King Solomon would always say, "This, too, will surely pass. The roller coaster will swing up." I added the roller coaster bit for him. I can imagine him saying that part, too.

What comes to mind to say next is to let them share together the work they are doing. It is in Share Time that I wake back up to the power of writing with kids. I am pulled out of the slumber of not trusting. I am moved, inspired, and juiced up. All Share Times aren't this way, but there are enough to remind me.

Share Time I got from Nancie Atwell. I like it and have kept the name. In my room, it is share by choice. Share Time for us has come to be a very special gathering. It's the "aw right" if we do it and "maan" if we don't. We find out that Al Capone really means something to Eduardo. We ponder why people have to be homeless. We find that Adelina feels life is "beautiful and confusing" and that some of us share that feeling. We want to know why you chose that idea or where it came from. When you talked about the blood transfusion, you made us shiver. And sometimes we just sit and stare at each other and no one is talking. Uh oh. Time to trust again.

How does all of this happen? Well, there are many ways to get there, but one very important common denominator stands out: safety. I put a high premium on making it safe for young people to share their writing in a group. If they are reaching deep to express themselves and bringing that to language, then it is a must that they be taken care of when coming to share in a group. No matter what they bring. With each writer I

> *Writing is as alive as the human beings who do it.*

make sure we focus. I am always talking about how we have to take care of each writer who comes up to share. It is part of the ritual at the beginning of Share Time that I remind us of safety. If you can't be a part of making it safe for everyone, then we invite you to leave. Quickly.

Safety doesn't come quickly. It builds over time as our relationship does, as we start to trust each other. When Kyle read his first story about his grandmother, we could feel ourselves come together, drawn together by this most intimate and trusting sharing. It didn't happen overnight that Kyle would trust the group enough to tell us his story, to share with us out loud as he worked out this tragedy in his life. It took time and more of that trust stuff. We had reached a point of safety. I stopped and pointed that out to the group at the time. I made sure that students understood that what we had as a group, our ability to be safe together and take care of each other, had given Kyle the room to share. It was quite an accomplishment for us as a group of writers sharing with each other. They come to understand. They also forget, as was the case when the unrelated giggle came at the wrong time. It, too, is part of the process.

I try to keep my hands off their writing, and I send that message during Share Time. (I am often tempted to put my hands all over their writing. I can hardly help it; it was part of my upbringing as a teacher.) I reflect on what moves me, catches my attention. Whenever anyone, including myself, is giving input or feedback, I am always reminding the authors that they can take it or leave it. What we are saying to you is just how we see it. We have this little rule: Never say "should" in Share Time. I enjoy watching the kids catch themselves or each other.

"You should take out the part . . . ."

"You *could*," comes a chorus of voices correcting the one giving input.

"You could take out the part . . . ."

With safety comes a willingness to trust and reveal, to express the real issues and concerns that are always moving around inside of children. To explore out loud. To work out. Esteban heard Kyle and got himself stirred up. Then he wrote. Without the Share Time, I just do not think it would have happened. Without the safety that we have built over time, I know it would not have happened.

So what else would I say? Close the doors and let them write. Get out of their way (see "trust"). Do it a lot, every day. Let them do it in different places, inside and outside. We once wrote on the city bus going to the public library. We had everybody worried, with all these twelve-year-olds watching them and writing in spiral notebooks. Give your students notebooks, journals, or something to write in that is theirs: a free place to write where no one is going to mess with it. It is part of letting them write.

I sometimes play this game to help me see what might be good to do in a classroom. Imagine yourself with a group of people who are going to write together. How would you want it to be? How would you want the time together to go? Well, of course, you would write. You would write a lot. Would you put together a bunch of checklists and tell yourselves the steps to get through the process? Would you want someone telling you that you can't type on the computer until you have done your handwritten final draft? Don't get me wrong. I use checklists, procedures, and process—all those things. They come and they go, along with my concerns about using them. But the moment I find them getting in the way of how someone wants to get said what he or she needs to get said, a little alarm goes off inside. Sometimes I hear it.

I put a high premium on making it safe for young people to share their writing in a group.

How else would you want it if it were you in a writing group? You would want to move at your own pace. You probably would not mind someone looking in on your pace. Maybe a deadline here and there. There is nothing like completing a piece of work. Sometimes I give deadlines to certain kids. It works for some. Sometimes. It's what has me sitting through the weekend writing this now.

You would want to work with each other, comparing ideas, grabbing each other, "Hey, listen to this!" and getting help. You would probably find yourself talking about really good literature and trashy novels. They would inspire you. Jason would never have come out with his *The Town of Flatwater* if he had not fallen in love with William Steig's *Dominic*. You would definitely want to choose your own ideas and topics. Who wants to write something that is only important to someone else? Just because you think that life is "beautiful and confusing" doesn't mean that I do.

Keep thinking about how you would want it. It is good practice to put yourself in their shoes and think about how you would like it to be. Which brings me to the last thing I want to say. It has to do with getting into their shoes. How do you yourself get up *inside* language and stir your own pot? How do you bring yourself to get *inside* the language? For me, the answer is obvious. I write. I mess around and write earnestly, too. I keep notebooks, daybooks, journals, whatever I might be calling them at the time. I write to discover, to express,

to sort out, to create. Sometimes it is for an audience and other times it is definitely not. What I learn while I am writing gives me a wealth of personal knowledge and experience to draw from when I work with young writers. I share my writing and discoveries with the kids. I have noticed that it is part of the trust building. I am a writer with successes and frustrations just like they are, and I try to share both.

Does this mean we all should be writers to teach writing? I can hear my kids saying, "Not we all *should*, but we all *could!*" I used to think so, but I am not so sure anymore. For me, it is important. But that is for me. My way is not yours. Yours may be through the literature that you pore over, the poetry that moves you, or the biographies of famous people that you read. But whatever your way, it seems very important that you are stirring your own pot, that somehow you are getting up *inside* of language, of yourself.

And so here we are. I have shared my views right from the rickety rackety seat of this roller coaster. By the time this comes out, I'll be on some other curve, swooping along with all my buddies: the people whose ideas I embrace and steal, my fellow teachers who give me strength as we scratch our heads together, and most important, another group of children continuing to explore themselves. There we will be, hopefully remembering to trust, striving to say something important for ourselves and sharing it together. And just remember, the view at the top is grand. I just forget sometimes.

Suggestions for Share Time

An idea I currently use is to gather for Share Time in a circle with two chairs at the top of the circle. One is for the author, the other is for me. We sit next to each other. I have noticed that this gives a little extra boost of confidence and safety. I put the author in charge of his or her time up there. I always begin Share Time with a general statement that goes something like this: "Remember that we are all writers here gathering to share our work. We want to make sure that we respect each writer as you would want to be respected. We want to make it safe for anyone who comes up to share and for anyone who gives ideas and feedback." I remind them how important their own writing is to them and ask them to remember that when someone else is up here sharing. Together we make it safe.

When a writer comes up to share, I always ask him or her, "What do you want from us as an audience? How do you want to use us?" They will then say what they want. For example, they might say, "I want you to tell me what you think about the ending" or "I just want to share it. I don't really want feedback." I think this gives them more ownership. When Kyle first read, he only wanted to share.

Sometimes I ask some kids in the audience to keep notes on any feedback or suggestions that the group might offer on a particular piece. Having those written responses makes it easier for the writer to remember and use the ideas. I always remind the writer that these suggestions and comments are the viewpoints of other writers; the author is free to decide how (or whether) to use them. It is always the student's final decision.

Sometimes I have the students keep a response paper in their writing folder so that they can jot down what they might want to talk about in a person's writing as it is being read—something they liked about the way the writer gave them a feeling, etc. This seems to focus them and helps out in those times when we all stare blankly at each other.

Lingering Questions

- How do I let go and at the same time understand what thirty-three writers are doing?

- How can I come to trust better the whole process, trust that Albert's talking about the Suns' basketball game last night is really part of his process?

- How can I better manage or be aware of what is going on without creating too many overwhelming accounting systems that drive me crazy and stifle the process?

- How can I keep moving and priming the pump for all of the students as they write?

- Where and when do I exert pressure, demand, expect more?

- How do I keep it fresh without overwhelming myself, trying to reinvent every moment?

- How can I have more compassion for myself and the fact that many of these lingering questions are unanswerable?

IMAGINATION AND PASSION: RICH SOURCES OF AUTHENTIC TEXT

Colleen Buddy

Third-grade teacher, Eagle Ridge School, Evergreen, Colorado

It is the second week of school. A gentle buzz creates the backdrop of our multi-age classroom of six, seven, and eight year olds. The children are in the throes of learning. Kasey, Darrah, Andrea, Rick, and Brandon gather round to read a big book of poetry together. Pairs of children fill all available corners reading, writing, chatting. I marvel at their engagement and industry.

Seven-year-old Nelson and I sit together on the floor knee-to-knee. Nelson wears a plastic pair of wolf teeth. As I begin to interview Nelson about reading and writing, he removes the play teeth from his mouth. Nelson tells me about his writing. "Writing is different for me," he says. "Like last year, my teacher wanted me to write about my life, like things in my life. I don't like that." I feel my face grow warm. Nelson could be talking about me. I pause. "Hmm," I say, "Why not?" "Well," he says, "I like to use my imagination. I live in the world of my imagination. So that's what I like to write. I think it's more interesting." I'm sure my face is aglow now. Don Graves, Lucy Calkins, Don Murray and others have taught me the importance of writing from what you know and see, writing from what puzzles and intrigues you, writing from your own experience. I wonder if my notions about personal experience as the source of powerful writing is perhaps limiting the potential of young writers, writers like Nelson who live in the world of their imagination. I set aside the writing interview questions and begin composing new questions to dig deeper into Nelson's notions about the world of his imagination and how it works with writing. We continue our talk. "How is it more interesting?" I ask. "It just is. It takes me places I want to go. I can become anybody, and I can have lots of adventures." Then I ask, "What is the imagination?" Nelson says, "Imagination is the source that makes the ideas bigger and bigger. Like let's say you're going to write a book and you get a little idea. That's like a seed. You put it in your imagination and it gets bigger and bigger and better and better as it goes along . . . ."

Although Nelson is the first child to tell me he lives in the world of his imagination, I am sure I have taught countless others. In my mind I see images of Quinn, Aimee, Bumni and others. Quinn's world was the world of dinosaurs. Aimee lived her life playing out the role of different heroines found in fairy tales. Bumni engaged in ongoing conversations with her imaginary friend, Tusa. I did not encourage the children to explore the worlds of their imagination in writing. Had I silenced the children, insisting they write from their personal experience, from what they see and know? I grimace.

My interview with Nelson ends, yet I carry his words with me for several days. I record them in my notebook. "I live in the world of my imagination." Nelson's words have my full attention and I am filled with questions. If Nelson lives in the world of his imagination, how do I make room for it in our classroom? Can imagination and reality coexist? What are Nelson's beliefs about fiction and nonfiction? My two-pronged challenge begins to take shape: to help Nelson come to know he can live in the world of his imagination and draw on its passion as a rich source for his literacy, and to nurture, extend, and enhance his passion for the imaginative in his reading and writing.

When thinking of Nelson's remark, I am reminded of Dewey's words ". . . we hear much nowadays about the cultivation of the child's imagination. Then we undo much of our talk and work by the belief that the imagination is some special part of the child that finds its satisfaction in one particular direction—generally speaking, that of the unreal and make-believe, or myth and made-up story. Why are we so hard of heart and so slow to believe? The imagination is the medium in which the child lives . . . ." I do not wish to undo or squelch the life Nelson lives in his imagination. I want to honor it, value it, and harness all its power, and put it to work for Nelson and his literacy development. How can I come to know the medium in which Nelson lives and capitalize on it to support his growing literacy?

I decide there is much to learn from Nelson. Nelson can also teach me about the world of the imagination. I know he will teach me in extraordinary ways, not only about *his* world but also about the worlds of Quinn, Aimee, Bumni, and other children. It is through Nelson I

hope to revisit and reframe my notions about authentic text, and the roles imagination and passion play in creating authentic text, either in reading or writing. These questions come to mind:

1. What are the roles of authenticity, passion, and imagination in literacy?

2. How can I help Nelson and other children define who they are and who they might become through the interplay of passion, imagination, and literacy?

3. In what ways might my new learnings connect to our classroom?

Authenticity, Passion, and Imagination

Authentic, according to Webster, is that which can be believed, real, genuine. A number of synonyms come to mind as well: natural, honest, orthodox, and evidential. I reconsider my notions of authenticity. To me, authentic text is real text, text born out of personal experience, text that is meaningful and purposeful to the author. It may also serve a passion. This text comes in many forms. It might be a love letter to grandpa or an editorial; it might be a grocery list or a sign on a six year old's bedroom door admonishing a little brother: "Kep owt. I men ET!" I find my view of authentic text somewhat limiting as I watch Nelson. He is a warrior in battle. He is a dragon breathing fire. He is Huck Finn on the great Mississippi. He is filled with passion as he plays out each scenario. He lives the

To me, authentic text is real text, text born out of personal experience, text that is meaningful and purposeful to the author.

world of his imagination. His writing is reminiscent of his imaginative play as he creates authentic text from this world.

Long ago there was a very suspicious cave. When it was winter time, a lonely princess was coming upon the cave. There was a rumor that there was a dragon. As she came upon the cave, there was a dragon in the cave. The princess scrambled to the castle. The dragon was mad. He was real mad.

Nelson relies on his world of imagination and his passion for dragons to create authentic text.

Tied closely to the notion of authenticity are Eleanor Duckworth's notions about the having of wonderful ideas, which she considers the "essence of intellectual development." She further considers the essence of pedagogy as giving a child the occasion to have wonderful ideas and to feel good about having them.

Nelson explores his wonderful ideas during our Math Workshop, where he builds castles and fortresses to demonstrate and extend his understanding of patterns in math. Authentic and wonderful ideas work in harmony with each

> So when Nelson composes texts and is drawing his bucket from the well of the imaginative world in which he lives, is he writing authentic text as he knows it? Indeed he is.

other. Clearly, Nelson is having wonderful ideas and is feeling good about them as he invites Steven, Brandon, and Nicki to view his work. Next he composes authentic text as he creates sophisticated dialogue for the imaginary (yet authentic) knights, kings, and heroes. Watching Nelson immersed in the world of his imagination, I come to realize that authentic text, imaginative text, begins

with passion, a fervor about someone or something. In a follow-up interview, I ask Nelson about passion and writing. He tells me, "Passion is liking something with your whole self. If you have a piece of writing and you really care a lot, you'll write it better. You'll spend more time and write it better because you'll think, 'I really love this.'"

Nelson's current passions—wolves, dragons, knights, and kingdoms—sow their own seeds of possibility, sprouting conceptual roots that will grow and bloom or wither and die as he explores the world of his imagination in writing. I begin to see through Nelson's play how the worlds of authenticity and imagination merge.

Imagination, according to Webster, is the act or power of forming mental images of what is not actually present. It can also be the act or power of creating new ideas by combining experience. All acts of composing then, either reading or writing, are by nature acts of the imagination. So when Nelson composes texts and is drawing his bucket from the well of the imaginative world in which he lives, is he writing authentic text as he knows it? Indeed he is.

Nelson brings to life the mental images he has. When he wears his wolf teeth, he is authentically living the world of his imagination. In a note to Brittney and Andrea, Nelson writes, "If you can play, meet me at my den under the stairs on the first playground at first recess." His passion for wolves also arouses his anger at the depiction of the wolf in fairy tales. "It's not fair," he insists, "and it's not true either. If I could just talk to all those authors, I'd tell them what an injustice they've done to the whole species." It is in this passion that Nelson plucks a seed of possibility and plants it. He grows what seems to be endless sources for his writing. Are they authentic? For him, most definitely. Through his stories, Nelson is living the life of his imagination. He is reconstructing his world of play and is creating a world that is most pleasing to him. And isn't that the point and power of literacy?

Extensive reading and writing about wolves has nurtured Nelson's literacy. He has read several fiction and nonfiction texts on wolves, including *The Land of Gray Wolf*, *The Wonder of Wolves*, *Jim Ugly*, *Julie of the Wolves*, *Wolves for Kids*, *Amazing Wolves, Dogs, and Foxes*, and others. Nelson also pours through newspapers, cutting out articles about wolves. I suggest he begin a scrapbook. "Good idea," he says, and we three hole punch several sheets of 11" x 18" construction paper. I envision this scrapbook as a bridge . . . a bridge that connects Nelson's life in his world with another world that exists outside of Nelson . . . a shared world.

Nelson has written several texts as well, using a variety of genres including poetry, exposition, letters, and folktales. Drawing has also served as a powerful way for Nelson to represent his world. All are endeavors to create meaning in his life. All nurture his life in his imagination.

Nelson writes this poem in his poetry draft book:

> Wolf, wolf run away
> Oh no
> Today is hunting day.
> Look out Here comes the dogs
> Vicious hunting dogs they are.
> Eek, They're shooting at you
> See, there's a place to hide
> They're gone.

Duckworth speaks of two aspects to providing occasions for wonderful ideas. The first is the willingness to accept ideas. The other is creating a setting that suggests wonderful ideas to children. These ideas come alive for me when Nelson writes in his journal: "I dicided I am going to hibernate this winter but I will go hunting when food is avalibal . . . sighned Sharpclaw." That day Nelson spends time living in the world of his imagination, hibernating under his desk with his journal, author folders, and books. He is defining through his literacy just who he is in this world. I accept his decision to hibernate, knowing his imaginative setting may suggest new ideas to him. It is in this setting that he composes still another wolf piece.

Nelson's world of imagination is nurtured by his parents as well. At the beginning of each year, I invite the parents of the students in my class to write a letter to me about their child through their eyes. Nelson's father writes, "Nelson has always liked to go fast. He loves action and motion. He loves to pretend he is a character associated with action—a Ninja Turtle, a pirate, a pilot, etc. He loves to draw and make stories. He likes the past (dinosaurs, knights) and the future (space explorers, space aliens) but doesn't deal too much with the present (for instance, he doesn't make up stories about his family, friends, home) . . . . Please give Nelson the freedom to pursue his interests. . . ." In another journal entry, Nelson writes, "Me and dad made a big shield with a dragon on it. We made a snow castle. Later me and dad hiked in our snow shoes. We have to chase the gobblins away." Together, Nelson's parents and I support the world in which he lives.

Nelson also brings his imaginary world into the classroom, shares it with the children, and they respond with gusto. After sharing a piece of writing about the habitat and diet of wolves, Nelson invites all the children to meet him at his den to play wolves. At recess, Nelson organizes the children into packs. He gives them names, assigns Alpha

Drawing has also served as a powerful way for Nelson to represent his world. All are endeavors to create meaning in his life. All nurture his life in his imagination.

leaders, and sets up territories. The passion spreads. Many children begin checking out books from the library about wolves. They, too, begin writing stories of wolves, poems about wolves. They embrace the world of wolves. Nelson brings them into the world in which he lives, the world of the imagination, and they read and write and draw in packs around the classroom. It is then that I first observe the children coming together as a whole community and it truly is because of Nelson and his world. They are coming to know each other, caring for each other through the power of passion. It is shared play triggered by a boy's passions and his teacher's respect for this that turned this classroom into a community or, in Nelson's words, a pack.

Nelson's passions are played out in the world of his imagination. He defines who he is through his play, his reading, and his writing. His literacy helps him know himself more deeply. His literacy helps him take a stance and be known in his world.

Bibliography

Calkins, L.M. (1990). *Living between the lines.* Portsmouth, NH: Heinemann.

Dewey, J. (1956). *The child and the curriculum/The school and society (2nd ed.).* Chicago: University of Chicago Press.

Duckworth, E. (1987). *The having of wonderful ideas and other essays on teaching and learning.* New York: Teachers College Press.

Fleischman, S. (1992). *Jim Ugly.* New York: Greenwillow Books.

George, J. C. (1974). *Julie of the wolves.* New York: HarperCollins.

Graves, D. (1991). *Build a literate classroom.* Portsmouth, NH: Heinemann.

Ling, M. (1991). *Amazing wolves, dogs, and foxes.* New York: Knopf.

Locker, T. (1991). *The land of gray wolf.* New York: Dial Books.

Robinson, S.C. (1989). *The wonder of wolves: A story and activity book.* Niwot, CO: Robert Rinehart Publishers.

Tolkien, J.R.R. (1938). *The hobbit.* Boston: Houghton Mifflin.

Wolves for kids. (1991). Minocqua, WI: NorthWord Press.

Daily Schedule

8:50 – 9:15 Message board. Children read message board and write in Living Books—either focused writing or free writing. Children take lunch count, attendance and go to the library.

9:15 – 10:00 Opening. Calendar. World news (children bring in articles). Literature focus and strategy instruction. Strategy instruction is either reading comprehension or writing.

10:00 – 10:50 Literary Focus.

Monday and Wednesday students are in invitation groups with teacher. Invitational groups can be focusing on an author, discussing a piece of work ready for publication, a reading share, a writing share, or providing time for assessment. The teacher invites children to informally chat about reading or do QRIs or assessments. Children not in the invitational group read independently during the time.

Tuesday and Thursday children's book clubs meet.

There are four book clubs in class—all socially based. The teacher is the invisible person with the clipboard.

Friday—children choose a reading strategy (drawn from Pearson and Dole) on Monday and work on that strategy and a response (through art, speaking, writing, or creating your own response) throughout the week. The work on the strategy and response is done at home—Fridays are the time for a big group share of strategies and responses.*

*This is organized this way because the school has a homework policy and all classes have to have some homework—so ours is based around strategies and responses.

10:55 – 11:35 Specials—art, PE, and music each for one week at a time.

11:40 – 11:55 Author's chair or literature circles where children share reading or writing.

12:00 – 12:40 Lunch.

12:45 – 1:00 Author focus for one week or two weeks. Read aloud and study works of one author.

1:00 – 1:50 Math workshop modelled after morning time with literary focus. Children have independent time working with manipulatives and invitational groups. M, T, W, and F.

Thursday the class goes to the library.

1:50 – 2:10 Jobs or choose. 3 days a week do jobs—such as meteorologist, botanist, scientist, poet. Keep the job for a week, done in partners.

2:15 – 2:30 Recess.

2:30 – 3:30 Theme focus.

3:35 – 3:40 Mystery box. Children can bring in anything as long as it is something they can teach us about—encourage the mystery box to relate to the theme focus. Short teacher of the day reads (does duties of day)—pass out care bears for those students who have been especially helpful to each other.

Just on Friday—write exit notes (reflections on the week—what went well, what would you like to change, etc.).

Ways of Creating Authentic Text

As I reflect on the lessons I have learned because of Nelson, I consider what they mean for our classroom. They have resulted in a number of subtle and not so subtle changes, the most powerful of which is my own awareness and attention to the roles of passion and imagination in creating authentic text. As I change and broaden my notions about the power of passion and imagination, our classroom changes, too. Here are some ways I have connected my new understanding to our classroom.

Interviews

Many of us use reading and writing interviews to come to know children and their literacy. While interviewing Nelson, I added several questions on the spot to gather more in-depth information about the role of imagination in writing. This allowed Nelson to blaze the trail in his interview and I simply followed him down his path.

Passion Register

Periodically we come together to simply talk about our passions. We share our new passions and record them on a Passion Register for public display. In this way, children come to know each other and can be on the lookout for new articles, books, and events related to each child's passions. Passion-based learning groups also emerge.

Occasions for Imaginations

I have carved out of our daily schedule a half hour block of time structured specifically for nurturing the imagination. In our classroom it is called Choose. It is a time that honors the inventing of knowledge through a focused use of the imagination, passion, and play. Blocks, paints, books, unifix cubes, tiles, and other materials are available to the children for their imaginative endeavors.

My Living Book

To encourage children to play out and record the texts of their imaginations, we have just begun to keep Living Books. The concept of Living Books was conceived by my friend and colleague Randi Allison, and is based on a notion from Murray's work on day books. It is a place for us to keep notes, pictures, quotes, ideas, drawings, questions, book club passions.

Scrapbooks

Scrapbooks are another way to honor a child's passions. Nelson's scrapbook was an 11"x18" book on white construction paper held together by metal rings. Here he collected and created text, photographs, and illustrations of wolves. Other children then requested scrapbooks, though not everyone has chosen to use one. Encouraging children to keep scrapbooks lets them know we value their passions.

Focus on One Child

Nelson reminds me of the importance of focused classroom inquiry. His statement, "I live in the world of my imagination" caused me to pose questions and rethink notions. Focusing on one child as a springboard for my own learning helped me think more deeply about my teaching.

Lingering Questions

- How might I create occasions to nurture "the having of wonderful ideas"? (Duckworth's language)

- What systems/rituals in our classrooms inhibit or squelch children's passions and imaginations?

- Where do curriculum, imagination, and passion intersect? What is their relationship to each other?

- What are authentic outcomes of passion-based learning?

- How do I structure passion-based learning groups so they are focused and engaged, yet inclusive of the children's agenda?

In the last thirty years, there have been radical changes in the field of language arts. Most of this change has come about because we know so much more now than we did then. By collectively asking "How?" and "What?", we have come to understand how language is learned and how it is used. We have learned what we can do to support ourselves and others as language learners. This increased knowledge base has affected how we think about language arts, how we talk about language arts, and how we act on what we know. We talk now of classrooms that support literacy learning, of the need for people to see themselves as readers and writers, and for people to choose to read and to write. We even have a new word for people who do not make that choice; we refer to them as aliterate.

In this volume of *Primary Voices K–6*, Donald Graves, Marsha Winship, Susan Stires, Tom Tracy, and Colleen Buddy share with us their experiences, thoughts, and ideas about writing. In so doing, they push our thinking into territory that is newer still. "Why do we write?" they ask. And then they share with us the answers they have worked out for themselves. We write, they suggest, in order to understand and in order to be understood. We write because we have a need to do so. We write because we are passionately connected to the world we live in and to the worlds we create.

Caring passionately, Donald Graves tells us about B. J. Sherman who wrote to "make sense" of having to move from his mother's house to his father's. Tom Tracy explains how Kyle's writing helped him deal with the death of his grandmother. Colleen Buddy describes Nelson's decision to write a story in which the wolf is the hero. Susan Stires explains about Joe's connection to the "windbegin." Marsha Winship shows us the power of letting children pursue their own interests when writing.

Their reasons, their explanations for writing, are noticeably different from the reasons and explanations that were offered a decade ago. They are different because they encompass a need, a want, a desire, a passion that we have only recently acknowledged. These new reasons help us understand aspects of writing that we have not understood before. They help us to understand what drives the writing, what powers the re-visioning, what it means for a text to have voice. Too, they allow us to ask new questions, questions about learning to write, questions about supporting others as writers.

We found ourselves, for example, thinking about the relationship between revision and passion. Are the students who are "passion hot" about their writing the same students who are able to be "critical cold" and to revise and revise and revise until their piece meets their vision? Is the reverse true, that you cannot be "critical cold" unless you are "passion hot?" Is that what causes revision to bog down? We wonder about time. How much time do writers need to discover what it is they need to say? To find out what they are "passion hot" about? To make the "critical cold" changes they need to make? How will we know what is too much time and too little? How will we know if the time is worth giving? We wonder about curriculum. What are we really supposed to be teaching? Just what is the function of school? Should we try to "cover" the content in the curriculum guide?; use an inquiry approach, helping students to discover their own questions?; strike some sort of balance between the two? How should we balance our writing with the other demands on our time? We wonder about organization. Does there need to be a time called

Diane Stephens

Kathy Meyer Reimer

Karen Smith

What these articles suggest is that, as literacy educators, we are just beginning to ask the right questions.

"writing"? Or is that something that should be happening all day? If we give it a time, are we honoring that which published authors do for themselves (set aside time to write) or are we creating artificial boundaries?

Most of all, we wonder and worry about teaching. Donald Graves suggests that to help students connect writing to their lives we need to "begin with our own literacy." He asks us to be writers ourselves and to share our struggles with our students. We know that means sharing the things we are "passion hot" about. It means giving ourselves the time to find out what those things are. Where do we find the time? Draw the boundaries? What if we are working on something that is too personal to share? And what are we supposed to do during writing time if we are the kind of writer who needs silence and privacy in order to write? Do writing teachers have to write in public?

It would be possible for us, as editors, to end this section by moving from the realities of hard questions to the fantasy, the fiction, of easy, store-bought answers. But what these articles suggest is that there are no neat and tidy answers. Indeed, what these articles suggest is that, as literacy educators, we are just beginning to ask the right questions. We all want children to be "passion hot," to write because they need to write. And we want those children to continue to see

themselves as writers and to write into adulthood. We want that for ourselves as well. And we are not really sure how to do that. We do have a sense of how to begin. We believe Don when he says we need to start with ourselves and that writing is about connections and choice. We believe Marsha when she says if learners don't venture into the unknown, they won't grow, change, learn. We believe Tom when he tells us that we need to stir that deep down pot within ourselves. We believe Colleen when she tells us that what is authentic is passionate. We believe Susan when she tells us as visual thinking, writing helps us learn.

So now, what each of us needs to do for ourselves is to find courage and a way to begin. If we haven't written, we could pick a time to start. If we have written, but not shared, we could pick a place and a person and read what we've written. If we've written and shared, but kept our writing out of the classroom, we could pick a piece and a time and bring our text and ourselves into the classroom. It's scary just to write these words. We can hear Susan telling us that visual writing identifies the creator and points in their direction. That makes us feel vulnerable. But we know that it's necessary to move forward with the fear. Our students deserve to learn that learning is authentic, that it connects to their lives, that it is driven by passion and by caring. And, scared or not, it's our job to help them.

Bibliography

Atwell, N. (Ed.). (1990). *Coming to know: Writing to learn in the intermediate grades*. Portsmouth, NH: Heinemann.

Bagge-Rynerson, B. (1992). This fish is so strange to me: The use of the science journal. In T. Newkirk (Ed.), *Workshop 4: The teacher as researcher* (pp. 88–99). Portsmouth, NH: Heinemann.

Burk, D., Snider, A., & Symonds, P. (1991). *Math excursions 1*. Portsmouth, NH: Heinemann.

Burk, D., Snider, A., & Symonds, P. (1991). *Math excursions 2*. Portsmouth, NH: Heinemann.

Burk, D., Snider, A., & Symonds, P. (1992). *Math excursions K*. Portsmouth, NH: Heinemann.

Cairney, T. (1990). Intertextuality: Infectious echoes from the past. *The Reading Teacher, 43*, 478–484.

Doris, E. (1991). *Doing what scientists do: Children learn to investigate their world*. Portsmouth, NH: Heinemann.

Fulwiler, T. (Ed.). (1987). *The journal book*. Upper Montclair, NJ: Boynton/Cook.

Giacobbe, M. E. (1986). Learning to write and writing to learn in the elementary school. In A. R. Petrosky & D. Bartholomae (Eds.), *The teaching of writing: Eighty-fifth yearbook of the National Society for the Study of Education*. Chicago: University of Chicago Press.

Graves, D. H. (1989). *Investigate nonfiction*. Portsmouth, NH: Heinemann.

Heard, G. (1989). *For the good of the earth and sun: Teaching poetry*. Portsmouth, NH: Heinemann.

LINX learning system. (1993). Waldoboro, ME: The Science Source.

Martin, N., Newton, B., D'Arcy, P., & Parker, R. (1976). *Writing and learning across the curriculum, 11–16*. Upper Montclair, NJ: Boynton/Cook.

Pappas, C. C., Kiefer, B. Z., & Levstik, L. S. (1990). *An integrated language perspective in the elementary school: Theory into action*. New York: Longman.

Skinner, P. (1991). *What's your problem: Posing and solving mathematical problems, K–2*. Portsmouth, NH: Heinemann.

Whitin, D., Mills, H., & O'Keefe, T. (1990). *Living and learning mathematics: Stories and strategies for supporting mathematical literacy*. Portsmouth, NH: Heinemann.

Wilde, J. (1988). The written report: Old wine in new bottles. In T. Newkirk & N. Atwell (Eds.), *Understanding writing: Ways of observing, learning, and teaching* (2nd ed.) (pp. 179–190). Portsmouth, NH: Heinemann.

Winograd, K. (1992, November). *Strategies and techniques that support student written problems*. Address to National Council of Teachers of English, Louisville, KY.

HEINEMANN

Eddie's Cat

Eddie's cat has kept me company for the past quarter century. The faded pastel with its brown and white body and white tail occupied spots, some sunny, some not, on the walls of several rented flats. In 1975 he graduated to the first wall I actually owned, a white wall in a basement flat in London's North Kensington where every summer the noise of the Notting Hill carnival filled the street outside

and flowed down the stone steps to the basement flat. A few years later he moved to his first house. A two-up, two-down flat-fronted Regency house with cast-iron balconies outside the two upstairs windows. A historic house, John Keats had lived there briefly during the summer of 1820, long enough to have had his first hemorrhage there. ("Yes love, we did have a plaque but it got blown away during the war," said the old lady who owned the house before me.)

These days, and for the past thirteen years, Eddie's cat has cast his quizzical gaze on his native land from the other side of the Atlantic—three thousand miles from St. James Primary School, Muswell Hill, North London, where in my first year of teaching I taught the seven-year-old Eddie. Or rather, failed to teach him. Why was a child so well able to express himself verbally and artistically, seemingly at such a loss when asked to write, or read, or do math? My year of postgraduate teacher training hadn't prepared me for Eddie. It hadn't prepared me for much, in fact. It certainly hadn't prepared me for the sense of isolation I would feel every morning as I entered that empty classroom and stared at the wooden desks with their metal runners and attached benches (no easy feat to rearrange those pieces of furniture from

straight rows to groups). My colleagues were no help. They must have resented the young new teacher who spurned the reading scheme and had the ridiculous notion that children could learn to read from library books instead. And seated in groups rather than in rows.

At the beginning of the summer term the school moved from its Victorian red brick building to a new site. When the teachers first visited the new school building and saw that the old desks were to be replaced with trapezoid tables, two of which would fit together to provide seating for a group of six children, they became more animated than I had seen them all year. How could these tables be arranged in rows? Where would the children store their books? Fortunately a solution was soon found, but not before one teacher had gasped with horror ". . . but, we will have to teach them all individually." That was when I realized my fascination with children's learning might find a stronger voice out of the classroom and in publishing.

Every time I look at Eddie's cat I am reminded of that time, and of what I didn't know then, and of what I still don't know now. But I do know that if wise teachers write good books about teaching and learning, books that are based on children and how they learn, and how teachers can best support that learning, then struggling teachers won't feel quite so isolated. And nor will seasoned teachers who may be the only person in their building trying to make changes in their teaching. Through reading about how another teacher has worked with a child like Eddie they may get insights into how to reach their *own* Eddies.

Philippa Stratton

Editor-in-Chief,
Heinemann

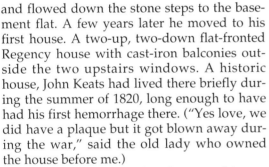

PrimaryVoices K-6

Volume 1 Number 2 • NOVEMBER 1993

Revising for Meaning

Responding to Language

Monitoring Learning

Understanding Conventions

Preparing for Meaning

Constructing Meaning

MEANINGFUL CHANGE

Improving Teaching and Learning

NATIONAL COUNCIL OF TEACHERS OF ENGLISH

CONTENTS

Thanks to our 1993–94 Sponsors
Heinemann Educational Books, Inc.   Scholastic, Inc.

Primary Voices K–6 is published four times a year in January, April, August, and November by the National Council of Teachers of English, 1111 W. Kenyon Road, Urbana, Illinois 61801-1096. Annual subscription is $15. Single copy, $6.00 (member price $5.00). Add $3 per year for Canadian and all other international postage. Remittances should be made payable to NCTE by check, money order, or bank draft in United States currency.

Communications regarding orders, subscriptions, single copies, change of address, and permission to reprint should be addressed to *Primary Voices K–6*, NCTE, 1111 W. Kenyon Road, Urbana, Illinois 61801-1096. POSTMASTER: Send address changes to *Primary Voices K–6*, NCTE, 1111 W. Kenyon Road, Urbana, Illinois 61801-1096. Application to mail at second-class postage rates is pending at Urbana, Illinois.

 Printed on recycled paper

A MESSAGE FROM THE EDITORS

When we were asked to put together this issue of *Primary Voices K–6*, we were excited about the chance to share with a much larger community some of the ideas that we explore monthly in our Rutgers Literacy Curriculum Network. We welcomed the opportunity to reflect on some of our ideas with the care and thoughtfulness that writing about them requires. Finding a central topic was quite simply a matter of identifying what it is that brought our Network of fifty school districts together in the first place, and what it is that keeps us going—change. Ironically, it is the search for meaningful and constructive *change*, a key factor affecting English/language arts education today, that emerges as the most consistent and unifying element binding us together.

Our Network gives us the chance to learn from some of the finest researchers in our field. This is critically important. We want our change to be well-informed. Equally important, however, is the opportunity to learn from one another. We find that the new understandings we generate as we share one another's successes and pitfalls are helpful and encouraging. For most of us, the need for professional support is made especially critical through the realization that we are moving into areas for which we have a solid research base but relatively few blueprints or models.

One of the most important lessons we have learned about making change in education is that a single teacher working alone can make significant and positive change for the students he or she teaches. Groups of teachers, working together and with parents, administrators, university professors, and students, can make significant changes for many more students. We decided to use this opportunity to ask Network members to write about their change experiences. Our intent is to further explore the connections people have made across classrooms, school buildings, and districts throughout the State of New Jersey as they attempt to improve teaching and learning. This issue of *Primary Voices K–6* allows us to take our conversation beyond the borders of New Jersey, to continue the dialogue with others facing similar challenges in the broader language arts community.

Dorothy S. Strickland
Joanne K. Monroe
Judith J. Wood

Dorothy S. Strickland

Joanne K. Monroe

Judith J. Wood

NETWORKING FOR CHANGE: THE RUTGERS LITERACY CURRICULUM NETWORK

Dorothy S. Strickland

Professor of
Reading, Rutgers,
The State
University of
New Jersey

Looking for Change?
Take a Second Look!

The following was shared by Barbara Burns, a student of mine at Rutgers University, who opted to observe in several "whole language" classrooms as part of a class project. In one school, she was advised by the principal that visiting the two second-grade teachers would be very useful. He explained that since these teachers were already far along the road to whole language, a great deal could be learned from them. Indeed, my student did learn a great deal from this visit. Neither of us believes that it was quite what the principal had in mind, however.

Both of these teachers had physically inviting classrooms. Student desks were arranged in clusters. Children's work adorned the walls. Bookcases and other materials were arranged to create centers of activities. A book corner with an abundance of literature, a nature center, and a well-equipped art area were evidence of the kind of thoughtful planning required to achieve a print-rich, child-centered environment. Barbara spent one full morning in each of these classrooms. She learned very quickly that the two classrooms, so similar in appearance, were diametrically opposed in the kind of education being offered.

Perhaps the best way to characterize the classroom of Teacher A is by its variety and shared control. Children were observed working as a whole group, in small groups led by the teacher or by a child, and in one-to-one teacher–child or peer conferences. On display were many individual pieces of children's work, as well as charts and graphs used to record information related to topics under study. Barbara was most impressed by the children's ability to "take charge" of so many aspects of what occurred. When asked how she managed to get them to this point, Mrs. A. answered with a chuckle, "Very slowly!"

Teacher B, on the other hand, conducted a very skills-based, teacher-controlled program despite the physical appearance of her room. Indeed, a closer look at the children's work on the walls revealed a series of very similar "best" papers on display. When asked why the centers were not in use, Teacher B explained, "These children are not ready to learn via centers. They need much more whole group instruction." As a result, except for one very brief recess period, the children spent the entire morning working at their desks with Teacher B directing every aspect of instruction.

Both teachers talked about how their teaching had changed in recent years and both professed to love whole language. When asked about the staff development they had received in order to teach this way, both teachers mentioned the two staff development days offered each year by the district. They also mentioned some workshops at a nearby university they had attended. With further probing, Barbara learned that Teacher A also belonged to a study group that met on a regular basis to read and discuss new ideas and share concerns. Barbara reported being surprised that, of the two teachers, it was Teacher A who was the more tentative about her progress. She readily acknowledged that although she generally felt good about what she was doing, there were many things that simply were not working as well as she had hoped and many questions that remain unresolved.

Barbara's report led to one of the most interesting class discussions of the semester. We talked about change: What does it really mean to change? Is the process the same for everyone? What is the difference between real change and superficial change? What can account for a principal who cannot tell the difference? How is it possible for people to sincerely believe they have changed, when they obviously have not? What must be in place for genuine change to occur? Is there a danger in encouraging people to make surface level changes before they really understand the philosophy that underlies what they do? The questions went on and on. The discussion was made even more interesting by the fact that most of these students were, themselves, undergoing a process of change. Indeed, most were being asked to become a very different kind of teacher from those they had known and (for the most part) respected in the past.

At the end of our discussion, we summarized a few of the key ideas we could all agree on:

1. For change to be effective, it must be focused.

2. Change for its own sake is meaningless; there must be a vision.

3. Change takes time and reflection.

4. Change requires encouragement and support.

5. Curriculum change is never completed.

Barbara's report served as a catalyst for us to summarize and crystallize many of the ideas we had shared throughout the semester. For some, it appeared that this may have been a real turning point, as they began to think and talk about the teacher they wanted to be.

New Directions in the Language Arts Curriculum

Throughout the United States, school districts are wrestling with the same questions that we struggled with in our class discussion. Many are attempting to move toward more holistic instruction. As with most things, they are finding a great deal of variability among schools within a district and among the classrooms within a school. Some of the variability is the natural result of moving in an instructional direction that, by its very nature, is not standardized. Some variability is the result of the need to address genuine dilemmas, such as the mismatch that frequently occurs when instruction changes but the assessment and reporting of student progress do not. Some of the variability can be attributed to the lack of ongoing, in-depth staff development needed to enable teachers and adminis-

Is there a danger in encouraging people to make surface level changes before they really understand the philosophy that underlies what they do?

trators to shift from a paradigm that requires adherence to a strict manual of instructions to one that gives *them* the responsibility for making key instructional decisions.

Curriculum Coordinator, Key Catalyst for Change

Wherever school districts are changing their curricula, you can be certain that the Language Arts Curriculum Coordinator, or someone with a similar title and duties, has the major responsibility for seeing that the desired change does occur. Faced with the task of providing services to large numbers of schools, teachers, and students, these individuals are constantly making major decisions that eventually affect the entire school district. Highly trained, many with doctoral degrees, these administrator/supervisors are key instructional leaders in their districts. They are expected to keep the district current, but not radical or faddish; provide structure, but allow for individual flexibility; set direction, but make sure everyone shares in the decision making; and assuage reluctant teachers and administrators, while nudging them to keep an open mind. In many districts, the curriculum coordinator may even be the individual who acts as a key liaison to the School Board and to parent groups in order to involve them in the process. Little wonder that most say it is no longer enough to be well informed in the English language arts. They must be astute about the change process as well.

Because their job responsibilities are rather unique within their districts, many coordinators have found it helpful to form networks across district lines. Establishing ties with others who face similar challenges serves to keep them informed and revitalized.

The Rutgers Literacy Curriculum Network

The Rutgers Literacy Curriculum Network is a network of school districts interested in exploring literacy initiatives related to literature-based curricula, process approaches to reading and writing, whole language philosophy and practice, literacy across the curriculum, and assessment. Aimed primarily at the curriculum coordinator, the Network serves as a vehicle for sharing information with curriculum personnel, administrators and supervisors, and classroom teachers from school districts throughout New Jersey.

The Network acts as a catalyst to support staff and curriculum development, materials selection, and the general knowledge base at the district level. Activated in September, 1990, over fifty school districts throughout New Jersey are involved. Those involved in the Network meet monthly to interact with nationally known speakers as well as local educators who are engaged in work of interest to the group. Speakers have included Bess Altwerger, Ethel Buchanan, Ralph Fletcher, Jane Hansen, Bill Harp, Donna Ogle, Ralph Peterson, Linda Rief, and Carol Santa.

Other activities include discussion study groups; after-school workshops; and the sharing of information about upcoming events, effective workshop presenters, and publications of mutual interest. Many of the members have presented workshops in each other's districts and many have arranged for teacher visitations across districts. Cross visitation not only serves as an excellent staff development tool, it allows curriculum coordinators to highlight some of the good things going on in their districts.

Little wonder that most say it is no longer enough to be well informed in the English language arts. They must be astute about the change process as well.

What We Are Learning about Change

The lessons we are learning in our Network are many. Here are some key factors we keep in mind.

1. *Change takes time.* Planning must involve multi-year intervals. Along the way, people need time to exchange views and solve problems together. The tensions that emerge as people strive to learn new skills and behaviors are a necessary part of the process. We have learned to be wary of artificial "surface trappings" indicative of superficial performance rather than real change. Simplistic statements such as, "I'm whole language, I don't use basals," make us shudder.

2. *A shared vision is essential.* Shared decision making and continuing dialogue help people to feel they are part of the process. While it is important to learn what other districts are doing, eventually each district must construct its own reality of what it wants to be. For some, it may appear to be "reinventing the wheel." Involvement in the process, however, helps create the much needed will to change as it informs the why and how of change.

3. *Focus on specific areas of concern.* It is important to systematically focus on specific areas of concern within the shared vision of where you want to be. Massive, multifaceted changes may prove overwhelming. We noticed that the implementation of a process approach to the teaching of writing caused many teachers to question and change the way they taught reading. When teachers truly understand the theoretical base for their practice, new areas of inquiry and opportunities for change naturally evolve.

Of course, we center on knowledge as a key element of change—the growth of our own knowledge and our ability to help others become better informed. Since we value our time together, we

> **When teachers truly understand the theoretical base for their practice, new areas of inquiry and opportunities for change naturally evolve.**

rarely use it to voice our frustrations about fiscal constraints, internal district politics, and faculty inertia. Certainly, these factors exist in all our districts to some extent. But, we also see a growing sense of professionalism among the teachers with whom we work. Increasingly, we are observing and participating in classrooms where teachers and students are excited about teaching and learning. Children talk about books and authors with great enthusiasm and assurance. Written stories and reports are completed with great care for both content and the conventions of written composition. Students are reading and writing because they want to, not simply because they are required to.

After visiting these classrooms we come away saying, "There is something special going on here. We want to support it and make it spread throughout the district." We remain hopeful about the possibilities for significant, enduring change. We feel that our Network is one key element in making it happen.

Lingering Questions

1. How can language arts coordinators help teachers and administrators recognize the difference between surface-level and genuine change in teaching practices?

2. To what extent can key issues, such as the degree of shared control in the classroom, be the decision of individual teachers? Established by building principals? District coordinators?

3. Can a genuine theoretical shift occur through dialogue alone, or does it require some type of action? Will teachers, who have yet to make even superficial changes in their teaching, be able to make theoretical shifts?

TAKING THE CHALLENGE: ONE DISTRICT'S JOURNEY THROUGH CHANGE

There is extraordinary unanimity surrounding the belief that American education should change. Ten years ago, *A Nation at Risk* launched a vigorous, decade-long debate over schools and their relationship to the social, economic, and intellectual health of our nation. After so long, after so much said, so little has changed. Can schools meet the challenge? Can schools change? *Yes*.

This is the story of one district's journey through a major shift in English language arts education, K–12. It has required a major paradigm shift in how students learn. It has required new curriculum, new instruction, new materials, new assessment, new reporting, and it has required significant support for both the professional and parental communities. It began approximately fifteen years ago; it hasn't ended.

What did we learn along the way from theorists in the field and our own experience in change? We developed, among other things, a shared perception that change is needed.

Developing a Shared Belief Structure

In 1978, our Superintendent did a follow-up study of graduates of our high school. Generally, graduates felt very positive about their experience—with one glaring exception. They felt they were not taught to write at the level demanded by college work. This galvanized the English department and its new leadership.

Through a grant from the federal government, a committee from within the high school English department began to learn. They read widely; they spent time learning from, among others, Janet Emig, Nancy Sommers, and James Moffett. They experimented in their own classrooms; they took the talk-time necessary to build a shared belief structure about how students come to know how to write.

The publicity that grew out of this grant and the effort it funded generated another site where change was perceived as needed. The Assistant Superintendent for Elementary Education was feeling some pressure about writing instruction at the elementary level. He turned to an elementary teacher who was completing her doctorate in English Education under Janet Emig. Under this teacher's leadership, a group of elementary teachers spent a year reading, listening, experimenting, and talking. While most elementary teachers felt they knew how to teach reading, most felt less secure about the teaching of writing. Here was a recognized need to change. As they read, talked, and listened, a common belief structure emerged about how students learn, what they should learn, and how they are best taught and assessed. Through the leadership of the elementary teacher and the high school department chair, the staff was given, as one of them put it, the "gift of time" to read and reflect as professionals.

Defining Informed Practice

Both the elementary and high school groups now faced the task of sharing the

E. Everett Kline

Assistant Superintendant, School District of South Orange and Maplewood, New Jersey

new belief structure with the staff, translating the new beliefs into written curriculum, and developing a meaningful assessment.

To develop a more widely shared belief structure among all staff, the elementary committee members distributed a few selected readings to the staff. They conducted a workshop where, in grade-level breakout sessions, there were articles discussed, important ideas identified, and consideration given as to how these ideas should inform practice. A university-level educator circulated among the groups and spoke to the assembled elementary faculties, affirming the important ideas he had heard in the sessions. The New Jersey Writing Project was held, on-site, tuition free, for four summers.

At the high school level, the group used department meetings to discuss similar materials. Student work was collected and discussed. Ultimately, this work became the basis for new texts in the department's writing program.

To this model was added a new component. Informed practice was demonstrated for every elementary teacher and every high school teacher. Time was provided after each session to reflect on how the theory learned in earlier discussions informed the practice of the classroom lesson.

Both committees set to work writing their new curriculum. As this task began, mistakes began to emerge. Two curricula were written. While informed by common beliefs, there was no district-wide coordination. More serious, what of grades 6–8, the middle schools? There the staff had been given no opportunity to explore and, through exploring, to question their beliefs. As public praise grew for the high school and elementary efforts and as central administration belatedly grafted the middle school onto the high school effort, it appeared to the

6–8 teachers that they were under assault from all sides. Naturally, strong defenses against change arose in the middle schools.

As program development proceeded, the question arose: "Is it working?" The Board president queried: "It all sounds very heady for the participants, but is it making a difference with kids?" An assessment mechanism was called for. Here, the leadership of the two committees collaborated. Student achievement and student attitudes were to be analyzed. It was quickly acknowledged that if standardized tests were to be used to measure achievement, change would be sacrificed. New beliefs could not be seriously entertained if the assessment was informed by the very beliefs that staff members were being urged to abandon. Standardized tests would continue to have a place but *not* in the assessment of writing. Students were asked to write from a common prompt at the beginning of grade three and again at the end of grade four. Similar samples were gathered from students at grades seven and eight, and grades ten and eleven. This allowed the measurement of growth over two school years. At the end of the two years, a random sampling of the students was made and their papers from each of the paired grade levels were scored holistically and without knowledge of which papers represented the pre- and the post-learning experience. Student achievement was apparent (except at the middle schools). Student attitudes were gathered through interviews and surveys at the same times and in the same grades. The initial student opinionnaires were mostly encouraging. Students were telling us they liked to write (except in the middle schools). At one elementary school, writing workshop was the favorite activity; at another, it was second only to lunch.

It was quickly acknowledged that if standardized tests were to be used to measure achievement, change would be sacrificed.

Students were using journals to record and work through personal and academic problems.

Staff development had been initiated; a curriculum had been written; a modest assessment mechanism had been set out. Classroom practice was beginning to change.

Organizing for Change

As a result of a reorganization in the central office, a single assistant superintendent for instruction and learning assessed the state of curriculum as a whole in the district, with a particular eye to providing the necessary support for this project. Understanding that elementary teachers and administrators cannot address multiple, unrelated program changes at one time, the decision was made to drop several initiatives already underway and to focus on the writing program. This meant saying no to good ideas but it was necessary to focus if fundamental change was to happen in language arts.

Second, a committee of teachers, program leaders, and building administrators were charged with developing a model for the development, implementation, and evaluation of all curriculum, K–12. They were told to focus on what a student should know and how it came to be known, and to place at least as much attention on implementation and assessment as on development. They were given three months.

Third, in addition to focusing program and staff development funds on writing, technical assistance was redistributed to increase equity. The high school retained its department chair; for the K–8 grades, we hired a director of English language arts. Through the creation of the K–8 director, we linked middle school to the more child-centered elementary schools.

Linking Change

As informed practice found its way into more classrooms, teachers at the elementary level began to question how reading was being taught. "If writing workshop acknowledges that students must make meaning and do so best with rich, relevant experiences, something is wrong with the way we teach reading."

To support these questions and insights, a small, voluntary, summer workshop on reading was offered; over half of the elementary staff applied for less than twenty spaces. Next, a new forty-five hour, after-school course was offered by the new director of language arts. The local university offered three graduate credits. The course linked the changes in instruction about writing, reading, and speaking. The teachers began with knowledge in the field; they saw practice modeled in the course, in their own classrooms, and in visits to colleagues. They planned collaboratively. They were coached as they taught their first whole-language lessons. Every term, we offered one section of this course; we always ran two and had a waiting list.

The district signaled that this approach to English language arts was a district priority. Building budgets were reviewed and, when necessary, revised to make sure that the phenomenal amount spent on workbooks was now being redirected to make each classroom an integrated language arts classroom.

To link this budget-building process and the staff supervision process more closely to the program change, all building level administrators, the superintendent, and the assistant superintendent were given a workshop spanning eight half-days on what one should see in an integrated language arts classroom. The administration became that necessary ingredient for ensuring teachers an excit-

"If writing workshop acknowledges that students must make meaning and do so best with rich, relevant experiences, something is wrong with the way we teach reading."

ing, collegial community engaged in positive change in each building. Finally, report cards and special education IEPs were revised to better reflect the new approaches.

At about the same time, an assessment of the K–12 mathematics curriculum was begun. It was guided by the new model for curriculum development and was informed by the same theory of learning as had informed the language arts changes. This time change was much easier. As one excited elementary teacher said, "This is just a math workshop. It's just like reading and writing." Through linked change, no paradigm shift was required; only practice was modified and in very understandable ways.

Correcting Early Mistakes

A new Language Arts Leadership Team of teachers, principals, and parents was appointed by the director and department chair to write an integrated language arts curriculum, K–12. They, too, read and listened, in this instance to Toby Fulwiler, Ralph Peterson, a local story teller, and a library/media specialist in children's literature. They developed guiding principles that would become the organizing strands running across all grades in the new curriculum. Figure 1 names the six strands and indicates the interactions among them.

The marginalized middle school staff remained unchanged. The Assistant Superintendent and Director of Language Arts, K–8, formally met with each middle school principal in that principal's building. The Assistant Superintendent directed the principal to develop, with staff, within three weeks, an action plan for implementing an integrated language arts curriculum at that level. The director offered help. Shortly thereafter, the middle school staff began to join the forty-five hour course. Ultimately, they, like

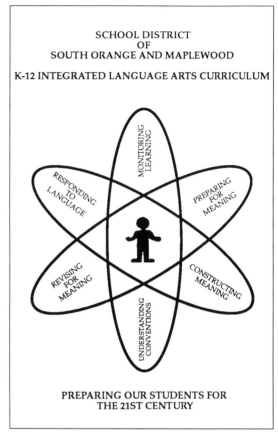

SCHOOL DISTRICT
OF
SOUTH ORANGE AND MAPLEWOOD

K-12 INTEGRATED LANGUAGE ARTS CURRICULUM

MONITORING LEARNING

RESPONDING TO LANGUAGE

PREPARING FOR MEANING

REVISING FOR MEANING

CONSTRUCTING MEANING

UNDERSTANDING CONVENTIONS

PREPARING OUR STUDENTS FOR
THE 21ST CENTURY

Figure 1.

their elementary level colleagues, brought the special education teachers into this mainstream.

The Test

The staying power of the emerging paradigm was illustrated by the fact that it withstood changes in administrative staff and, at one point, public alarm at the lack of spelling books, workbooks, and permanent reading groups. The teachers and building principals rallied. "We can never go back." Teachers, administrators, as well as students, clearly articulated the value of the change to student learning. The public was persuaded. The Board of Education unanimously approved the new curriculum. The change was formally acknowledged.

Summary

We had been changing for a decade. Were we done? No. We had learned that curriculum is *never* finished. We are now working to develop a better portfolio assessment process, K–12. We are working, through a grant, to integrate contemporary poetry into the curriculum. We are, again, revising the report card.

That has been our journey. To review it here is of little value unless we can identify the underlying principles of change that should be remembered anytime curriculum revision is undertaken. Helpful in synthesizing our experience has been the work of Michael Fullan, Gene Hall, Bruce Joyce, and Beverly Showers. Collectively, they cite the need to address the following three questions that all teachers have as they confront change:

1. *What is the change and what are the theoretical underpinnings that guide it in practice?*

They tell us that clarity is necessary if accurate vision of the change is to be widely shared and implemented. They tell us theory is necessary if the knowledge is to become transferable for use in any class or any new set of circumstances. In our experience, we read and listened to Moffett, Emig, Sommers, Fulwiler, Peterson, etc. It was important that we began with the reading, not the consultant. This enabled us to set our agenda and invite the consultant into our context. Further, we found that we needed time to talk after we had read. We learned that, as Alan Purves tells us, "It takes two to read a book."

All parties must be a part of addressing the question: teachers, administrators, and parents. All of them must be given a variety of entry points as they begin the change process. Entry points we used were readings and staff development—for the entire staff, for all grade levels, and for groups who shared a common interest or need. Some staff had to be directed to enter the change process. Yet, all are valid entry points; all will probably be needed.

2. *What does the change look like in practice?*

Here the critical terms are modeling and demonstration. Fullen et al. tells us these are necessary so that teachers can see the change in concrete form and be reassured that it is, in fact, possible. They tell us that an answer is necessary so that the effect of the change on students can be seen. Only then can the value of the change be established. Only then will the professional really "buy in." Modeling and demonstration are necessary so that teachers can come to develop an increasingly concrete and shared language regarding the change. Only with this shared language can the teachers begin to talk about the change and come to share a vision.

We modeled in classrooms and at every inservice session. In the debriefing sessions that followed every presentation, we linked the theory to what had just been seen. In addressing the question, we again included teachers, administrators, and parents.

3. *How can I do it and get better?*

Here the critical terms are practice and coaching. The research of Fullan et al. shows that a change in behavior frequently precedes a change in beliefs. As a behavior is practiced, it gradually becomes internalized. When coaching is supplied by knowledgeable people in a risk-free environment, teachers receive the psychological support to deal with the anxiety change can bring. The degree to which fundamental changes in attitudes and beliefs take place is directly

It was important that we began with the reading, not the consultant. This enabled us to set our agenda and invite the consultant into our context.

related to the time spent practicing a new behavior and to the frequency of support.

In our experience, we hired a Director of Language Arts, K–8, and assigned coaching responsibilities to this person and the high school department chair. The job description for the director indicated that a minimum of one-half of that person's time must be spent demonstrating and coaching. Recently, we recognized that we needed more; thus, we reorganized to provide an English language arts lead teacher at both the elementary and middle school levels. The lead teachers demonstrate and coach.

In addition to these three questions, the researchers suggest that there are several parameters on the process:

1. *The district's focus must be narrow and clear.* We had to cut the number of projects under way in the district. We had to generate peer and central office pressure for change.

2. *Multiple changes should be linked.* We made sure that the same learning theory informed our change in language arts and mathematics. We made sure that the presentations regarding every program contained a common litany regarding how children learn. We worked to link change in the curriculum to instruction, budget, supervision, reporting, building leadership, and special students' individual educational plans.

3. *More money will be required for curriculum implementation than for curriculum development.* We read, we talked, we researched—in the summer, after school, and during the day; the whole staff and small grade-level and shared-needs groups. We underwrote attendance at conferences. Every building budget contained staff development money for this effort. We had to target language arts as a high budget priority so that the teachers

entering the change would have the richness of materials necessary for them to find meaning and satisfaction in its implementation.

4. *Change takes place within a larger, systemic context.* If change in one part is to succeed, other institutional changes will be required. We had to change our text materials, our assessment process, our classroom strategies, and our administrative structure.

5. *There is a political component to curriculum development and implementation.* At one point we almost lost our program because we ignored the parents' need to understand and be reassured about the change. As Dorothy Strickland states in her lead article, "Shared decision making and continuing dialogue help people to feel they are part of the process." The teachers at Crim School ("Learning Is a Family Affair," p. 23) recognized this when they began their Family Language program. Seeing the development of motivated learners based on a "scaffold" of parents, peers, and community members, these teachers remind us that making the parents our partners increases our chance of success.

6. *Curriculum is never finished.* We continue to identify what we need to know. We continue to learn from Grant Wiggins, Sharon Olds, Galway Kinnell, and Tori Derricotte. We continue to learn from each other.

7. *Recognize that change takes time.* We began almost a decade and a half ago.

To the questions of Fullan, Hall, Joyce, and Showers, I add two more questions I feel compelled to answer:

1. *Why did it take so long if the research on change is so clear?*

... these teachers remind us that making the parents our partners increases our chance of success.

I'm indebted to Michael Fullan for providing George Bernard Shaw's answer to this question, "Reformers have the idea that change can be achieved by brute sanity." It doesn't happen that way. Be assured, however, that subsequent changes are taking place in about one-third the time. We've linked change, and we've learned how to do it better.

2. *Has it all been worth it?*

Yes. At those moments when I get most discouraged, I remember back to what a group of fifth graders told a parent meeting about what it means to be writers. I remember the story told to me by a special education teacher about one of her students bringing a book to share with her because the student wanted to discuss it with someone. I remember the students in a class who, when asked what group they would be in if the class reinstated permanent reading groups, all answered that they would be in the top group. That's confident growth. It's been worth it.

Bibliography

Fullan, M. (1991). *The new meaning of educational change.* New York: Teachers College Press.

Fullan, M. (1985). Change processes and strategies at the local level. *The Elementary School Journal, 85,* 391–419.

Hall, G. E., & Hord, S. M. (1987). *Change in schools: Facilitating the process.* Albany: The State University of New York Press.

Hall, G. E., & Loucks, S. F. (1977). A developmental model for determining whether the treatment is actually implemented. *American Educational Research Journal, 14,* 263–276.

Hall, G. E., & Loucks, S. F. (1981). Program definition and adaptation: Implications for inservice. *Journal of Research and Development in Education, 14,* 46–58.

Joyce, B., & Showers, B. (1982). The coaching of teaching. *Educational Leadership, 40,* 4–8.

Joyce, B., & Showers, B. (1982). Transfer of training: The contribution of coaching. *Journal of Education, 163,* 163–172.

Miles, M. B. (1983). Unraveling the mystery of institutionalization. *Educational Leadership, 40,* 14–36.

Lingering Questions

1. What steps, if any, should be taken when some members of a faculty reject theory and research and stand apart from the prevailing shared belief structure in the district?

2. School districts are notorious for producing big plans and short deadlines, requiring enormous energy from everyone concerned. In a time of shrinking financial resources and increasing teacher responsibilities, how can faculty be inspired to devote that kind of energy? Who should be responsible for providing that inspiration?

POSITIVE CHANGES FOR CHILDREN

Therese M. Bialkin

Third-grade teacher, Jackson Academy, East Orange, New Jersey

Michele Giordano

Third-grade teacher, Jackson Academy, East Orange, New Jersey

I*s that all there is?* That song title, made famous decades ago, comes very close to summing up the way we felt about our teaching just a few years ago. As beginning, primary grade teachers, our enthusiasm and excitement could not be rivaled. We expected hard work and we approached it eagerly. We worked hard to learn all that we could about our students and their community, to acquaint ourselves with school and district expectations, and to establish ourselves as professionals. As graduates of local teacher education programs, we felt reasonably well prepared. Yet, as with most beginning teachers, those early years posed enormous challenges for us.

We both began teaching more than a decade ago, a time when school districts throughout the United States were heavily focused on the basics. Urban school districts, such as ours, were under tremendous pressure to improve student performance on standardized tests. Many felt that the surest and quickest way to raise test scores was to offer a curriculum that emphasized isolated skills and teacher-centered, direct instruction with strict time constraints for each curriculum area. It was not uncommon for us to leave school at the end of the day, loaded down with totebags full of worksheets and workbooks. We were working hard! Our students were working hard! Indeed, most of them *were* acquiring the skills that we presented. Unfortunately, much of the learning was devoid of a sense of purpose and joy—elements we knew were essential to the creation of lifelong learners. We knew there must be a better way.

Ironically, it was only after our routines settled into place and we felt a growing sense of confidence about ourselves as professionals, that we both—quite independently—began to question some of our teaching practices. We knew that our students were capable. Yet, the curriculum we were providing did not allow them to demonstrate their abilities to the fullest. We also knew that we were capable of more creative and inspired teaching. Yet, in many ways, the curriculum we had worked so hard to master seemed to discourage individual teacher creativity and initiative. We began to explore possibilities—together. Now, as third grade teachers, two years into our journey of change, the initial excitement and enthusiasm we felt as beginning teachers has returned, but in a very different way.

First Steps

It was easy to identify the first problem we would tackle together. We both had difficulty apportioning the time available in a typical school day among all the subjects we were required to teach. In order to reduce the time spent on some subjects without reducing the quality of the instruction, we devised a form of "semi-departmentalization." We divided the curriculum between us with one of us teaching science and math to both classes and the other teaching social studies and language skills. With classrooms right next door to each other, this was a relatively easy innovation.

After a year's experimentation, it was clear that our teaching had changed dramatically. Narrowing our focus gave us time to make our lessons more exciting and challenging. In general, we were better prepared. Moreover, teaching this way required us to communicate with each other frequently in order to coordinate our activities. Still, we were not satisfied. Our collaboration and discussion led us to realize that we could improve our lessons even further by working together to integrate the subjects we were teaching, rather than teaching them in isolation. Having some familiarity with whole language, we felt that this was the direction that would offer us the most help. We also knew that we had a lot to learn.

Moving toward Whole Language

Over the years, we had attended several workshops dealing with various aspects of whole language philosophy and practice. We continued to attend as many workshops as we could. We also shared articles with one another; and we talked with other professionals about what they were doing. We enlisted and received the administrative support of our principal, Gladys Calhoun. From the very beginning, her support has been an essential part of our success.

One of the most important activities affecting our change was the initiation of a whole language study group by our district reading and language arts supervisors, Norma Nichols and Ruth Gillman. The group was established to provide

support to teachers, like ourselves, who were interested in changing their teaching. We met once a month to discuss new insights, ideas, and problems encountered as we attempted to move toward the use of whole language. We read and discussed Regie Routman's *Invitations: Changing as Teachers and Learners*. These meetings helped us to know that the concerns we were experiencing were not unique to us. Our ideas about integrating the subject areas with the language arts were reinforced. During the summer of 1992, we began to do some serious planning.

Teaching through Themes

During our initial planning, we selected five theme topics, established goals for each theme, and brainstormed ideas for integrating subject areas and for establishing a learning environment that was natural and flowing, not forced. We decided to use a variety of children's literature (tradebooks), rather than a textbook, as the major source of reading material. A story related to the theme would serve as the catalyst for framing our work.

Acquiring the literature we needed proved to be our first major challenge. We wanted a minimum of one book per child for each of the five themes. The challenge was met through a series of collaborative efforts. Our principal and the Office of Curriculum provided partial funding. Additional funds came through the use of monies allocated for the purchase of workbooks; a student-managed plant sale; and through the use of bonus points earned through student book clubs, such as Troll and Scholastic. Other teachers donated excess tradebooks and several publishers sponsored us through the donation of trial materials. Once we had obtained the necessary literature, we began each theme using a variety of instructional techniques.

Mapping the theme. We usually start each theme unit with a brainstorming activity. This involves the creation of a semantic map of the theme we are going to explore. We collaborate with students to list on the map the subjects and content we expect to cover in the unit. Copies of the map are distributed to students and referred to as we move through the unit.

Introducing the theme story. Each story is introduced with a prediction activity. For example, students may be asked to observe only the illustrations in the literature. A prediction list is then created from ideas that students volunteer, such as where they think the story takes place, what might occur in the story, and so on. These ideas are compiled on a chart. Students are required to justify their predictions with evidence gathered from the pictures or story title. After reading the story, the chart is used to evaluate all of the predictions made.

Reading the story. In order to accommodate the various reading abilities of individual students, we employ a number of different reading strategies. One of us may read the story aloud to the less proficient readers before they read it on their own. More able students may be initially assigned to read independently, while other students may be linked with a reading partner.

Reading is done in an informal setting with students lying on the carpet or gathered around the teacher in comfortable positions. After the reading, students respond to the story in their literature logs. These responses are later shared and discussed in small groups. The discussions focus on subject-area content, reading comprehension, and literary understandings in an integrated way.

Follow-through and follow-up. The brainstorming and story-reading activities serve as a commonly shared experience for all of the students. This is followed by a variety of lessons and experiences that may involve the whole group, small groups, and individuals. Here are three examples:

Extended reading and writing. Each day, we read aloud to students from materials related to the current theme. Students are also given time for independent reading in theme-related materials. The reading is followed by discussion as well as opportunities to write. Each child has a journal and a literature response log to write down their reactions to the reading, create a poem or story, or to record some interesting facts. Students are given time and assistance for the revision and editing of material that will eventually be published. Whenever possible, computers are used to publish books using different word-processing programs.

Cooperative learning. We use a variety of cooperative learning strategies throughout each unit. One cooperative learning technique we employ is called "Envelope." Varied levels of comprehen-

We collaborate with students to list on the map the subjects and content we expect to cover in the unit.

sion questions relating to the literature (or content) under study are written on the front of the envelopes. Students work together to discover the evidence in the story that supports the answer to the question written on the front of the envelope. The answers are written down and placed inside the envelope, which is then rotated to another group for evaluation. This is followed by a very high level class discussion, as students verify or challenge certain answers and return to the text for supporting evidence. Most often the questions are originated by the teacher, but as students become more familiar with the process, they enjoy developing questions themselves as a small-group or homework activity.

Grouping for specific strategies and skills. Strategies and skills, such as vocabulary or word analysis, are integrated into the various lessons. Based on our observation of student needs, skill groups in these areas are formed. Groups are changed daily as students progress. The literature always forms the nucleus of these lessons. For example,

one skill lesson originated from our observation that a number of students were having trouble recognizing and reading dialogue. A lesson addressing this problem consisted of helping children to identify specific lines of dialogue in the story. Having demonstrated that they could isolate the dialogue from the remaining text, we had them choose characters, identify all the dialogue for their character, practice reading it, and perform it as a play.

Pulling It All Together

Providing an integrated curriculum for students, while keeping track of the various disciplines, is a common dilemma for teachers using theme-based instruction. What follows are some examples of science, social studies, math, and language integration for a theme commonly taught in third grade. For purposes of record keeping and accountability, we labeled the activities in terms of specific subject areas. However, each activity overlapped into all the others.

Science. During our unit on Native Americans, students learned the importance of corn for the survival of many tribes. Students were shown real, fully grown corn plants. They learned the parts of the corn plant, grew their own corn, dissected corn seeds and looked at the baby plant under a microscope.

Language arts. After reading a number of Native American legends in class, students worked in groups to create their own legends, complete with illustrations. The stories were bound and made into books for everyone's reading enjoyment.

Social studies. Students investigated Native American homes, crafts, and tools. They created their own simulations using various materials and then wrote about them.

Mathematics. Students used corn seeds to conduct estimation activities.

All Day Learning Stations

Every Friday, we institute what we call our "All Day Learning Stations." Students are rotated through a series of learning stations, working cooperatively in small groups. They are grouped heterogeneously. This, in itself, is unusual in our school, where students are typically divided into groups according to academic ability. Our third grade classes contain a mixture of students with varying academic abilities, ranging from very fluent readers to several students who are more than a grade level behind in reading.

The make-up of each group is not absolutely fixed throughout the year. As we see fit, students are moved to different groups to allow them to gain experience working with other members of the class as well as to allow us to find the combination of students that produces the best results academically and socially.

Station assignments for the whole day are written on the board. Due to the size of each class, ten stations are required to keep group sizes to a maximum of six students.

At a station, each group is required to complete a task associated with our theme and requiring the use of children's literature. The tasks are designed so that they can be generally completed within the fifty minutes allotted to each group. While the students are working diligently at their stations, we act as facilitators, moving from station to station, monitoring progress, and offering assistance. After the time is up, groups rotate to the next station to begin a new task. Students are able to work through three stations in the morning, and then complete two more stations after lunch. On the following Friday, the remaining five stations are completed, using the same routine.

This scheduling leaves about thirty minutes at the end of the day to get together with the entire two classes and reflect on the day's progress. We use this time to discuss solutions to problems that may have occurred, share opinions of tasks assigned, listen to feedback from teacher observations, and sometimes use our journals to log personal evaluations. These sessions have proven to be invaluable in improving the listening skills of our students and ourselves.

A very bold innovation for us and for our school, the "All Day Learning Stations" have opened our eyes to what children can do when they are given greater control over their own learning. The children are learning more; they are thoroughly engaged in their tasks; and, contrary to what most teachers would think, there are virtually no discipline problems.

Assessment

Student evaluation is an ongoing process. As the need arises, students are given formal tests concerning information and skills taught within our theme. Daily classwork is also assessed by observing student behaviors and by measurable academic progress. In addition, we keep anecdotal records of academic and social progress for discussion in parent, student, and teacher conferences.

Reflections

These past two years have been enormously challenging and rewarding. It is true that our teaching has changed. But perhaps more importantly, we have changed the way we view ourselves as professionals. Taking greater control over what we do has meant that we work much harder, but we believe we also work much better. As we look back there are several things that really account for the success we have had so far. Our commitment to individual accountability and team planning is essential. We spend time together planning our weekly lessons and our Friday sessions so that we both understand the entire learning program and how it all fits together. Planning initially took a great deal of time. As the program developed, we found that less time had to be spent once the framework was in place.

Another key element is the support and talent of some of our colleagues. Gwendolyn Cottingham, our librarian, has proved to be an essential part of our program. She has created, at our request, a list of books available in our library covering our chosen theme. She also helps to provide literature for classroom read-alouds, silent reading, and student research projects. She even supplied her personal slides taken on her trip to Africa when we were studying African folktales.

The Music, Art, French, and Physical Education teachers also make themselves available to enhance the learning process. With advance notice, these professionals will develop their lessons specifically to relate to our current theme. The special talents of all these people are invaluable to our program.

We feel that we have progressed a long way toward achieving our goals and we are continuing to plan some interesting new activities for the upcoming school year. We are aware that research has shown that it can take as many as five years to develop a comprehensive whole language program. Keeping this in mind, we continue to monitor and adjust our learning environments to make them the best they can be for our student learners and for ourselves as professionals, continuing to learn. We are excited about what the future holds because we know that the change has been a positive one.

Friday Schedule for "All Day Learning Stations"

9:00–9:30   All students meet in one room for whole group conference (station directions, etc.). Each group is assigned to one of the ten areas.

9:30–12:00   Students rotate through three of the 40-minute stations with five-minute clean-up between each.

12:00–12:30 Lunch

12:30–2:00   Students rotate through two additional stations.

2:00–2:30   Whole group processing (discussions and reactions about the day's activities)

2:30–2:35   Dismissal

A repeat of the same ten stations will occur the following Friday in order for students to work through all of them. Below is an example of some possible station arrangements. Stations vary as they relate to our chosen theme.

1. Computer Station: Teacher selected integrated software
2. Listening Station with headphones
3. Arts & Crafts Station
4. Hands-On Science Lab Experiments
5. Writing and Publishing Center
6. Computer Station: Free choice from network menu
7. Social Studies Research
8. Math Manipulative Station
9. Reading/Language Strategies
10. Student/Teacher Writing Conferences

Classroom Floor Plans for "All Day Learning Stations"

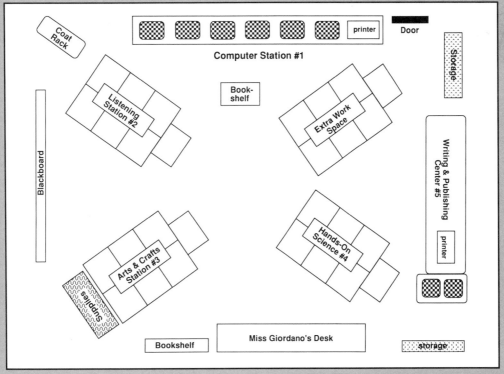

Mrs. Bialkin's Classroom

Miss Giordano's Classroom

Lingering Questions

1. Should a successful innovation created by classroom teachers be implemented across a school district? If so, under what circumstances and how?

2. How can children, who are only familiar with teacher-centered classrooms, be helped to adjust to the expectations of a whole language classroom?

3. How can teachers reconcile the need to encourage children to make their own choices with the need to maintain quality time on task during independent activities?

Resources That Supported Our Change

Glazer, S. (1992). *Reading comprehension.* New York: Scholastic Professional Books.

Goodman, K. (1986). Basal readers: A call for action. *Language Arts, 63* (4), 358–363.

Johnson, W., & Johnson, R. (1991). *Cooperating in the classroom.* Edina, MN: Interaction Book Company.

Newman, J., & Church, S. (1990). Myths of whole language. *The Reading Teacher, 44* (1), 1–7.

Routman, R. (1991). *Invitations: Changing as teachers and learners.* Portsmouth, NH: Heinemann.

LEARNING IS A FAMILY AFFAIR: ARTICULATING CURRICULUM CHANGE TO PARENTS

"My daughter impressed me with her creativity and her writing skill. We're so glad we participated in the Family Language program."

"What I liked was that everyone explored the same topic creatively. I want to sign up for another Family Language session so that I can see more of this approach."

"This isn't at all the way school was when I was a child. It's quite a change and I like it."

What kind of school project generates this type of positive feedback and supportive community response? The answer is an innovative program called Family Language. Developed by Crim School in New Jersey's Bridgewater–Raritan Regional School District, the Family Language program brings together parents, teachers, and students in a community setting and provides them with the unique opportunity to cooperatively explore whole language in action. The sharing of ideas that results enables the members of their community to better understand the changes that have been taking place in the ways their students learn to read, write, and reason.

Involving the Community in Change

Like many other schools, Crim School is changing. From the materials the teachers use to the way they organize the learning environment and evaluate growth, their classrooms are different from what they were ten years ago. They are different from what most parents experienced, different from what has always been considered basic and traditional. The change didn't come about because of the purchase of a new reading series or the piloting of a new science program. It occurred because of a deep philosophical belief that students are most successful when they are immersed in a print-rich environment that issues invitations to learning. The teachers at Crim School know that when classrooms are interactional, learning is more meaningful. In their classrooms, students are active learners, working cooperatively with adults who demonstrate activities, structure the environment, and provide instruction that helps them complete tasks on their own.

Because "learning is a family affair" to Dr. Marie Simone and the members of her staff at Crim School, they are especially attuned to the critical role family plays in supporting learning and shaping the environment of the classroom. They firmly believe that parents, peers, community members, and teachers provide a scaffold that supports the development of motivated and successful learners. This belief is reflected in the school's commitment to forging a partnership with parents in the learning process. Over the years, the staff has made a conscious effort to weave the parents into the fabric of the school tapestry in many traditional, as well as innovative, ways.

In an effort to extend this home–school cooperation and collabora-

Judith J. Wood

Elementary Teaching Specialist, Adamsville School, Bridgewater, New Jersey

Christened Family Language, and patterned after its predecessors, it is designed to bring whole language into the home and the home into whole language.

tion, Jane Fidacaro, a second grade teacher at Crim School, became involved in the Rutgers Consortium for Educational Equity. Through Jane's participation in the Consortium, Crim School became a part of a national program called Family Math. Crim's involvement in this program began a pattern of unique family learning projects. As a result, Family Science and Family Math became a part of Crim's community outreach program. It was the success of these two projects that engendered the most recent of Crim's parent–school partnership programs. Christened Family Language, and patterned after its predecessors, it is designed to bring whole language into the home and the home into whole language.

Responding to Community Needs

Family Language at Crim School originated in response to community interest in the changes taking place in the classroom as a result of the whole language

movement. Since whole language has its roots in the ways that families help children learn, the staff realized that the most natural way to support whole language learning in the classroom was to make parents their partners in the learning process. Because the strategies, materials, and activities being used in the primary classrooms of the children differed greatly from what most parents had as a part of their own educational experience, the staff recognized a need to provide parents with an understanding of the philosophy and methodologies of the holistic approach. Since it is usually easier to relate from a position of experience, it was decided that the best way to inform, model, and establish a mutual support system was to engage parents directly in the learning situation. It became a primary goal of the Family Language project to provide parents with a simple, direct means of experiencing integrated learning first hand. Our general plan for organizing a Family Language session appears in Figure 1.

Format for Family Language Presentations

OPENER: An activity designed to establish the theme and immediately involve the participants in a collaborative endeavor.

OVERVIEW: A formal presentation designed to establish background on the philosophy and methodology of whole language using the opening activity as an illustration.

CURRICULAR ACTIVITY: An activity designed to integrate reading and writing across the curriculum.

FAMILY FOLLOW-UP: In order to demonstrate how families can support learning in the classroom, participating families are given "homework" assignments based on the activities of the evening. They are also encouraged to sign out books from a specially prepared library of materials which they can share at home.

CLOSURE: The parents are debriefed. Lesson objectives are spotlighted and skills identified. Parental questions are addressed.

Figure 1. *Organizational plan for Family Language event*

The Family Language Experience

An evening of Family Language is like stepping into a first-grade whole language classroom. The multipurpose room, transformed for the evening, is set up with reading and writing centers as well as small group and large group work areas. As parents and their first grade children assemble in the "classroom," they are immediately engaged in an opening activity related to a theme that organizes the evening's events. For example, if the evening revolves around a friendship theme, each family unit is asked to brainstorm traits they value in a friend, record them on a cut-out of a gingerbread person, and decorate the cut-outs. The cut-outs are then united to form a friendship circle encompassing the participants. As the families share their creations, the group converses about the importance of friendships. A graphic organizer, such as a web, is then used to organize a discussion of what a friend is.

Immediately following this opening activity, the participating families are assembled for a formal discussion of whole language philosophy and methodology. During this discussion, the opening activity is used as a model for spotlighting the integration of speaking, listening, reading, and writing activities in a whole language classroom. The effective use of cooperative and collaborative learning strategies is also highlighted. As this work session concludes, the project team sets the stage for the remainder of the evening's activities by listing for the parents the techniques and strategies the activities will illustrate.

Stepping back into the "classroom," the families continue their work with the topic of the evening. During this segment of the program, the participants engage in activities that illustrate how reading and writing can be integrated across the curriculum. If the tropical rainforest is the theme for the evening, the family units are invited to close their eyes and visualize the animals they hear as they listen to a tape of tropical forest sounds. This leads them into a brainstorming session during which all of the animals they would expect to find in a tropical rainforest are identified. The animals' names are recorded on slips of paper and dropped into a pith helmet. Each family unit then draws a slip from the helmet. Working cooperatively, family units discuss their animal's features, create a drawing of the animal, and place it on a rainforest mural that had been created earlier by the students in their art class. An appropriate rainforest poem is then read and used to teach blends and rhyming words. A sing-a-long to the tune of "The Bear Necessities" leads the parents into their "homework" assignment for the evening.

The "homework" assignments given to the participating families help to extend the sharing and the learning beyond the confines of the school building and the evening's program. Each assignment is designed to involve the family units in using language at home in ways that are creative and meaningful. For a communication theme, parents and their children are given the assignment to create T-shirts with a special message. These shirts are then brought back to school to be shared with classmates and tied into the thematic unit as it continues in the classroom. An integral part of the homework assignment is the selection of books to be signed out by the families and shared at home. These books, carefully selected by the project team, tie into the theme and provide parents with a vehicle for recapturing the events of the evening in their own homes.

Perhaps the most important part of the program for the parents is the debriefing session that brings each evening to a close. It is at this time that the lesson objectives are spotlighted and the skills

An evening of Family Language is like stepping into a first-grade whole language classroom.

that have been developed are identified. Parents are encouraged to ask questions and voice their concerns. High interest issues such as phonics instruction, invented spelling, and the use of whole texts instead of basals and workbooks are addressed. A special effort is made to

The school merged with the home to create a community of learners.

illustrate the ways in which parents can employ whole language strategies in the home to support the learning taking place in the classroom.

The best part of the evening for the families and the project staff is the refreshments that follow the debriefing session. Also tied to the theme, this portion of the program provides the parents with an informal forum for talking about what they saw and heard during the evening. The atmosphere of sharing and caring established during the evening is extended into the night. If a program can be measured by how long its participants linger over friendship fruit salad or animal crackers and Gatorade, then Crim School can label its Family Language program a success.

Establishing a Blueprint for Success

A project as successful as Crim School's Family Language program requires a great deal of planning and collaboration. Many factors must be carefully mapped out in advance. For this reason, the planning for Crim's project began during the summer months when Project Coordinator Jane Fidacaro, Principal Marie Simone, and Curriculum Reading Specialist Alberta Evans met with the five

first grade teachers to target the program's goals and outline its format. Experience with previous projects had taught the team that participation is more effective than demonstration. This knowledge led them to design an authentic classroom experience for the first grade families targeted for the program. Learning experiences incorporated into the evening were designed to be typical of the everyday activities of a whole language classroom. Every effort was made to replicate the classroom learning experience in a realistic and relaxed way.

Establishing a blueprint for the entire project became a priority. The format for the five sessions needed to be standardized so that each presentation provided the families with a logical and systematic introduction to what whole language is and how integrated learning occurs. This need for a strong unifying plan led to the selection of themes with which first graders and their families could relate. The use of the thematic approach allowed the project team to pattern the activities in a sequence that led to an understanding of why holistic learning is so powerful.

Factors such as time and class size were also given special consideration. The project team studied family routines and the pattern of community participation in school activities. From this data they concluded that more parents would be able to attend the program with their children if "school" sessions were held in the early evening. Since the team felt it was essential to provide a means for stimulating social interaction between family members and among family units, numbers became important. Class sizes needed to be kept workable. For this reason, the participating groups were kept small enough to facilitate collaboration, yet large enough to accommodate all of the participants.

Work on the development of activities and materials for the program continued throughout the summer and into the beginning of the school year. When the first grade teachers—Lois Elfvin, Ellen Gulick, Bette Hance, Jennifer Sloane, and Muriel Stillwell—introduced Family Language to the parents during Back-to-School Night in late September, the project was met with interest and enthusiasm. Beginning in October, Thursdays were set aside for Family Language. On those evenings, the members of the project team, the first grade students, and the participating family members assembled for "school." They thought about, talked about, wrote about, drew about, and sang about ideas related to each evening's theme. In pairs and in collaborative groups, the families and the members of the project team studied science, math, social studies, and the language arts thematically. The school merged with the home to create a community of learners.

A Recipe for Success

What makes Family Language at Crim School such a success? Is there some magic recipe? Not really. Their success is built on the traditional principles of hard work, careful planning, and commitment. What does set Crim's program apart from others of its kind is the rapport the school has with the community. Because it recognizes the importance of the home as the primary educational institution of the child, it places family participation in the school in a position of paramount importance. The staff at Crim School realizes that schools can learn from families and they structure their school programs to support effective home–school communication. The parents of this school community know that the professional staff values what they do to be supportive of the school and their children. The entire school community has learned the importance of collaboration and sharing.

Because of the tremendous success of the Family Language program at Crim School, the project team is presently designing two new programs which extend the scope of the project. Both of these new programs are targeted for parents and their children of grades three and up. The Living Literature program will involve parents and their children in the sharing of literary works. The Writer's Workshop will involve families in the writing and publishing of their own creative materials. Together, these new programs will carry on the tradition of making learning a family affair at Crim School.

Lingering Questions

1. What can be learned from family literacy to help us do a better job of articulating the curriculum to parents?

2. What sort of learning results for teachers while they are preparing and implementing family literacy?

3. A perennial problem in home/school relations, is the fact that those parents most in need of being involved don't come to parent meetings. How does family literacy address this problem? Is there a need to examine ways to encourage involvement from more or different families?

4. How can family literacy be evaluated? What types of evaluation tools will generate parental input and make a positive impact on the program?

5. How can family literacy be extended to other schools? Other grade levels?

In this issue of *Primary Voices K–6*, we examine the topic of change in language arts education as it has been experienced by people in a variety of school districts and roles. Change has brought us together; were it not for the current explosion of new knowledge and its implementation in the schools, the Rutgers Literacy Network would not be the vital organization it is, and those of us who have contributed to this issue would not be linked in the ways we are. We would not have this story to tell.

We might expect that a university professor, an assistant superintendent, two teachers working together in an urban school, and teachers from a suburban district who are working to involve parents would have very different ways, perhaps even conflicting ways, of looking at instructional change. What is more interesting, however, is to look at the common characteristics of change that all of our writers, despite their differences, reveal in telling about change as they experienced it. The common characteristics that I have identified are not the only ones evident in the four articles, but they have helped me clarify some of my own ideas about change

Talk. It takes more than one person to make a change. All four of our writers refer to the need to talk, to share, to exchange and build upon ideas if we are to change our ways of thinking and doing. Even making small changes, such as trying a new teaching strategy, seldom happens without talk. So much of the work we read about in our language arts and reading journals suggests ways that individual teachers working quite independently can make personal changes in their teaching. Many of us read the articles and think, "Oh, that's a great idea! I'm going to try that!" and find that we've forgotten about it before we can implement it. We become so much more likely to try a great idea when we've taken the time to tell a colleague about it and talk about how we're going to go about trying what we've read. If our colleague says she's going to try it, too, the chances of implementation grow even more, because now we have a partner to whom we're almost obligated.

When the change we're trying to make is a big change that involves more than one classroom and more than one teacher, as did the changes described by Ev Kline, Judy Wood, and Therese Bialkin and Michele Giordano, the need for talk is obvious. However, as Dorothy Strickland points out, some big changes involve only one person, like the philosophical shift a teacher must make in order to release some of the responsibility in her classroom to her students. Very few of us can make that sort of a shift without talk. We need to clarify our ideas before we can use them for change, and talk is how most of us manage to do that.

Purpose. No one changes without a reason. Ev Kline stated that his district's high school English department was "galvanized" to change the way writing was taught by a 1978 follow-up study of their graduates, who "felt they were not taught to write at the level demanded by college work." Therese Bialkin and Michele Giordano "knew there must be a better way" to teach when they recognized that much of the learning in their third grade classrooms was "devoid of a sense of purpose and joy." Judy Wood reported that the teachers at Crim School launched Family Language "in response to community interest in the changes taking place in the classroom as a result of the whole language movement." For some graduate students in Dorothy Strickland's class, a discussion of the differences between surface level changes versus fundamental changes of teaching theory led to new understandings of the roles of learner and teacher.

Joanne K. Monroe

Language Arts Supervisor, Flemington–Raritan Regional Schools, New Jersey

When teachers make their own decisions to change, for purposes that are clear to them and personally held, they are able to make the changes without the sense of pressure that seems to accompany changes that they make in response to building or district level demands. Ev Kline points to the need for "a shared perception that change is needed" and the amount of staff development time and effort that was required in his district to bring the faculty to that shared perception. As Dorothy Strickland states, the time invested in building this shared perception is critical, because it "helps create the much needed *will* to change as it informs the why and how of change."

All of us who meet together as members of the Network are the people in our districts who are charged with insuring that all of the students we serve are receiving the most appropriate instruction we can offer. We applaud and support the independent investigation being done by teachers. We also recognize that we must move all teachers in the district, even those who do not independently experience a personal purpose for change, toward more student-centered teaching. We have all learned that helping teachers see a personal purpose in the changes we are working toward is an important aspect of our jobs. We need to remind ourselves frequently that, in Dorothy Strickland's words, the "tensions that emerge as people strive to learn new skills and behaviors are a necessary part of the process."

Time. All five authors state quite explicitly that making significant changes in the way we teach takes time. We all need to keep referring to the importance of time in change-making because while we recognize it on a cognitive level, we have real difficulty with it on an emotional level. We feel frustrated by the amount of time change requires; we may even feel guilty when we recognize the need for a

change and see that we haven't yet been able to meet it. It is only by continually reminding ourselves and one another that change is a long-term plan that we can stay with it and make change happen.

Responsibility. When we think about making change in the teaching of language arts, a great deal of the change we are making is a shift of responsibility. In moving the student to the center of the teaching, we release some responsibility from the teacher to the student, and a great deal of responsibility from the textbook publisher to the district and to the teacher. When the teachers of Crim School used a reading series and language arts texts as the basis of their instruction, they had no need to involve parents in the way that they do with their Family Language program. As they assumed more responsibility for designing instruction, they recognized that they needed to "make parents partners in the learning process."

Therese Bialkin and Michele Giordano saw that at the same time they took greater control over their teaching, they were able to give their students "greater control over their own learning." The delight that Therese and Michele felt as they watched their students "thoroughly engaged" and learning is evident in their article. In the Flemington–Raritan Schools, we have found the model for the gradual release of responsibility from teacher to students (Pearson, 1985) to be a helpful guide. The model reminds us that, ultimately, it's the students, not the teacher, who have to do the work for the learning to be effective.

Barbara Burns, Dorothy Strickland's student, was impressed when she saw a classroom where the children were able to "take charge" of many aspects of their learning. She knew what she was seeing: A classroom where students were given a chance to become independent readers

"...tensions that emerge as people strive to learn new skills and behaviors are a necessary part of the process."

and writers. When we talk about changing language arts instruction, this is what we are talking about.

Reflection. Change continues when we compare where we are to where we started. Ev Kline's district was able to look back to their change process and improve on it to initiate further change. Therese Bialkin and Michele Giordano's reflection on the progress they had made allowed them to look forward to additional change with feelings of excitement. When the teachers at Crim School reviewed the success of their Family Language program, they designed Living Literature and Writer's Workshop to extend family involvement in their school's language arts program.

As Dorothy Strickland indicated, the same is true for our Network. We know we have more work to do before we achieve "significant, enduring change." That doesn't stop us from acknowledging and celebrating the change we've seen to date. What we've learned from our change is that we are capable of growth. Once we come to know ourselves as teachers who are learners, we know that we will continue with our work and our change.

Reference

Pearson, P. D. (1985). Changing the face of reading comprehension instruction. *The Reading Teacher, 39*, 724-738.

U.S. POSTAL SERVICE
STATEMENT OF OWNERSHIP, MANAGEMENT AND CIRCULATION
(Required by 39 U.S.C. 3685)

1. Title of Publication: PRIMARY VOICES
1a. Publication No.: 000000

2. Date of Filing: September 1, 1993

3. Frequency of Issue: January, April, August, November
3a. No. of Issues Published Annually: 4
3b. Annual Subscription Price: $15.00

4. Location of Known Office of Publication: NCTE, 1111 W. Kenyon Road, Urbana, IL 61801-1096

5. Location of the Headquarters of General Business Offices of the Publisher: NCTE, 1111 W. Kenyon Road, Urbana, IL 61801-1096

6. Name and Complete Address of Publisher, Editor, and Managing Editor: NCTE, 1111 W. Kenyon Road, Urbana, IL 61801-1096; Karen Smith, Carol Schanche, NCTE, 1111 W. Kenyon Road, Urbana, IL 61801-1096, Miles Myers, NCTE, 1111 W. Kenyon Road, Urbana, IL 61801-1096.

7. Owner: NCTE, 1111 W. Kenyon Road, Urbana, IL 61801-1096

8. Known Bondholder, Mortgagees, and Other Security Holders owning or holding 1 percent or more of total amount of bonds, mortgages or other securities: NONE

9. No Change Preceding 12 Months

	Ave. No. Copies Each Issue During Preceding 12 Months	Actual No. Copies Single Issue Published Nearest Filing Date
10. Extent and Nature of Circulation		
A. Total No. Copies Printed (Net Press Run)	6000	6000
B. Paid Circulation		
1. Sales through dealers and carriers, street vendors and counter sales	-0-	-0-
2. Mail Subscriptions	4360	4360
C. Total Paid Circulation (Sum of 10B1 and 10B2)	4360	4360
D. Free distribution by mail, carrier or other means, samples, complimentary, and other free copies	-0-	-0-
E. Total distribution (Sum of C and D)	4360	4360
F. Copies not distributed		
1. Office use, left over, unaccounted, spoiled after printing	1640	1640
2. Returns from news agents	-0-	-0-
G. Total (Sum of E, F1 and 2—should equal net press run shown in A)	6000	6000

11. I certify that the statements made by me above are correct and complete.

12. For completion by publishers mailing at the regular rates (Section 132,121, Postal Service Manual) 39 U.S.C. 3626 provides in pertinent part: "No person who would have been entitled to mail matter under former section 4359 of this title shall mail such matter at the rates provided under this subsection unless he files annually with the Postal Service a written request for permission to mail matter at such rates."

Signature and title of editor, publisher, business manager or owner:

Katherine Hope, Business Manager

In accordance with the provisions of this statute, I hereby request permission to mail the publication named in Item 1 at the phased postage rates presently authorized by 39 U.S.C. 3626. (Signature and title of editor, publisher, business manager or owner) Katherine Hope, Business Manager

Collaboration and Change

Darling-Hammond, L. (1993). Reframing the school reform agenda. *Phi Delta Kappan, 74,* 752–761.

Educational Leadership. (May, 1993). Themed issue: The changing curriculum, *50* (8).

Fullan, M. G. (1993). *Productive educational change: Going deeper.* New York: Falmer Press.

Fullan, M. G., & Miles, M. B. (1992). Getting reform right: What works and what doesn't. *Phi Delta Kappan, 73,* 744–752.

Fullan, M. G. (1991). *The new meaning of educational change.* New York: Teachers College Press.

Lieberman, A. (1992). School/university collaboration. *Phi Delta Kappan, 74,* 147–156.

Lieberman, A., & McLaughlin, M. W. (1992). Networks for educational change: Powerful and problematic. *Phi Delta Kappan, 73,* 673–677.

Lieberman, A. (Ed.). (1990). *Schools as collaborative cultures: Creating the future now.* New York: Falmer Press.

Maeroff, G. I. (1993). Building teams to rebuild schools. *Phi Delta Kappan, 74,* 512–519.

MacGinite, W. H. (1991). Reading instruction: Plus ça change . . . . *Educational Leadership, 48* (6), 55–58.

Sarason, S. (1982). *The culture of the school and the problem of change.* Boston: Allyn and Bacon.

Teacher Research, Reflection, and Action

Cochran-Smith, M., & Lytle, S. L. (1993). *Inside-outside: Teacher research and knowledge.* New York: Teachers College Press.

Feeley, J., Wepner, S., & Strickland, D. S. (1991). *Process reading and writing.* New York: Teachers College Press.

Goswami, D., & Stillman, P. R. (1987). *Reclaiming the classroom: Teacher research as an agency for change.* Portsmouth, NH: Boynton/Cook.

SCHOLASTIC INC.

Can More Than Coincidence Be Following Me?

Something odd is definitely going on. Either some mysterious force is causing more coincidences in my life, a genetic glitch has set in, or there are benefits of getting older that no one told me about. It's not that I don't like it. As a matter of fact I welcome that little frisson that accompanies each startling connection. But the most disconcerting of these surprises are wreaking havoc with my well-established notions of how the world works.

Little did I ever suspect that NCTE, Karen Smith, and Dorothy Strickland would set me off in a tailspin. Here's what happened: Terry Cooper, editor-in-chief of Scholastic Professional Books, asked me what I thought of the idea of trying to find out about sponsoring an issue of *Primary Voices K–6*, and when I said "Great," she dashed off a letter to Karen. Before Terry's letter could find its way from Greenwich Village in New York City to the NCTE offices in Urbana, Illinois, Karen was on the phone, calling to discuss our sponsorship of the next issue, which had been taken out of sequence. Obviously, there was little to discuss, except the coincidence and my agreeing to write this message to readers, after reading the manuscript on "Perspectives on the Changing Language Arts Curriculum" prepared by Dorothy Strickland and others involved with the Rutgers Literacy Curriculum Network.

Well, I read, and that "little frisson" turned into waves of shock. Karen's call. An issue out of sequence. The Changing Language Arts Curriculum. Dorothy Strickland. And me. This had to be more than coincidence.

Dorothy Strickland came into my life in the 1970s, when she traveled from her office at Columbia University to advise Deborah Kovacs and me on a speculative early childhood project. Although the project never got past the development stage, I learned a lot about early literacy that I thought I would know forever. After all, Dorothy Strickland had been my teacher.

Early in the 1980s I left direct involvement with school-based education behind for a while to start a magazine for families using computers. Before long I realized how much I missed my old life and my old lifeline, contact with kids and teachers and people like Dorothy, so I began to attend more and more Scholastic meetings. And one day, there was Dorothy, sitting around a table with Bruno Bettelheim and others, at a meeting of our Early Childhood Division. But what was Dorothy saying? The language and references were new, and all that stuff about early reading that I thought would be true for an eternity had evolved beyond recognition. Dorothy, the master teacher, had gone on learning. That revelation was a major awakening for me.

In 1989, when Scholastic bought Instructor magazine, and I was asked to head it and a new professional book publishing program for teachers, I felt a little nervous and a lot out of touch with the schools. My own teaching was far behind me. My friend Jeremiah Kaplan advised me to travel, to talk to teachers, and that's what I did. As I went from state to state and school to school I felt like Rip van Winkle. Teachers and schools were in the midst of profound change that I had never dreamed possible. Thousands of you, most notably in the language arts, had grabbed hold of your own fate and transformed the experience of schools for millions of children.

I wish I could be one of your students. My own schooling was probably a lot like yours. Discrete blocks of time for discrete subject areas. No connections. No concept of ourselves as writers. We were just doing exercises, assignments, almost always the same from class to class and year to year. I doubt that I can ever think of myself as a "writer." It's a miracle that so many of you do, that you can put down onto paper all your wonderful adventures and discoveries as you learn *with* your children, perhaps the greatest revelation of all. I feel privileged to have the opportunity to publish just a few of your personal stories. And I feel especially lucky to have shared in this amazing coincidence.

Claudia Cohl

Vice President and Publishing Director, Professional Publishing Division, Scholastic Inc.

PrimaryVoices K-6

Volume 2 Number 1 • JANUARY 1994

CHALLENGE FOR CHANGE

Theme Cycles

NATIONAL COUNCIL OF TEACHERS OF ENGLISH

CONTENTS

Thanks to our 1993–94 Sponsors
Heinemann Educational Books, Inc.   Scholastic, Inc.   DDL Books, Inc.

Primary Voices K–6 is published four times a year in January, April, August, and November by the National Council of Teachers of English, 1111 W. Kenyon Road, Urbana, Illinois 61801-1096. Annual subscription is $15. Single copy, $6.00 (member price $5.00). Add $3 per year for Canadian and all other international postage. Remittances should be made payable to NCTE by check, money order, or bank draft in United States currency.

Communications regarding orders, subscriptions, single copies, change of address, and permission to reprint should be addressed to *Primary Voices K–6*, NCTE, 1111 W. Kenyon Road, Urbana, Illinois 61801-1096. POSTMASTER: Send address changes to *Primary Voices K–6*, NCTE, 1111 W. Kenyon Road, Urbana, Illinois 61801-1096. Application to mail at second-class postage rates is pending at Urbana, Illinois.

It is the policy of NCTE in its journals and other publications to provide a forum for the open discussion of ideas concerning the content and the teaching of English and language arts. Publicity accorded to any particular point of view does not imply endorsement by the Executive Committee, the Board of Directors, or the membership at large, except in announcements of policy, where such endorsement is clearly specified.

Copyright 1994 by the National Council of Teachers of English. Printed in the United States of America. ISSN 1068-073X.

 Printed on recycled paper

A Message from the Editor

*P*rimary Voices K–6 was designed to give voice to different learning and teaching communities. In this issue, the voices you hear are those of bilingual and whole-language educators who have been implementing theme cycles in their schools and classrooms. The lead article represents many years of collaboration between Bess Altwerger and me. For us, the tension between theory-in-practice and practice-as-theory has been paradoxically a constant nemesis and impetus for our collective growth; for our need to create a community of educators with whom we could collaborate; and for the challenge to evolve beyond our present knowing, thinking, and doing. Our article sets the stage by rethinking learning and teaching, laying out the theoretical underpinnings of theme cycle, outlining its practical aspects, and reexamining the integration of curriculum.

Elena Castro's piece, "Implementing Theme Cycle: One Teacher's Way," provides readers with a veteran teacher's perspective. Elena has been pioneering and developing theme cycles since 1985. She started by learning from educators like Kitty Kaczmarek, Gloria Hidalgo, Terri Romero, and Lisa Hoffman in Glendale, Arizona, and has greatly contributed to the evolution of theme cycles.

Marty Andrews-Sullivan and Esther Negrete, new to this concept, detail the struggles they experienced in implementing theme cycles. Their article makes clear that theme cycles have structure, and that teachers who use theme cycles actively engage children as teachers and learners.

Bill Cudog's article is a story of change and challenge. As a principal, Bill has had to change his ideas about what a principal is or should be. He has rethought his ways of "leading"—making decisions; allocating funds; and communicating with staff, parents, and children. In this new role, Bill works alongside the teachers in implementing theme cycles across the grade levels.

Karen Dockstader-Anderson's students exemplify democracy in action as they learn to use the principles of democracy to negotiate their curriculum. Their quest takes them beyond the classroom as they connect with officials and businesses from local to international levels.

Lupe Ramirez's story that appears in the Reflection section of this journal is the story of a first-year teacher's dreams and intentions, and her confrontation with the hard reality of the status quo that is basically a rude awakening for us all.

We see a need to challenge some of the currently held beliefs about learning and teaching. We hope this issue helps teachers rethink their ideas about teaching and learning, that it invites critical dialogue and reflections, and that it serves as a catalyst for change.

Sinceramente,

Barbara Flores

Barbara Flores

THEME CYCLES: CREATING COMMUNITIES OF LEARNERS

Bess Altwerger

Teacher educator, Towson State University, Maryland

Barbara Flores

Teacher educator, California State University, San Bernardino, California

Theme cycles are our way of rethinking curricular integration. The concept grows out of our ongoing commitment to student-centered education, authentic language and literacy, and collaborative learning and teaching. For us, theme cycle is a dynamic, ever-changing framework for thinking about life in our classrooms. In a theme cycle, learners (both teachers and students) are at the center of learning, asking critical questions, engaging in meaningful problem-posing and problem-solving, and creating and recreating knowledge. Teachers and students select and negotiate topics of study, and based upon the collective knowledge of the class, they delineate questions and issues of interest, seek out resources, and plan learning experiences. Because each classroom community has a unique store of knowledge, interests, and available resources, theme cycles are nontransferable. In fact, theme cycles challenge the idea that knowledge of any form can or should be "forwarded" like so many products on an assembly line.

Engaging in theme cycles helps students to become confident and resourceful learners capable of constructing knowledge, tackling complex problems, and critically examining issues. Incorporating theme cycles into the classroom requires rethinking teaching, learning, and curriculum. In this paper, we share with you our rethinking and describe some of the critical features of theme cycles.

Rethinking Learning and Teaching

Most of us have been socialized to believe that teaching and learning are separate and dichotomous events performed by different persons in the classroom; the teacher is responsible for teaching, the students are responsible for learning. Content is mandated and then transmitted to students by teachers through carefully planned and sequenced instruction. Students are expected to learn the information presented, and demonstrate their knowledge via various assessments that are, again, determined by others. Traditionally, the roles of teacher and learner are clearly defined so that learners have little or no input into what they learn, how they learn it, or if they learned it. The teacher, of course, never steps into the role of learner, presumably already possessing the content knowledge to be taught. Thus, knowledge becomes a gift bestowed upon the learner by the teacher. It is seen as something others have; something created by someone else.

Paolo Freire, the Brazilian educator, calls this pedagogy "banking education." According to Freire: " . . . education, thus becomes an act of depositing in which the students are the depositories and the teacher [textbook] is the depositor. Instead of communicating, the teacher issues communiques and makes deposits which students patiently receive, memorize, and repeat" (Freire, 1970, p. 58).

The theme cycle attempts to move away from this banking education stance and toward a "pedagogy of knowing" (Freire, 1970; Berthoff, 1987) in which the teacher is co-learner, and the students are co-teachers. Together, a community of learners and teachers is formed. Teachers value the ideas, questions, and ponderings that take shape and change as students engage in thinking about their world.

The theme cycle, then, provides teachers with a framework for transforming the classroom into an exciting learning environment, where everyone participates in the experience of coming to know their world.

Rethinking Integration

The notion of integration as an organizational and conceptual tool is not new to the area of curriculum development. For years teachers have seen the efficacy of integrating the various subject areas. One common way in which teachers have achieved some level of integration is to "pull" various subject areas into a unit of study around a particular subject area topic (see Figure 1). In this model, a teacher who recognizes the relevance of social studies, math, art, or music to a science unit such as weather might plan weather-related activities in those subject areas. These may be scheduled during science time or during times designated for the other subject areas. For example, students might study weather in various geographical locations using map skills to locate these regions (social studies), singing weather-related songs such as "Frosty the Snowman" (music), drawing

pictures of their favorite season (art), or graphing seasonal preferences (math). However, teachers who attempt to integrate the curriculum in this manner often feel a responsibility to cover the prescribed skills and topics within the other subject areas. Therefore, the unit-related activities may be seen as peripheral rather than critical to the theme. This type of integration places a burden on teachers when they do their scheduling, and increases the pressure to fit in "the really important stuff." This naturally acts as a deterrent to integration on any large scale.

In another approach to integration, broad units based on concepts such as "system" or "change" are developed in order to link prescribed topics of study within the various subject areas (see Figure 2). For example, the teacher might choose to have the students study how the United States changed from an agricultural to an industrial society, how seasons change, or how characters change over the course of a story. Although this way of integrating may offer opportunities for a multidisciplinary approach to

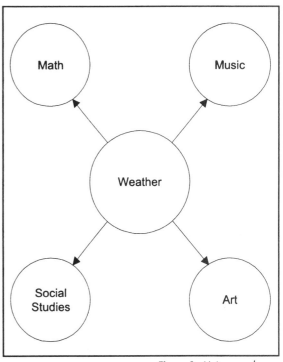

Figure 1: *Unit around Subject-Area Topic*

theme topic studies, many teachers feel that both they and the students have to do some imaginative stretching to see the relationships between subject area topics and the theme topic.

Regardless of which approach one takes, we believe that these conceptualizations of integration are flawed in two important ways:

1) subject areas are conceived as static bodies of knowledge, composed of objective sets of critical facts and skills, carefully defined and sequenced for systematic transmission to students, and

2) knowledge is viewed as externally developed by others, packaged into digestible units, and delivered to students.

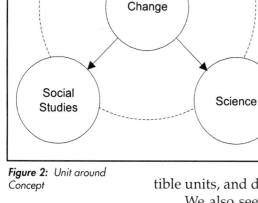

Figure 2: *Unit around Concept*

We also see as problematic the separateness of the various subject areas. In the real world, solving complex problems requires the investigative tools and strategies of a variety of disciplines. These models of integration, however, prevent the simultaneous and integrative use of content areas. Looking back at Figures 1 and 2, you will notice that all the subject areas are clearly self-contained. In these models, the autonomy of each subject area is maintained, and the theme topic is used merely as an organizing device for the teaching of the established content.

In contrast, within a theme cycle, the topic does not operate in service to the subject areas, but rather the subject areas operate in service to the theme topic. Those subject areas that can offer investigative and informational resources critical to the theme topic are selectively utilized.

Theme Cycles vs. Theme Units

Many people ask us why we chose to adopt the term "theme cycle" rather than the standard term "theme unit." We chose the term "cycle" to reflect what we perceive to be the recursive and spiraling process of knowledge construction. Unlike the traditional theme units, which are often disconnected and unrelated to subsequent units, theme cycle studies often develop into subsequent studies, as new and related questions and problems are posed. Further, the learning process itself is cyclic (see Figure 3). Each step of the theme cycle generates new steps:

1. Collectively tapped knowledge of the negotiated topic leads to collaboratively posed questions and problems.

2. The questions and problems lead to the selection of appropriate and fruitful learning experiences.

3. The learning experiences suggest methods and materials, as well as functional uses of literacy and other sign systems.

4. Creative and meaningful presentation of learning leads to new areas of investigation.

In the theme cycle, the students are involved in the entire process of theme development from deciding on topics, to planning learning experiences, gathering materials, researching information, and presenting what was learned. Students work in collaboration with the teacher as well as with each other in order to learn how to learn.

Topic Selection: The theme cycle begins with the negotiation of topics based on the children's need to know, curiosities, and interests. The teacher helps the children consider what could be

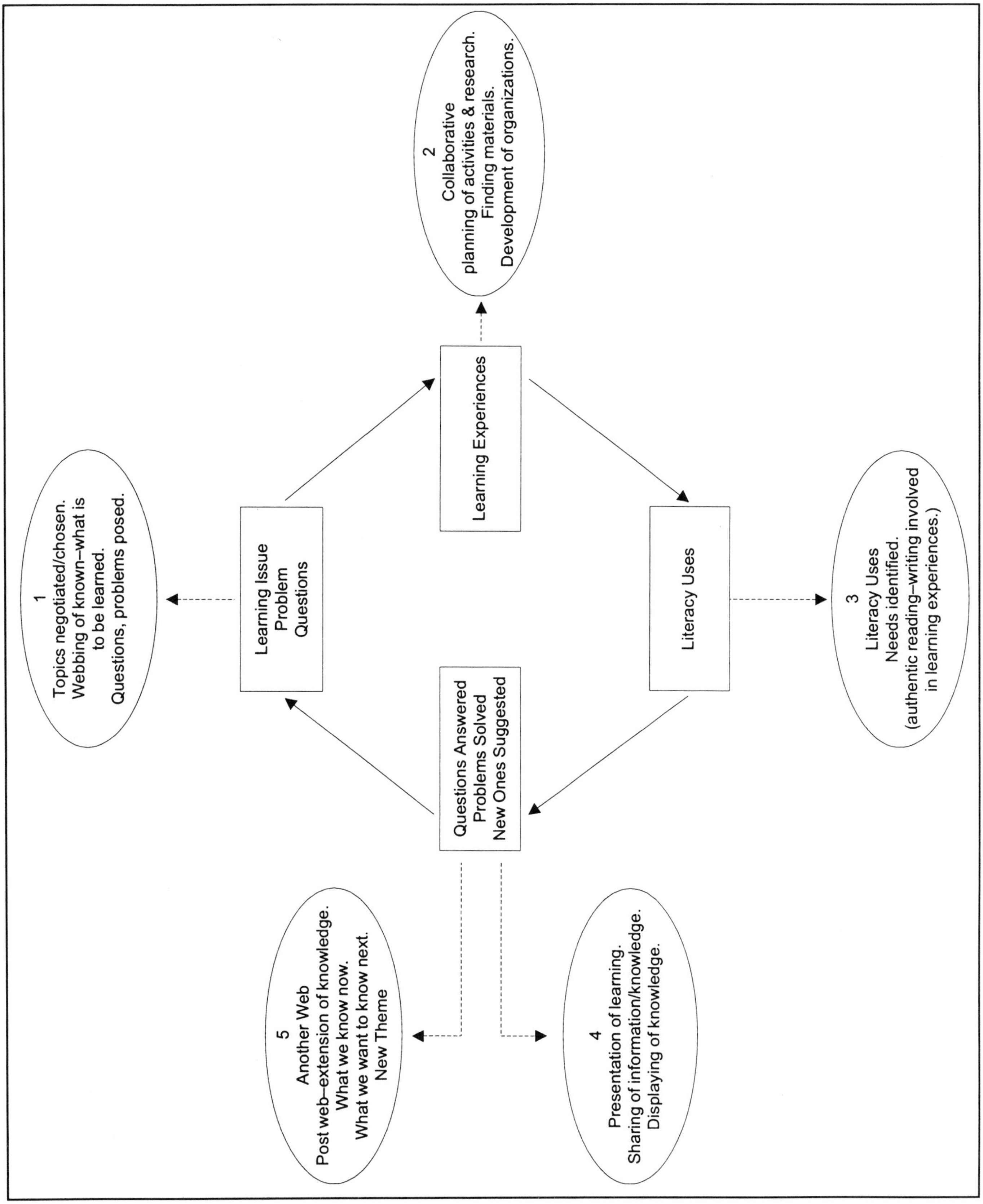
1
Topics negotiated/chosen.
Webbing of known–what is
to be learned.
Questions, problems posed.
Learning Issue
Problem
Questions
Learning Experiences
2
Collaborative
planning of activities & research.
Finding materials.
Development of organizations.
Literacy Uses
3
Literacy Uses
Needs identified.
(authentic reading–writing involved
in learning experiences.)
Questions Answered
Problems Solved
New Ones Suggested
4
Presentation of learning.
Sharing of information/knowledge.
Displaying of knowledge.
5
Another Web
Post web–extension of knowledge.
What we know now.
What we want to know next.
New Theme

Figure 3: *The Learning Process Using Theme Cycles*

learned from such a study and what types of resources are available. Once a topic is chosen, the teacher records what the children already know about it on a "What We Know" chart. This chart includes children's thoughts, experiences, assumptions, and even misconceptions about the topic. Each child's contribution is accepted and recorded. Sometimes a web is created to depict both the major and subcategories that emerge.

Posing Questions: Next, the children pose questions, problems, or curiosities they have about the topic. These, too, are recorded on a chart. It is not unusual for children to generate fifty to sixty questions. These questions or problems provide the understructure and the guide posts for the theme cycle. They are used by the teacher and children to co-plan the learning experiences that will be necessary to fully explore the chosen topic.

Co-planning Experiences: In this part of the theme cycle, the teacher helps the children figure out ways to solve their problems and questions. They may decide to have outside speakers, interview experts, or conduct surveys in the community. These experiences provide the children with an opportunity to explore, discover, analyze, and critique various aspects of the topic at hand. The knowledge base, tools, and learning strategies associated with the disciplines of science, social studies, math, etc., are used as needed.

Identifying Literacy Uses: Once potential learning experiences are decided upon, the teacher and students brainstorm authentic ways to use reading and writing. For example, students may decide to read a variety of texts, keep learning logs, write letters, graph and chart information derived from the data collection, record and transcribe interviews, and/or write reports.

Presenting New Knowledge: Presenting one's new knowledge is an essential part of the theme cycle process. A variety of sign systems (Harste, 1993) such as music, art, media, literacy, drama, can all be used to present the new knowledge about the topic. Through sharing and presenting, new questions and issues emerge. These often lead to a new area of study. Thus, the theme cycle continues.

Changing Our Classrooms

Changing and transforming beliefs, assumptions, and practices related to the teaching/learning process is a difficult, yet exciting task. Traditionally, change was thought to be brought about through staff development programs presented to teachers in a transmission-like mode. However, teachers, like all learners, need to be in charge of their own learning. Faced with the challenge of simultaneously creating new knowledge and constructing new social contexts in the classroom, teachers need to form their own community of learners. They need to take risks, pose and solve problems collaboratively, and engage in dialogue with others (administrators, curriculum specialists, teacher-educators, parents) who can contribute to their learning.

The best way to learn about the theme cycle, then, is to engage in it yourself, and along with your colleagues, embark on an exciting journey of discovery, reinvention, and change.

References

Berthoff, A. (1987). Forward. In P. Freire & D. Macedo, *Literacy: Reading the word and the world* (pp. xi–xxiii). South Hadley, MA: Bergin & Garvey.

Freire, P. (1970). *Pedagogy of the oppressed.* New York: Herder & Herder.

Harste, J. (1993). Inquiry-based instruction. *Primary Voices K–6*, Premier Issue, pp. 2–5.

IMPLEMENTING THEME CYCLE: ONE TEACHER'S WAY

At the end of the first week of school, I asked my third-grade students what they were interested in learning this school year. Raul said he wanted to know what had caused the hurricane in Florida. Andres said he wanted to learn all about music and how music is made. He said he had always wondered how people learned to play instruments.

Vivian said she wanted to be a scientist when she grew up so she wanted to learn all about energy and inventions.

As the students shared their ideas, I wrote them on chart paper so we could have a permanent record of their choices. As the flow of ideas continued, I interjected a few of the topics I have to teach because they are part of the state framework. Once we finished the brainstorming process, the students and I voted on nine themes for the year, assigning each one a month of the coming school year (see Figure 1). For this article, I have chosen our theme cycle on insects to serve as an example of the theme cycle process.

We began our study of insects by tapping our collective knowledge. The day before we embarked on our theme cycle, the students' homework assignment was to list five things they already knew about insects and five things they wanted to know. This helped get everyone prepared for the sharing session. This is a very important part of the theme cycle process because it values the knowledge that the students bring to the theme, and it shows that each student's voice counts. During the sharing session, I recorded our questions and curiosities on two charts, one entitled *What We Know about Insects* and the other entitled *What We Want to Learn about Insects*. All facts, questions, and assumptions were accepted and recorded. Our class is bilingual; therefore, we had charts in English and in Spanish (see Figure 2). The items on the list were then grouped into four categories: insect characteristics, systems, interdependence, and change.

Elena Castro

Third-grade bilingual teacher, Dool Elementary School, Calexico, California

THEME CYCLES ROOM 42 1992-93		
MONTH	**THEME**	**ISSUE/CONCEPT**
September	Natural Disasters	Energy Environmental changes Co-existance Patterns of change Cause/Effect
October	Music	Appreciation Patterns Evolution Measurement
November December	Imperial Valley	Perseverence Historical background Environmental changes
January	Cultures	Interdependence Tolerance Appreciation Cooperation Ancestry
February March	Wild Animals	Extinction/Endangered Characteristics Categories Interdependence Stability
April	Insects	Systems and Interactions Characteristics Interdependence
May	Inventions	Evolution Dependence Invention vs discovery
June	Human Body	Systems within Abuse Energy

Figure 1. Themes for the Year

Spanish

Lo que queremos aprender de los insectos
1. ¿Cuáles son cochinos?
   la mosca y la cucaracha son cochinos
2. ¿Cuáles cambian de colores?
   El insecto Palo cambia de colores
3. ¿Qué tan recio corren?
   Algunos coren resio como la cucaracha
4.
5.
6.
7.
8.
9.

English

What we Know about Insects
1. Some insects fly. yes
2. Some lay eggs. yes
3. Some insects have eight legs. no
4.
5.
6.
7.
8.
9.

Figure 2. "What We Know" Charts (It is important to note that the English chart is not a translation of the Spanish. The questions on each chart are usually different.)

The students easily generated fifty to sixty interesting questions about insects. From the questions and categories, I organized learning experiences (see Figure 3) that enabled students to construct the knowledge they were seeking. These learning experiences occurred in a variety of groupings (whole group, half-class groups, small groups of 2–8 students, or individually) and in workshops and learning station settings.

We were interested in knowing where insects lived, what insects ate, how they moved, and which insects were harmful or beneficial to people. The children consulted a variety of resources to answer their questions about particular insects. Their findings were recorded on a matrix (see Figure 4).

The students also wanted to know how, if at all, insects were like people. They wondered if insects had jobs, families, wars, or feelings. We began to read about the social insects such as bees and ants. We read books, both expository and narrative, and talked about how each bee in a hive has its job and how the queen bee is the ruler. The students were excited to learn how bees recognize each other, how they communicated, and how the queen bee is served by soldiers who protect the hive from intruders. We compared the bees and ants, using a Venn diagram, and we also compared and contrasted the bees with ourselves. We discussed the responsibilities of the male and female in the bee colony as compared to our perception of human male and female responsibilities. Each child shared and presented what they thought were their own and their mother's and father's responsibilities to the family.

Another of the learning experiences in the insect theme cycle was for each student to do a research project on one insect. Students were free to choose which insect they wanted to research. Such in-depth studies allow for individ-

Theme Cycle: _Insects_

Initiating Activity: _"Talking Mural"_
Culminating Activity: _Insect Cookies / Butterfly release_

Key Concepts/Cognitive Skills: _Interdependence_ _Characteristics_ _Systems/Interactions_

	Science Center	Math Workshop	Art Center	Teacher's Workshop	Listening/Interest Center	Writing Center	COLLABORATIVE ACTIVITIES
	Activity Description	Activity Description	Activity Description	Activity Description	Activity Description	Activity Description	
Week #1	Identify parts of a grasshopper. Hypothesize what size what each part is used for. — Science Log	Using pattern blocks create an insect. Identify: · 3 body parts · 6 legs · antennae	Symmetry: Paint one side of a butterfly using tempera. Fold to create symmetry	Research — Selection of insect — identifying sources	Listen to "What is an Insect" — Outline characteristics of an insect.	Writing Prompt — "Giant Insect Invades City"	① Talking Mural ② Resource Chart — insects ③ Habitat Chart ④ AIMS - Comparison spider/ insect
Week #2	Matrix— Identify for different insects · habitat · what it eats · where it lives · harmful/ beneficial — science Log	Measurement of different size beetles. Organize by using >, <, =	Use glue on cardboard to draw with insect. Cover with (foil) Decorate with Marker pens. Add habitat	Read "Diggericks" by Lobel — Discuss Limerick structure. — Students write their own limmericks	Listen to "Interesting Insects" — Write and draw about interesting facts.	Research: — using sources to write 1st draft.	⑤ Groupings of Insects ⑥ "What's In Your Jar"— Students bring an insect — they describe in writing
Week #3	— Observe and record metamorphosis of a butterfly — Science Log	Graph the kinds and amounts of insects found at home (yard). Name the different habitats	"What Hatches From Your Egg?" Draw insect eggs on white shape. Cut out yellow egg. Write self. Write insect	Insect ABC Book (audience: K-partners) Brainstorm insects for each letter. Research into each insect.	Listen to "Honeybees and Ants" Using Venn diagram compare and contrast	Research — Peer editing and teacher editing	AIMS: ⑦ Mealworm metamorphosis — graph change over time ⑧ Presentation of Projects ⑨ "What I learned" Essays
Week #4	— Observe and record metamorphosis of a butterfly — Science Log	Measure the wing span of different butterflies. Write conclusions	Metamorphosis Pop-up book — Illustrate and describe stays of metamorphosis	Read "Honey-Bees" — Map out information — Collaborative Text on what was learned. — Discussion comparisons comparisons to humans	Listen to "Insects that Help and Insects that Harm" — Interdependence — how do we help and hurt each other (insects/man)	Research: final draft and illustration	**Suggested Read-Aloud TITLES:** _James and The Giant Peach_ _Very Hungry Caterpillar_ _Grouchy Ladybug_ _The Monarch Butterfly_ _Honeybees_ _Bugs_

Carpenter 1992.

Figure 3. Learning Experiences

Spanish

Nombre __Marisela L__

Insectos

Nombre del Insecto	¿Dónde vive?	¿Qué comen?	¿Cómo se mueve?	¿Es dañoso o bueno para la gente?
Chapulín	En las plantas	Plantas	brincan y caminan	son dañosos porque se com las cosechas
Campamocha	En plantas donde esta caliente	Comen Insectos	Caminan	Ayuda a la gente porque se comen a los incectos malos
Escorpión	Vive en la tierra	Comen Insectos	Caminar	Es dañoso porque su piquete es venenoso
Mariposa	Vive en aire y plantas	El nectar de las flores	Vuelan	Ayudan a que las flores crescan
Abeja	En las Colmenas	El nectar delas flor	Vuelan	Ayadan a las plantas
Cucaracha	En casas y plantas	Cualquier cosa	Caminan	Son dañosas porque transmite enfermedades
Grillo	En rocas y Arboles	Comen Plantas	Brincan	pueden dañar a la gente
Mosca	En vasura o casas.	Comen Cualquier	Vuelan	tranmiten Enfermedades
Mosco	Cerca del agua	Chupan sangre	Vuelan	Son dañosos Porque transmiti enfermedades
Pinacate	bajo tierra	comen plantas	Camino	Son dañosos porque se comen

English

Science Center

Name __Karla Alteran__

Insects

Name of Insect	Where does it live?	What does it eat?	How does it move?	Is it harmful or helpful to man?
Grasshopper	grass.	plants.	crawls and jump.	harmful because they eat crops
Praying mantis	plants and warm plces	Insects	crawls	Helpful to person because they eat other insects.
scorpion	under ground	Insects.	crawls.	harmful because they are poisonous
butterfly	Air and Plnts.	Nectar.	Fly.	Helpful because they eat pollinate flower
bee	Hives.	Nectar.	Fly.	Helpful because the honey and wax
cockroach	homes and pa	Anithing	crawls.	harmful because they carry diseases.
cricket	Rocks	Plants.	hopping.	harmful to men.
housefly	Trash or house.	Anithin	fly.	harmful to man because transmet diseases
mosquito	water.	blood.	fly.	harmful because transment disease
beetle	Onderground	Insect	crawl	harmful to man because they eat up Plants

Figure 4

ual interests. Part of the individual research is presenting what they have learned, since I believe that the presentation of knowledge is as important as the students' search for knowledge.

The selection of which insect each student would research was made at the beginning of the cycle and the project took about three weeks to complete. Karla decided to study the centipede. She started by drawing her centipede and writing something she already knew about it. This was to be part of a "talking mural" bulletin board and later part of a class book (see Figure 5). Collectively, the students could see what knowledge they had brought to their research and how much more they had learned by the project's end.

Karla worked on her research project during workshop time and at her desk when her other tasks were completed. She began by writing what she knew and then recorded her questions about centipedes. She then looked for information in encyclopedias, books, magazines, cards, etc. Once Karla was done with her initial draft, she sought help from a peer editor and then from me. When Karla was done with her revisions and editing, she completed her final draft and illustration and the report became part of our class research book on insects. (See Figure 6).

One of the goals of the theme cycle is to integrate the different content areas and disciplines within the theme but not to force this integration. In our classroom, we try to find the natural connections through learning experiences at an Art Station, Math Station, Listening

Figure 5. *Karla's Initial Work on Centipedes*

Station, and a Science Station. One activity at the Math Station was to measure and compare the wing span of different butterflies. We had caterpillers at the Science Station, so that we could observe and record the process of metamorphosis.

At the Art Station, we made a pop-up book, illustrating the steps of metamorphosis: At the Listening Station, we listened to a book about bugs. We learned that all insects are bugs, but not all bugs are insects. This helped us clarify our assumptions about insects.

Through their research, the children as a group became interested in habitats. Therefore, we all began to read about insects that occupy particular habitats. As we read, each insect was categorized on a chart according to where it lived (see Figure 7). This information was also

illustrated. It is important to remember that all these learning experiences were based on the questions the learning community generated at the beginning of the cycle as well as on the questions that emerged from their newly acquired knowledge.

Four weeks later, at the end of the insect theme cycle, the students each presented their research projects to their peers via talking murals, charts, matrices, books, and graphs. To bring closure to our cycle, we took all our newly hatched butterflies and set them free in our school playground; a few of us shed a tear. It was the end of a theme study, but for the butterflies, as well as for the children, it marked the beginning of a new cycle. To celebrate the end of a collective quest, we ate the insect cookies we made and talked about all we had learned during our study and about what we would be exploring next.

Reflections

The process of theme cycles is at once overwhelming and challenging, difficult and satisfying, and it is a step I will never regret taking. When I began to really listen to my students—to use their curiosities, to share their excitement in the discovery and creation of knowledge— I also began to understand my real role as a teacher. Creating a community of learners-as-teachers and teacher-as-learner is a big step toward democracy in action. I know now how much more children benefit from a classroom where they become active learners and teachers. I am no longer the center nor the source of all knowledge. My students' voices, curiosities, and needs to know have been empowered through the theme cycle process. I urge everyone to take that first step.

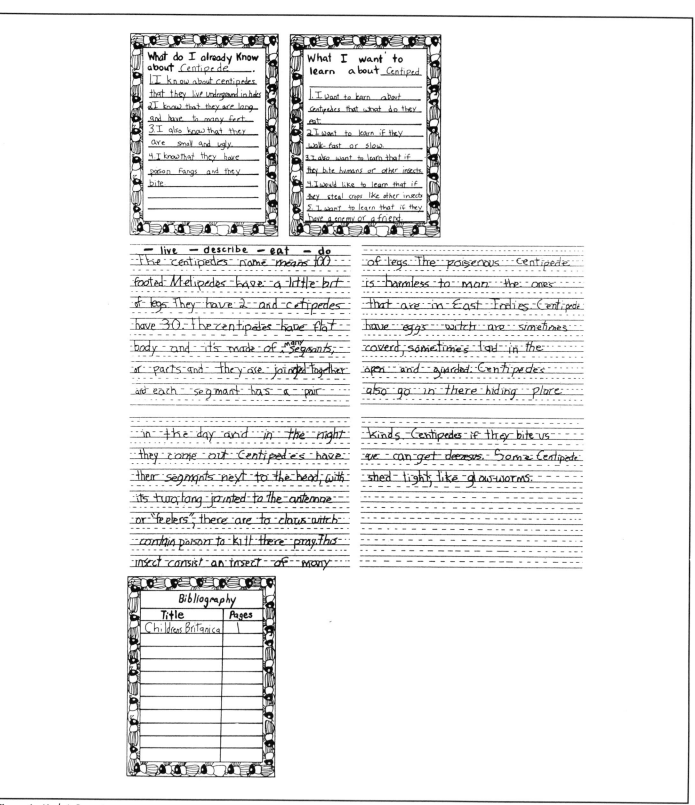

Figure 6. Karla's Report

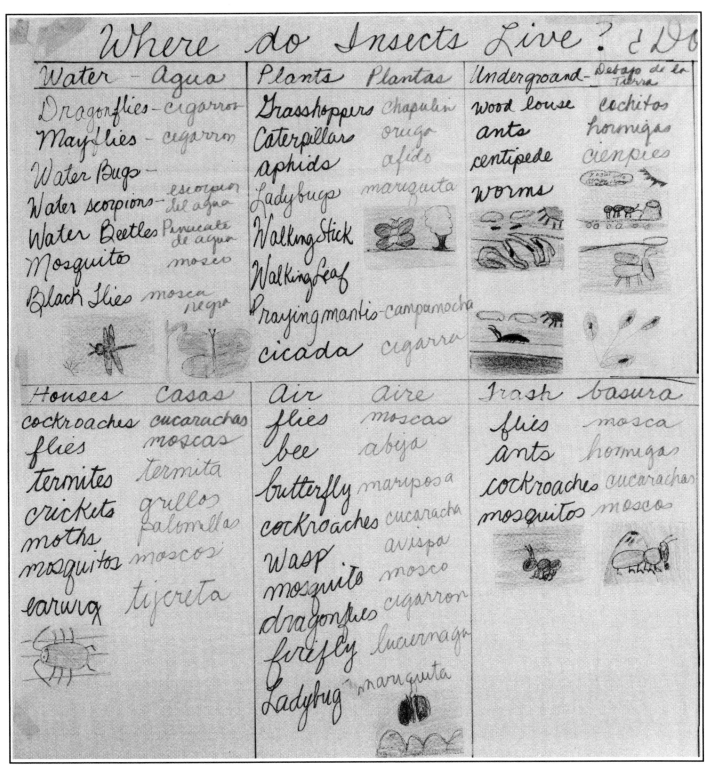

Figure 7. Partial Representation of Habitat Chart

Daily Schedule

8:10 – 8:30	Opening: Flag Salute, Roll Call, Bellwork, Collect Homework
8:30 – 8:50	Oral Language Development: Calendar, Current Events, Songs and Chants, Booksharing
8:50 – 9:10	Read-Aloud: Literature Studies
9:10 – 9:40	Whole Group: Science, Language Arts
	Wednesdays: Physical Education
9:40 – 10:00	Recess
10:00 – 11:45	Integrated Language Arts/Science, Social Studies, Art, Mathematics
	Four groups rotate to different learning stations and workshops. All work at stations is based on the theme cycle under study.
11:45 – 12:45	Lunch
12:45 – 1:10	D.E.A.R. Time: silent reading
1:10 – 1:40	Writer's Workshop
1:40 – 1:50	Recess
1:50 – 2:30	(M-W-F) Mathematics using manipulatives
	(T-Th) Physical Education
2:30 – 2:40	Learning Logs: Students reflect on what they learned for the day

This is the general schedule for Monday through Thursday. On Friday, instead of rotations, we do science experiments, cooking, super kid, and author's chair. We also incorporate the following:

Peer Reading and Writing:	Thursday 1:00 - 1:30	Kindergarten
	Tuesday 8:30 - 9:00	Fifth Grade
Computer Writing Lab:	Monday 8:30 - 9:30	
	Wednesday 10:00 - 11:00	
	Friday 11:00 - 11:40	
Library:	Friday 8:30 - 9:00	

Lingering Questions

1. How do I involve my students more in the planning and creation of the learning experiences?

2. How do we, as a class, involve the community more within the themes that we study?

3. How do I further incorporate social, political, "real life" issues into the theme cycle process?

Our Struggles with Theme Cycle

As beginning bilingual whole language teachers, we faced many challenges and experienced many struggles. Some were theoretical, some practical; some related to student resistance, some related to colleague relations; and some were just plain threatening to the status quo. We had underestimated the magnitude and the complexity of implementing a theory-in-action approach to teaching. We knew that 1) knowledge is socially constructed (Vygotsky, 1978; Diaz & Moll, 1987); 2) language and literacy are tools and need to be used for real and authentic purposes (Halliday, 1975; Goodman and Goodman, 1979; Edelsky, 1986); 3) children are "knowing subjects" capable of creating knowledge and constructing their world; 4) teachers are also learners and that the learner is also a teacher; and 5) theme cycle is one way of knowing (Altwerger and Flores, 1991). We understood that the theme cycle process is a way for teachers and children to reconstruct knowledge based on their needs to know. We had visited Elena Castro's classroom, and we knew what it looked like in action. What we didn't know was how much work was involved in the everyday "how-to-do-it."

Implementing theme cycle inevitably created a tension between beliefs and action. This tension, however, was generative. It caused us to continually ask ourselves new questions and shift our stance towards our students. We found that as we learned to respect our students' potential and thinking abilities, we grew more confident in orchestrating the theme cycle process. The struggles between theory and practice proved essential to our professional development.

In this article, we share some of the struggles we experienced as we moved away from a "banking education" view of learning/teaching to a more "pedagogy of knowing" view of learning/teaching (Berthoff, 1987). In so doing, we hope to demonstrate that "coming to know" theme cycles in a bilingual setting, as in any setting, is a saga of struggles, rewards, and satisfaction.

Students as Learners

One of our more formidable struggles was our students' resistance. These third and fourth graders were not accustomed to participating in their own learning. Their experience in school had been one of "no choice," i.e., the teacher tells you what to do and what to study. They dared not take risks, think for themselves, or be authors of their own learning.

At first, when we began tapping collective knowledge, the students' responses were generic and superficial. For example, in the theme cycle "Me and My Family," students would say, "We live in a house." "We have brothers and sisters." "We have grandparents, cousins, aunts, and uncles." It was difficult to value such generalities, but it was necessary in order to show them respect for their knowledge. We knew these efforts were seeds for the students' potential development. We continued to probe, asking about their curiosities and specific

Marty Andrews-Sullivan

Fourth-grade bilingual teacher, Live Oak Elementary School, Fontana, California

Esther Orono Negrete

Third-grade bilingual teacher, Warm Springs Elementary School, San Bernardino, California

topics of interest. Eventually, these seeds began to grow. Our initial steps—to guide, organize, and mediate the students' inquiry process (Harste, 1993), not to control it—helped the students realize that what they already knew was valued. By asking them about their interests, we demonstrated respect for the learning/teaching process.

As we evolved in implementing theme cycles, the children's inquiries showed more depth: "Why do people die?" "Why do parents divorce?" "How do we grow?" "Why do we grow?" "Why do some people not like other people?" These questions demonstrate how the children reclaimed their curiosities and voices. The theme cycle process restored and empowered our children's voices.

Getting the students to understand that the teacher is not the possessor of all knowledge was difficult. Sometimes it was necessary to make dramatic contrasts. One time, Mrs. Negrete taught the textbook (banking) way. The students, then, had to compare and contrast it with the theme cycle way. This critique enabled the students to qualitatively assess the differences between how learning and teaching were viewed, practiced, and evaluated in each situation.

The fact that the students engage in their own learning/teaching does not mean that they learn through osmosis or by themselves. We were still the authority, but not the authoritarian. Freire and Macedo (1987) make this distinction and state that the teacher is still in charge, but does not dictate facts, require memorizations, or just lecture for its own sake. The teacher teaches as a learner, while acting as a guide, facilitator, mediator, demonstrator, supporter, and organizer in helping students come to know.

The theme cycle process restored and empowered our children's voices.

Resources

Without adequate books, media, and resources, we knew our students' research would be limited. Consequently, we collected a wide variety of materials and books for our classroom library. We became scavengers, consultants to the school librarian, and familiar faces to the public librarians. We volunteered to be on the school book selection committee so that we could decide how funds would be spent to buy materials, literature, resource books, computer software, videos, and art supplies. Participation on the committee was an invaluable asset in acquiring bilingual materials, resources, and books. We also created many of our materials and translated several texts from English to Spanish.

Planning

Planning the theme cycle based on the questions and queries that our students generated was another major struggle. We were not used to organizing learning experiences based on students' needs to know. We found that the planning could be overwhelming and very frustrating for one person, so we worked together or with three or four colleagues. In that environment, ideas and creativity seemed to flow. We planned learning/teaching experiences that were for the whole class (read alouds, observing an event, storytelling), pairs of students (reading buddies, writing partners), small groups (authors' workshop, literature study), committees (research teams, issue/interest groups), and individuals (observation logs, learning logs, miniresearch).

We discovered that planning and implementing theme cycles gets easier with experience. We also found that when teachers collaborate and work together, their expectations are greater and the tasks are more challenging. Thus, planning has become more meaningful and more authentic. We do still have to resist the easy way out, such as using dittos as fillers. We do use worksheets, but they are based on the students' queries and are used to guide them in deepening their understandings. For example, in the theme cycle "Me and My Family," the students asked, "How many brothers and sisters do we have together?" To answer this question, we created a bar graph to illustrate the total number of siblings for our classroom. Next we created a worksheet that posed several questions based on the information on the graph. One of the questions was, "Are there more students with two brothers or more with three brothers?" These types of opportunities were deliberately structured to engage students in more complex thinking.

Planning also involved making decisions about the amount and quality of work the students would be required to do, especially at the learning stations. We found that sometimes the amount of work was too much for the time we alloted; other times it was not enough. We consulted with the children on what to do about this problem, and the group created a process for evaluating the quality and amount of work expected. This was a critical turning point for all of us; it helped us understand the need to balance, step back, reflect, and experiment.

Creating Community

Our goal was to create a community of learners. We wanted the classroom to become the students' workplace—a place where they could socially engage in creating and presenting knowledge and posing problems. In so doing, we were also encouraging them to discover new ways of learning, interacting, thinking,

and doing. We shifted the physical layout and use of space in order to get our work done. Because we had deliberately structured the theme cycle process to meet their needs to know and organized the physical space to accomplish these goals, the students all viewed themselves as learners. Politically we eliminated the hierarchy of learning by eliminating ability grouping. What evolved was a community of learners who were all capable of learning and who had access to knowledge; this is a significant socio-political by-product of the theme cycle process. This milieu, we believe, was created and sustained through the daily learning/teaching actions by both teachers and learners.

Closing Remarks

We have learned that:

1. teaching students by using theme cycles requires much preparation on the part of the teachers;

2. theme instruction allows for the integration of all the content areas;

3. theme cycles help students to see that everything is connected to something else;

4. students can learn how to make choices and decisions;

5. it is important to value students' knowledge and questions; and

6. as students become more confident about themselves as learners, they become more assertive, take more risks, and experience a rebirth in their curiosity.

We also have learned that as teachers we need to value all cultural and language backgrounds because each child brings a richness to the classroom from which everyone can benefit. We have come to realize that all children are capable of learning with the proper guidance

We also have learned that as teachers we need to value all cultural and language backgrounds because each child brings a richness to the classroom from which everyone can benefit.

and respect, and we have deepened our understanding of the importance of building on what children know. Through these experiences we have become kid watchers (Y. Goodman, 1978). We want our students to think, to discover, to generate knowledge, to pose and solve problems, to engage in debate, to work together, to learn. We believe that through the theme cycle, they do all these and more. We believe the struggle is worthwhile. We see the children's enthusiasm in their eyes, their smiles, their confident walk, and their voices.

We are just beginning our careers as teachers. We still have a long way to go, but we have also come a long way. We hope that by sharing our struggles with theme cycle, we have contributed in some way to the understanding of others.

References

Altwerger, B., & Flores, B. (1991). The theme cycle: An overview. In K. Goodman, L. Bird, & Y. Goodman (Eds.), *The whole language catalog* (p. 295). New York: Macmillan-McGraw Hill.

Berthoff, A. (1987). Forward. In P. Freire & D. Macedo, *Literacy: Reading the word and the world* (pp. xi–xxiii). South Hadley, MA: Bergin & Garvey.

Diaz, E., & Moll, L. (1987). Change as the goal in educational research. *Anthropology and Education Quarterly, 18* (4), 300–311.

Edelsky, C. (1986). Living in the author's world: Analyzing the author's craft. *The California Reader, 21,* 14–17.

Freire, P. (1970). *Pedagogy of the oppressed.* New York: Herder & Herder.

Freire, P., & Macedo, D. (1987). *Literacy: Reading the word and the world.* South Hadley, MA: Bergin & Garvey.

Goodman, K. (1986). *What's whole in whole language?* Portsmouth, NH: Heinemann.

Goodman, K., & Goodman, Y. (1979). Learning to read is natural. In L. Resnick & P. Weaver (Eds.), *Theory and practice of early reading* (pp. 137–154). Hillsdale, NJ: Erlbaum.

Goodman, Y. (1978). Kidwatching: An alternative to testing. *National Elementary Principal, 57,* 41–45.

Halliday, M. (1975). *Learning how to mean.* London: Edward Arnold.

Harste, J. (1993). Inquiry-based instruction. *Primary Voices K–6,* Premier Issue, 2–5.

Vygotsky, L. (1978). *Mind in society.* Cambridge: Harvard University Press.

Daily Schedule

8:10-8:30	All school run and pledge
8:30-8:45	Attendance and read aloud
8:45-9:00	Book sharing
9:00-9:30	1st Rotation
9:30-10:15	2nd Rotation

Recess 9:45-10:00 (during 2nd Rotation)

10:15-10:45	3rd Rotation
10:45-11:15	4th Rotation

Recess 11:00-11:10 (4th Rotation is 20 minutes)

11:15-11:45	5th Rotation
11:45-11:50	Clean up and prep for lunch

Lunch 11:50-12:30

12:30-1:00	Math
1:00-1:45	Science or Computers
1:45-2:30	Social Studies or P.E.
2:30-2:40	Journal "What I learned today"
2:40	Dismissal

Lingering Questions

1. How do teachers continue to awaken the children's curiosities, imaginations, and creativity in teaching/learning?

2. How will the inconsistent pedagogical philosophies affect the children (i.e., one year in a whole language classroom and the next in a traditional classroom?

3. How do we continue to develop in our understanding of learning/teaching?

4. How do we, as whole language teachers, recognize our knowledge plateaus so that we can go beyond our comfort zones?

Publishers and Distributors We Used as Resources for Bilingual Materials

1. Arroyo Books
   5505 N. Figueroa Street
   Los Angeles, CA 90042-4119
   213/227-1794
2. Children's Press
   544 N. Cumberland Avenue
   Chicago, IL 60656
   800/621-1115
3. Creative Edge Inc.
   80 Pineview Drive
   Amherst, NY 14228
   716/619-1100
4. DDL Books, Inc.
   6521 N.W. 87th Avenue
   Miami, FL 33178
   800/635-4276
5. Donars Spanish Books
   P.O. Box 24
   Loveland, CO 80539
   303/663-2124
6. Edumate Educational
   Materials
   2231 Morena Blvd.
   San Diego, CA 92110
   619/275-7117
7. El Correo de Cuentos
   P.O. Box 66521
   Pico Rivera, CA 90660
   310/695-2012
8. Global Village
   9537 Culver Blvd.
   Culver City, CA 90232
   310/204-4018
9. Hampton-Brown Books
   26385 Carmel Rancho Blvd.
   Carmel, CA 93923
   800/333-3510
10. Hispanic Books Distributors,
    Inc.
    1665 W. Grant Road
    Tucson, AZ 85745
    602/882-9484
11. Ianoconi Book Imports
    2220 Mariposa
    San Francisco, CA 92105
    415/255-8193
12. Jamestown Publishers
    P.O. Box 9168
    Providence, RI 02940
    800/872-7323
13. Jose Luis Orozco
    (Children's Spanish
    Songs/Rhymes)
    P.O. Box 9168
    Berkeley, CA 94707
    510/537-5539
14. Lectorum Publications, Inc.
    137 E. 14th Street
    New York, NY 10011
    800/345-5496
15. Libros Rodrigues
    P.O. Box 2854
    Oxnard, CA 93030
    805/488-8716
16. Los Andes Publishing
    Company
    8303 E. Alondra Blvd.
    Paramount, CA 90723
    310/220-2841
17. Madera Cinevideo
    525 E. Yosemite
    Madera, CA 93638
    209/661-6000
18. Mi Globo Publishing
    (Spanish Weekly Reader)
    15345 Midland Road
    Poway, CA 92064-2222
19. Modern Curriculum Press
    13900 Prospect Road
    Cleveland, OH 44136
    800/321-3106
20. National Clearinghouse for
    Bilingual Education
    1118 22nd Street, N.W.
    Washington, DC 20037
    800/321-6223
21. Niños
    303 Detroit, Suite 305
    Ann Arbor, MI 48104
    313/747-8934
22. Rigby
    P.O. Box 797
    Crystal Lake, IL 60037
    800/822-8661
23. Scholastic, Inc.
    730 Broadway
    New York, NY 10003
    800/392-2179
24. Shen's Books and Supplies
    628 E. Pamela Road
    Arcadia, CA 91006
    818/446-3237
25. Sundance Publishers
    P.O. Box 1326
    Littleton, MA 01460
    800/727-0664
26. Dale Rettinger and Associates
    P.O. Box 31296
    San Francisco, CA 94131
    800/285-1115
27. Zoo Books/Wildlife Education
    3590 Kettner Blvd.
    San Diego, CA 92101
    619/299-6034

Theme Cycle as a Vehicle for Transformation: One Principal's Story of Change

Bill Cudog

Principal, Dool Elementary School, Calexico, California

Since the mid 1980s, many schools have been engaged in building a more holistic and collaborative instructional model. In California, we have guidance from several state documents such as *The California State Frameworks, Program Quality Review,* and most recently *The California Task Force Reports,* i.e., *It's Elementary.* Armed with these guidelines and the latest educational research on teaching and learning, we, the staff at Dool Elementary School, decided to change to a more learner-centered approach to instruction. We wanted to organize learning and teaching experiences that would help our students make connections with the real world and would incorporate their knowledge, problem-posing strategies, problem-solving processes, critical reflection, and creative talents into the educational process.

For over eight years now we have been rethinking our educational paradigm and moving toward holistic ways of learning and teaching. This dramatic paradigm shift, including the use of theme cycles, has had a domino effect throughout the entire instructional program. It has directly affected ways of instructing students, ways of assessing student growth, ways of communicating with parents, and staff development.

This shift has also redefined my role as a principal. As curricular leader, my role shifted from not only coordinating the curriculum but also knowing and understanding the philosophy of theme cycles.

Curricular Leadership

Using theme cycles has helped us move toward instruction that:

1. redefines the role of teachers and students as co-collaborators and co-creators of their learning/teaching.

2. shifts instruction to a more authentic curriculum based on children's needs to know, interests, and curiosities.

3. creates opportunities for children to work in heterogeneous groups to share collective knowledge on what they know and to pose questions/problems about what they want to learn through the use of brainstorming strategies.

4. supports multiple ways of learning by allowing the children to explore, experiment, and question within real world contexts.

5. embeds and creates many genuine opportunities for the children to read and write for a variety of purposes and reasons.

6. generates possibilities for the integration of the content areas, i.e., integration across the curriculum.

7. respects and values the reinvention of knowledge, the learner-as-teacher and the teacher-as-learner, and the principal-as-partner.

8. raises issues about budget, governance and evaluation that move the school staff towards a team effort and shared decision making under the principal's leadership.

There are no quick fixes to implementing theme cycles. As the curricular leader, I used the "ready-fire-aim-method" to get the ball rolling. Taking this risk required that I believe in my colleagues and that I be willing to share the leadership role with them. As we stepped into this endeavor, I took cues from the teachers on issues related to staff development; acquisition of materials, books, and resources; budget; assessment; and our shifting paradigm. From the beginning, it was imperative to have actual student products to use as evidence for the work we were doing. We knew we needed to support the change from a concrete as well as a philosophical perspective. We relied heavily on our "site experts" in holistic instruction to support the rest of us as we created and shared knowledge and struggled with ongoing concerns and issues.

Staff Development

Providing ongoing professional staff development was crucial in developing theme cycles and making needed changes. We realized that in order to have lasting and meaningful change in instruction, we needed to make a longterm commitment to our professional growth. We also knew that this ongoing staff development must involve teachers, support staff, parents, and administration. Our first goal was to arrange for quality time, especially for the teaching staff, to plan, implement, and assess theme cycles. Currently, we

set aside three hours per week for staff to debrief, to share experiences from their classrooms, and to exchange ideas. This time allows us to learn from each other and to support one another.

Acquisition of Materials, Books, and Resources

Implementing theme cycles posed several administrative challenges. For example, we had to rethink how we order materials, supplies, and books. Traditional textbook orders no longer sufficed. Each year, we begin this process by prioritizing our needs and then collectively deciding how to spend our money. This decision includes deciding on the amount of photocopying we will do; the types of paper we want to purchase; the kinds of art, math, and science materials we need; and so on. Since themes are defined by students and teacher, ongoing communication with the classroom teacher is imperative. A multi-modality instructional program cannot succeed without supplies. Therefore, every effort must be made to support the classroom teacher in creating a rich environment.

Governance Structures

Making decisions about budget led to new governance structures. As more of the teachers began using theme cycles, we had a greater need to purchase consumables for science, math, and other hands-on experiences. Many of these

Therefore, every effort must be made to support the classroom teacher in creating a rich environment.

needs could not be determined on a yearly basis, so it became necessary to set up quarterly team meetings to discuss materials. These meetings ensured ongoing communication and allowed us to monitor the ordering of instructional materials, books, and resources throughout the entire year.

Team members were chosen from each of the grade levels. Their initial responsibility to order and monitor materials soon expanded to one of determining grade-level needs, concerns, and focus. In addition, these quarterly meetings became important in defining how we would report our progress in developing theme cycles; in devising ways to evaluate staff and programs, and in revising ways for assessing children's growth.

This school-wide decision-making process, which is based on a more representative and participatory governance structure, has created a sense of community and a forum for negotiating and for sharing responsibility. The ongoing communication also leaves the door open for voicing dissent or trying out a new idea.

Evaluation and Assessment

Developing vehicles for staff evaluation and student assessment that were consistent with theme cycles became a priority. We created two forms of teacher evaluation: one in which the teacher self-monitors and documents each theme cycle and the other in which the principal formally evaluates the teacher's varying tasks within the theme cycle. (See Administrative Connections at the end of this article.) The self-monitoring form (Theme Cycle Reporting Form) serves a record-keeping function. The formal quarterly administrative evaluation (Quarterly Instructional Monitoring) was jointly constructed by the teachers and me to capture both the process and the product of theme cycles.

Teachers' self- and collective assessments of the curricular characteristics of each theme cycle also help teacher evaluation become a more democratic process. Teacher representatives from each grade level summarize these characteristics by outlining: types of instructional experiences, materials, and resources (e.g., literature studies, fiction/nonfiction materials used); actions/behaviors (teachers' lesson plans, ways of talking, ways of teaching); and artifacts (students' products such as reports, narratives, "What I Know" and "What I Want to Know" charts). This collaborative process is meaningful and supportive because it is defined by teachers and administrators and is based on the intents, expectations, and actions of the children and teacher carrying out the theme cycle, not on those imposed from outside by district mandate. Having specific criteria that are negotiated by the staff eliminated the ambiguity we had felt in previous years. As an administrator, I felt that this was the first time in sixteen years that we were really addressing curricular needs.

Student Assessment

Traditional ways of reporting student progress, including the use of standardized test scores, were not aligned with our holistic philosophy of learning and teaching. Therefore, as we moved away from a sub-skill, isolated, rote memorization curriculum, it became necessary to develop methods of assessment that included both process and product. The traditional report card was first to be revised. We moved to a narrative format focused on documenting student growth. This was consistent with the school's new portfolio program that included student samples, questionnaires, surveys, and anecdotal records. Through portfolio assessment, we record, document, and demonstrate our children's growth. The advantages have been many:

1. We better understand children's progress.

2. Staff, students, and parents have become a more cohesive unit through the use of the portfolio.

3. We have developed expectations beyond the status quo—children's potential is far greater than ever imagined.

4. We, as staff members, feel more connected as we review documentation from previous years that details student growth across time, contexts, and grade levels.

5. Such documentation has served as a catalyst, challenging us to increase our expectations and to tailor instruction for specific students' needs.

6. By documenting our students' growth in math, literature, writing, science, and social studies, we have come to a better understanding of the relationship between teaching and learning.

7. Students and teachers use the portfolio to review their work and to celebrate their progress.

8. Parents' levels of understanding and expectations about the curriculum have markedly increased. They are now more knowledgeable about the use of theme cycles, as well as about other curricular components, such as scientific method, literature studies, writers' workshop, and learning logs.

Conclusion

Theme cycles have been a catalyst for change, a challenge to implement, and an impetus to create new ways of conducting school more collaboratively, more democratically, and more sanely. Theme cycles are not a panacea but they are the best pedagogy our staff has to date. Through the use of theme cycles, we have come to value choice, collective commitment, strong curricular leadership, a governance structure that facilitiates the process of change through shared decision making, parent involvement, and ongoing professional staff development.

We no longer fear change; we embrace it. We understand that change is a part of growth. We have learned that administrators, teachers, parents, and students working in concert can create a learning community that is responsive to the needs of our children. Redefining education so as to prepare our children for the world is no easy task. We all must accept the challenge and find solutions. Our children deserve it. We deserve it. And our nation needs it.

Theme Cycle Reporting Form

Theme _____

Focus _____

Literature Utilized	Key Concepts Learned
	Science:
	Social Studies:
	Math:
	Other:

Resources Utilized	Social Contexts Utilized

Type of Evaluation Utilized	Published Products

Quarterly Instructional Monitoring

Teacher _____ Grade _____ Monitoring Quarter _____ Date _____

Theme Cycles

_____
_____
_____
_____

Literature Materials
Used in Theme Cycle

_____
_____
_____
_____

Published Material

_____
_____
_____

Supplies/Materials Needed
to Implement

_____
_____
_____

Literature Studies

Title   Strategy used
_____

_____

_____

Math Concepts

_____
_____
_____
_____

Manipulatives Supporting
Math Concepts

_____
_____
_____

Inhibitors

_____
_____
_____
_____

Portfolios

1. Writing Prompts _____

2. Writing Process _____

3. Inventories _____

4. Book List _____

5. Other _____

Programs Used

_____
_____
_____
_____
_____

Comments/Focus

_____
_____
_____
_____
_____

Democracy in Action: Negotiating the Curriculum Beyond the Classroom

Karen Dockstader-Anderson

Seventh-grade humanities teacher, Lyndon Baines Johnson Middle School, Albuquerque, New Mexico

Since 1970, when I was teaching in Harlem, I have believed education is a political activity. It was twelve years later that I finally found a pedagogy to match this belief—whole language. It was then that Bess Altwerger introduced me to the writings of Paolo Freire, Henry Giroux, and Stanley Aronowitz, and combined it with Theme Cycle. I now had a paradigm matching my belief that, to function in a democratic society, schooling must take place in a democratic atmosphere. Since then, I have been developing and refining my actions in the classroom.

Two years ago, a theme cycle I had negotiated with my students had a deep effect on me—I became a vegetarian. We began the school year like most of my years begin, with discussions of different political systems. We talked about the differences among a democracy, a dictatorship, and a monarchy. I compare each system to the way our class could function. A democracy would be one in which many of the decisions during the year would be voted on and one in which we all would have an equal say, one person one vote. I would be queen of the class in a monarchy and all students would pay me homage. All decisions would be made by me in a dictatorship; students would have no choice and no voice. After this discussion, we voted on what kind of class we would like to have. As with every class during the last ten years, the students selected a democratic classroom.

In a democratic classroom, students and teachers vote on the topics to be studied. The first step is to brainstorm ideas; anything is acceptable and no judgments are made. I tell them they have a universe of universes, there are no limits. Anything we want to study will be written on the bulletin board paper. Students always test out the "no limits" idea by saying anything they think might be rejected. I write everything down from curse words to Disneyland. After they see I am serious, they begin generating ideas they think they really would like to study.

With my '90–'91 third-grade class we generated 200 to 300 ideas, and added to the list throughout the day. The next day we categorized the ideas based on commonalties. We came up with five major topics of study: animals, astronomy, electricity, toys, and geology. We also had a miscellaneous category for ideas that did not seem to fit anywhere.

Once the topics were decided on, we had one day to lobby for a specific topic. During this time, we talked about all the things we could think of to make a specific topic interesting, e.g., building a small house with electrical circuits for the electricity theme, making our own toys for the toy theme, or gathering a rock collection for geology. Many curriculum ideas were also generated during this time. I took notes on the different ideas and incorporated them into the chosen theme. We lobbied informally throughout the day but set aside a specific time for formal lobbying, keeping in mind our class rule against bribing or bullying each other during the lobbying and voting processes. We also talked about what really interested us and which topic could sustain our interest for an extended time. (My classes usually do two or three themes per year averaging twelve weeks each.)

At the beginning of the next week, we went over the topics and some of the ideas that were generated during lobbying, and then we voted. Each member of the class was given a ballot with all the topics listed. An outside person counted the ballots, in this case a student from a fourth-grade class. The majority voted for astronomy, with animals running a close second. The students suggested we study animals after astronomy rather than renegotiate at the end of the astronomy theme.

Students formed groups of three or four. Each student is responsible for the other students in her or his group. They support each other in completion of activities, read to one another, and catch each other up when someone is absent. All of the centers have written instructions and taped instructions based on student- and teacher-generated questions. Each group moves as a whole through the centers; no group moves until everyone in that group is finished with the center. This encourages support and cooperation.

In the next step, we webbed known and unknown information. The questions we asked determined content in each center. We then gathered materials and spent the rest of the week reading about astronomy and building on our background information. Our odyssey had begun. In our three-month study of

astronomy, we learned about astronomical units, gas and solid planets, light years, nebulae, rotations, and orbits. We also found out that we live on a middle-aged planet, five billion years old, and that our solar system is very young in stellar time. One of the students brought in an article from *Parade* magazine, "A Pale Blue Dot" by Carl Sagan. As we skimmed the article, we found out that Earth is one in a million, perhaps one in a billion. We looked at the pictures and began to bring our universal vision back home.

The journey home led us into our theme cycle on animals. We classified over 100 animals into phyla, classes, orders, families, genera, and species. Many of the animals we were interested in were endangered or almost extinct. When we looked more closely at the causes of endangerment, we came to the realization that a minority species was responsible for the destruction of animal habitats and the environment. That species was us. Interest moved to ecology. Several students asked to renegotiate the curriculum and change our overall focus. An overwhelming majority voted to study ecology. After our questions were webbed, we set up centers. I had twenty-six students in eight groups to move through twelve centers (see Figure 1). The centers took three to four days to complete. I developed the first eight centers and added the other four as students asked questions. As students rotated through centers, more questions were asked. "If one tree cleans 45 lbs. of air a year, how much air is being cleaned in

Students formed groups of three or four. Each student is responsible for the other students in her or his group.

CENTER CHECKLIST FOR ECOLOGY

NAME_____

CENTER   ROUGH DRAFT   COMPLETE
_____

AGUA PURA
_____

WATER USE
_____

EARTH HAPPENINGS
_____

KSE NEWS 1
_____

KSE NEWS 2
_____

RECYCLE, REUSE, REDUCE REFUSE
_____

RECYCLING SURVEY
_____

TREE PLANTING
_____

PLANT A SEED
_____

TREES: NATURE'S AIR CLEANER
_____

A CELEBRATION OF EARTH
_____

WATER POLLUTION
_____

_____

_____

Figure 1. *Center Checklist*

TREES
YOU FIGURE IT

NAME_____   DATE_____

USE THE "NUMBER OF TREES IN OUR YARDS" GRAPH AND ANSWER THE FOLLOWING QUESTIONS.

1. Who has the most trees in their yard? _____

2. Who has the least trees in their yard? _____

3. How many people recorded trees? _____

4. Use your calculator and find the total number of trees in everyone's yards.

    total trees _____

5. Now you are going to find the average number of trees we have in our yards. Do the following steps:

a. On your calculator, key in the total number of trees.

b. Then press the ÷ (divide) button.

c. Key in the total number of people that recorded trees.

d. Now press the = (equal) button.

    What is your answer? _____ is the average number of trees in our backyards.

6. Who are the people who have approximately 5 trees above or below the average number of trees? (For example, if the average is 10, list all the people who have between 5 to 15 trees.)

    _____
    _____
    _____
    _____
    _____
    _____

Figure 2. *Collaboratively Planned Activities*

our neighborhood?" We counted and graphed the number of trees in our yards and started answering some of our questions (see Figure 2). We collected water samples from our sinks, the ditches, and the Rio Grande, and filtered the water and measured the sediment. Our classroom became a research area.

The fall 1990 issue of "Kids for Saving Earth News" caused much discussion and action. One group of students wrote to President Bush requesting him to pass laws to protect the environment and endangered animals. Another group wrote to the Rainforest Action Network and requested more information. They followed up by writing and presenting a play about protecting the rainforests. A PSM (Public Service Message) on recycling and ground water pollution was written by another group and read over the intercom. We collected scrap paper from other classrooms and sent it for recycling. The groups began responding to the centers in more action-oriented ways.

Each center stimulated more questions and less satisfaction with the answers. Learning about ecology wasn't enough, taking small group action wasn't enough. We wanted to involve other students, the parents, and our community. We voted again. This time the vote was unanimous to hold the first "Alameda Earth Expo '91." Our negotiations continued to change and adapt to our needs.

The students formed a committee and presented the idea to the principal while I asked teachers if they were interested in working together with us on this project. We sent a letter home asking parents for help and ideas. We had support from all groups. Parent volunteers worked with us in the classroom, helped on field trips to the water treatment plant and the mayor's office. A parent and student used a computer to make 560 personalized certificates for everyone that participated in "Alameda Earth Expo '91."

Teachers and students brought in speakers on solar cooking, the New Mexico aquifer, the Rio Grande Conservancy, geologists, and environmental engineers. *The Albuquerque Tribune,* our local newspaper, sent a reporter to our room to talk about writing newspaper articles. A group of students formed a committee and solicited articles from the student body. They edited the articles, keyed them into the computer, and met with Tim Gallagher, editor of *The Albuquerque Tribune.* Tim agreed to publish their articles and had them go through the process of newspaper publication (see Figure 3).

Another group of students contacted radio stations and got permission to send PSM tapes to be played on the air. They solicited PSMs from the student body and chose a kindergarten class, a second grade class, and two students from their group to record their PSMs. They arranged a taping session with a local radio station and sent copies of the PSMs to radio stations they had contacted and had agreed to play their PSMs. While studying about Public Service Messages, a group learned about PSMs and TV. They asked a fourth-grade classroom to develop a PSM for TV. Channel 30, our city access channel, helped this class produce and film the PSM. It played on all our TV stations.

The awards committee designed a letterhead for our stationery, thank you cards, and a Defender of the Planet button. They also met with the Mayor and persuaded him to sign the 560 certificates of accomplishment. Each certificate was hand signed by the Mayor of Albuquerque, our principal, and a member of our class. Soon our entire school day was devoted to "Alameda Earth Expo '91."

Other classrooms began their own projects. One class planted a garden using plants from their own gardens. Two trees were planted in memory of a student and a teacher who had passed away that year. Several trees were planted to provide shade for classrooms. A fourth-grade classroom held fund-raisers and purchased two attractive garbage cans for the playground. The graffiti disappeared, the litter disappeared, and many students spent their recesses working in the gardens. Students from the local middle school came by after school and also helped in the garden. We were a community involved and focused on bettering our small corner of the world.

Students were writing plays, songs, and poetry about the environment, so we decided to have a day for "Alameda Earth Expo '91" performances. Students had to fill out a proposal describing what they would do for their performance, who would be in it, extra equipment needed, and how long it would take. This resembled the proposal forms teachers fill out to present at conferences. We

Learning about ecology wasn't enough, taking small group action wasn't enough. We wanted to involve other students, the parents, and our community.

Pupils promote conservation at 'Alameda Earth Expo '91'

Editor's note:

These articles were written as part of "Alameda Earth Expo '91" by third-, fourth- and fifth-grade pupils from Alameda Elementary School. The expo, which will be held from 9:30 to 11:30 a.m., Wednesday at the school, is a fair for pupils to share what they have done for environmental conservation.

Unfortunately, there were more articles and illustrations submit-ted than would fit. These are a few highlights.

"Alameda Earth Expo '91" is sponsored by The Clan of the Unicorn (Karen Dockstader-Anderson's third-grade class), and Motorola. They would like to thank Mayor Saavedra, Tim Gallagher of The Tribune, Karl and Charley at 105-FM, Edie Tulino, Channel 30, and Jeanne Postlethwait with Albuquerque Public Works Department.

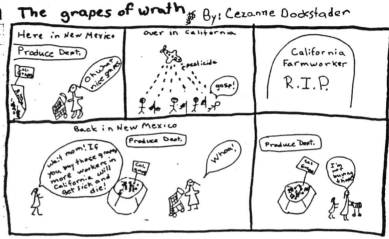

Cezanne Dockstader, fourth grade, created a mini-epic around pesticide use. Teacher: Anita Sandoval.

There's Nothing Like an Ice Cold Glass of Water — Or Is There?
By Leland Belmont, fourth grade
Teacher: Helen McCanna

Water can be a solid, liquid or a gas. Every drop of water we use is precious. ...

Albuquerque gets its drinking water from underground. The groundwater in the valley can sometimes be as close to the surface as two feet. In areas where the water table is higher it is easier to pollute our drinking water.

On the mesa, the water table would be found 300 feet below the surface, yet pollution can still seep down to the water table. We all have to be careful about what we put on the ground. ...

To keep our water clean you can: recycle oil at gas stations; make sure gas pumps don't leak; don't use too much chemical fertilizer; don't use pesticides or herbicides; and don't dump hazardous chemicals down the drain.

Remember: Together we can all make a difference.

The Recycling Quiz: How Much Do You Know?
By Soren Dockstader-Anderson, fifth grade
Teacher: Jim McCarthy

1. The average baby generates how many disposable diapers a year?
☐ 1 ton
☐ 200 lbs.
☐ 20,000 lbs.

If you checked 1 ton you're right. Using cloth diapers would save a lot of space in our landfills.

2. If you buy something for $11, how much goes to packaging?
☐ $11

Norman Michel, third grade, drew this in support of New Mexico's lobos. Teacher: Karen Dockstader-Anderson.

☐ $7
☐ $1

If you checked $1 you're right. You could keep throwing money away or write to the company and tell them to cut down on packaging.

3. What is the largest component of landfills?
☐ cans
☐ newspaper
☐ disposable diapers

The answer is newspaper. When you recycle newspaper you save trees and rain forests and the animals that live there. There are newspaper recycling bins all over Albuquerque. ...

Nick Sandoval, third grade, chose to show in pictures how the water cycle works. Teacher: Kay Ready.

Will the Lobo Be Only a Memory?
By Matthew McCabe, fifth grade
Teacher: Iris Wasson

"Only 40 Mexican wolves are known to exist in the world," according to the New Mexico Wolf Coalition.

But the howl of the lobo may return to the "wilds" of New Mexico. Since the early 1900s, the Mexican wolf and all other species of gray wolf were systematically eliminated from most of the United States.

People moved into the wolves' habitat and killed large-game herds which the wolves preyed on. Consequently the wolves began hunting livestock.

Government officials supported livestock owners by putting a bounty on each wolf killed. The result of those actions led to the near total extinction of the wolves in the Southwest. This brought mixed public reaction.

In the future, 30 to 40 wolves may be roaming the White Sands Missile Range, in southern New Mexico. This area was chosen by the New Mexico Department of Game and Fish because of its location. There is a lack of livestock, few people and it is the natural range of the wolves.

Some people object to the wolves being released into this natural habitat. They fear wolves may attack them and their livestock. Also traditional fairy tales have presented wolves as "big and bad."

The Mexican Wolf that once thrived in large numbers before this country was settled may become extinct in the wilds. Perhaps the lobo has a possibility of co-existing in small numbers with humans.

Student Editors
Claire Ortiz, third grade
Lydia Gutierrez, third grade
Therese Ortiz, third grade
Chris Swallows, third grade

Figure 3. Children's Articles Published in Local Newspaper

had proposals for lectures, rap songs, plays, poetry, charts, science experiments, and news reports.

My students were working behind the scenes, writing letters of acceptance to applicants, writing thank you letters to people helping us, organizing the schedule for the performances, and soliciting donations to cover the costs of paper and buttons. Students called and wrote to TV stations, radio stations, and newspapers asking them to cover the "Alameda Earth Expo '91" events. They sent invitations to the Mayor, the Governor, and the administration of our school system. They kept records of the people they contacted and of the people who responded. Each new effort created new problems. Much of our time was spent organizing and record keeping. We were constantly using our math and organizational skills.

Our year's work culminated on April 24, 1991, with the "Alameda Earth Expo '91" performances. We had 23 events, ranging from plays, lectures, songs, and storytelling. The library was set up with 20 science exhibits all relating to Earth's ecology. Over 100 students took part in the performances, with over 500 people from the school and community coming to watch. Our small cafeteria was packed with parents, teachers, students, community members, and reporters. My students and I saw all of our hard work come to fruition. On Thursday and Friday, the awards committee presented students, parents, teachers, and community organizations helping us with a "Certificate of Accomplishment in Recognition of Great Efforts to Protect and Preserve the Planet," and a Defender of the Planet button. It was a very moving experience for all of us.

We continued to work on this theme for the rest of the year. We wrote thank you letters, paid our bills, helped maintain the gardens, finished our centers, and talked about what we had learned and the changes we had made. I became a vegetarian along with a few other students. Several students said they would take shorter showers. The playground was litter-free. The most important lessons learned were summed up by several students when they stated, "We could talk to people in powerful places, like mayors and newspaper editors; we could write letters and call people and get action and they could work together to create change."

Education becomes powerful when everyone has a voice in the decisions and power is shared. When we trust our students to make wise decisions and to take control of their education, they can and do create change. They find their voices, they become empowered and prepared to take a role in maintaining a democratic society.

When we trust our students to make wise decisions and to take control of their education, they can and do create change.

Bibliography for Ecology

NON FICTION

Our Planet (series), *Troll Associates* 1990

by Zuza Urbova	Mountains
	Volcanoes and Earthquakes
by David Lambert	Forests
	Weather
by Richard Stephen	Deserts
	Rivers

The Sunshine Series: Science and Math, *The Wright Group*

by Colin Walker	Animals and Air
	Rain, Rivers, and Rain Again
by John Lockyer	The Humpback Whale
by Maggie Blake	The Emperor Penguin
	The Sea Otter

The Changing Earth (series), *The Wright Group*

Volcanoes and Earthquakes
Ice and Glaciers
Rivers and Valleys
Caves and Passages
Beaches and Coasts
Highlands and Lowlands

Animals on the Move (series), *The Wright Group*

Shape and Movement of Animals
Why Do Animals Move?
Walking and Running
Animals in Water
Animals in the Air
Jumpers and Hoppers, Climbers and Creepers

| *Doubleday* | The Doubleday Picture Atlas |
| | The Doubleday Children's Atlas |

Going Green by John Elkington et al., *Puffin Books* 1990

365 Ways for You and Your Children to Save the Earth One Day at a Time by Michael Viner with Pat Hilton, *Warner Books* 1991.

50 Simple Things Kids Can Do to Save the Earth by The Earthworks Group, *Scholastic* 1990.

Save the Earth! An Ecology Handbook for Kids by Betty Miles, *Alfred A. Knopf* 1974

The Albuquerque Tribune newspaper

World Magazine (past 15 years various issues), *National Geographic.*

Zoo Books (issues from 1983 to present), *Wildlife Education, Ltd.*

FICTION

Alladin Books

by Byrd Baylor	The Way to Start a Day
	Everybody Needs a Rock
	Hawk I'm Your Brother
by Paul Goble	The Gift of Sacred Dog
	Buffalo Woman

The Sky's the Limit by John Nichols, *W. W. Norton and Co.* 1990

Native American Legends (series), *Watermill Press* 1990

by Terri Cohlene	Ka-ha-si
	Little Firefly
	Clam Shell Boy
	Quill Worker
	Dancing Drum

Song of Sedna by Robert D. San Souci, *Doubleday* 1981.

Mother Earth Father Sky, Pueblo and Navajo Indians of the Southwest by Marsha Keegan, *Clear Light Pub.* 1988.

Rainforest Secrets by Arthur Dorros, *Scholastic* 1990.*

Heron Street by Ann Turner, *Scholastic* 1989.*

The Magic School Bus at the Waterworks by Joanna Cole, *Scholastic* 1986.*

Why the Whales Came by Michael Morpurgo, *Scholastic* 1985.*

A Tale of Antarctica by Ulco Glimmerveen, *Scholastic* 1989.*

*Used for literature studies; multiple copies of each title used.

Lingering Questions

I now team teach with Paula Maxmin in seventh grade at Lyndon Baines Johnson Middle School in Albuquerque and I find there are new challenges.

1. What happens if students choose topics not in the state curriculum?

2. How will Paula and I make sure we cover all areas in the core curriculum?

3. Most of our students will come to us with seven years of traditional schooling. Will it be harder or easier to negotiate the curriculum?

4. What will all of this look like in middle school?

Pedagogy can either empower or domesticate students and teachers. Theme Cycle is an attempt to move away from a debilitating banking education to a pedagogy of knowing. Lupe Ramirez's story of her first year's experience captures the struggles of a teacher who wants to move away from a domesticating form of pedagogy. Here is her account:

My educational career started many years ago when I worked in classrooms as a California Mini-Corp instructional aide. My job was to assist migrant students in the classroom.

This experience gave me the opportunity to work in whole language and traditional classrooms. I left the experience convinced that a holistic philosophy was the only way of teaching for me. In the whole language classrooms, I noticed how excited the students and teachers were about learning and teaching. Subsequently, I took courses from many teacher educators who taught about whole language and this reinforced my decision. I could hardly wait to graduate from the University, get my credential, and get my own classroom where I could begin to put into practice all the great ideas that were swimming around in my mind.

The day finally came in September of 1992. I started my first teaching assignment. I was to be a sixth-grade teacher at one of the local schools. I was so excited. I was finally going to have my own classroom!

My attitude was very positive on the first day of school. I felt exhilarated and ready to go. I was going to start off by asking my students what they wanted to learn about during the school year. After all, I had seen many students in other whole language classrooms get very excited when they went through the process of choosing themes for the year.

Teachers had given students choices and made them partners in the development of the curriculum. I remember one particular teacher telling her students to slow down and speak one at a time so that all the topics could be written down. I had even seen students as young as first grade brainstorm topics. So, I thought to myself, sixth graders should have no problem with this process. Wrong.

The minute I told my students that we were going to go through a process called brainstorming where they would select topics or themes, they looked lost. I asked, "What would you like to study about this year?" One student answered, "Social studies." Another one said, "Science." Still another said, "Math." Then, I asked them *what* in the area of social studies, science, or math did they want to study about. They said, "Whatever is in the book." I tried to explain that there was so much more to learn that was not in the math textbook or science textbook. Again, the lost look appeared.

I realized that for these students, learning meant open your books, read the chapter, and answer the questions at the end. I knew I was going to have a very difficult time bringing about change. Even so, I decided to try. Eventually, with my guidance, the students did select such themes as Sports, Countries, and Inventions. Tapping the collective knowledge and generating and posing problems or questions was very difficult for them. They were only used to answering questions, not asking them!

They also had difficulty working in small groups, pairs, or in workshops. They didn't trust this concept. They said that helping one another was cheating. I countered with another explanation, i.e., that it was cooperating, sharing, and reinventing knowledge together. After awhile, they began to get excited about

Lupe Ramirez

Sixth-grade bilingual teacher, Jefferson Elementary School, Calexico, California

some of the work. Occasionally, however, some would still ask for the social studies and science textbooks.

Seven months and seven theme cycles later, my students are getting used to the idea of collaboratively recreating knowledge based on their needs to know, their questions, and curiosities. They are studying sports and are especially excited about their collective knowledge and the new knowledge they are generating and acquiring.

I would be lying to myself and to you if I said everything was great now. Sometimes students still ask "When are we doing science? We haven't done science in a long time." They still think science only happens in the science textbook, math in the math textbook, and so on. My challenge continues.

I have learned a lot this year about teaching and learning. I have come to understand that we teachers indoctrinate students into our own beliefs about learning and teaching. Through our actions, expectations, and intentions, we mold these children so strongly that it is very difficult to break the mold. The mold that my students were in was rigid, mundane, and passive. Change is difficult, but not impossible. I have only just begun!

Lupe's story is living testimony to the domestication that Freire challenges us to question, but it is also a story of hope and possibility. Her students' resistance poses a challenge, but she doesn't give up. Theme cycle provided her with a key to undomesticate passivity, powerlessness, and indoctrination. Her courage, her will to succeed, and her convictions are lessons that we all have to relearn again and again.

We hope that this issue has been challenging, enlightening, and maybe even controversial. To move beyond our comfort zones and knowledge plateaus, we need forums such as this one.

Bibliography

Altwerger, B., & Flores, B. (1991). The theme cycle: An overview. In K. Goodman, L. Bird, & Y. Goodman (Eds.), *The whole language catalog* (p. 295). New York: Macmillan-McGraw Hill.

Berthoff, A. (1987). Forward. In P. Freire & D. Macedo, *Literacy: Reading the word and the world* (pp. xi–xxiii). South Hadley, MA: Bergin & Garvey.

Boomer, G., Lester, N., Onore, C., & Cook, J. (Eds.). (1992). *Negotiating the curriculum*. London: Falmer Press.

Diaz, E., & Moll, L. (1987). Change as the goal of educational research. *Anthropology and Education Quarterly, 18*(4), 300–311.

Freire, P. (1970). *Pedagogy of the oppressed*. New York: Herder & Herder.

Giroux, H. (1988). *Schooling and the struggle for public life*. Minneapolis: University of Minnesota Press.

Goodman, K. (1986). *What's whole in whole language?* Portsmouth, NH: Heinemann.

Goodman, K., & Goodman, Y. (1979). Learning to read is natural. In L. Resnick & P. Weaver (Eds.), *Theory and practice of early reading* (pp. 137–153). Hillsdale, NJ: Erlbaum.

Goodman, Y. (1978). Kidwatching: An alternative to testing. *National Elementary Principal, 57,* 41–45.

Halliday, M. (1975). *Learning how to mean*. London: Edward Arnold.

Harste, J. (1993). Inquiry-based instruction. *Primary Voices K–6,* Premier Issue, 2–5.

Lester, N., & Onore, C. (1990). *Learning change*. Portsmouth, NH: Heinemann Educational Books, Inc.

McLaren, P., & Leonard, P. (1993). *Paulo Freire: A critical encounter*. London: Routledge.

Shor, I. (1992). *Empowering education*. Chicago: The University of Chicago Press.

Shor, I. (1993). Education is politics: Paulo Freire's critical pedagogy. In P. McLaren & P. Leonard (Eds.), *Paulo Freire: A critical encounter* (pp. 25–35). London: Routledge.

Vygotsky, L. (1978). *Mind in society*. Cambridge: Harvard University Press.

Walsh, C. (1991). *Pedagogy and the struggle for voice*. New York: Bergin & Garvey.

Wells, G., & Chang-Wells, G. L. (1992). *Constructing knowledge together*. Portsmouth, NH: Heinemann.

DDL Books

We are delighted to sponsor this issue of *Primary Voices K-6*, especially since it focuses on Whole Language and bilingual children. At DDL we are committed to the publication of culturally authentic books that positively depict our United States Hispanic culture. Our objective is to offer Hispanic children the opportunity to see themselves, their culture(s), their language(s) represented in children's books. *When children do not see themselves in books, they do not exist.*

This issue on Theme Cycles makes an important contribution by introducing us to educators who share our commitment to a pedagogy that strongly advocates building on children's knowledge, language, and culture. We do not subscribe to the perspective that children know nothing coming into the classroom. Hispanic youngsters, as all children, have many strengths and we applaud those who consistently seek new and creative ways to build on those strengths. Teachers like Esther Negrete and Marty Andrews-Sullivan, whose struggles to implement theme cycles are detailed in this issue, are to be congratulated for their initiative and persistence. We applaud pioneers like Karen Dockstader-Anderson who have the courage to teach the principles of democracy by allowing students to negotiate the curriculum. As publishers and parents, we support the children, teachers, administrators, and organizations, such as the National Council of Teachers of English, who share our vision and commitment. *Our kids are the true beneficiaries of these efforts!*

One such example is the case of José, a migrant student in Elena Castro's class who, at age 8, entered third grade without knowing how to read or write proficiently in his primary language—Spanish. However, his teacher's pedagogical knowledge about literacy development was steeped in Whole Language, enabling her to organize, facilitate, and mediate this child's acquisition of read-ing and writing. She embedded his experiences not only in the theme cycle process, but also in many other authentic uses of written language. After 2 1/2 months, José was able to write alphabetically using invented spelling. By year's end, José was not only working at grade level, he was a confident, secure, and stable child. When teachers know how children learn, "miracles" happen.

As part of our **D**edication to **D**ual **L**iteracy (now you know why we are DDL Books), we have recently published an early literacy/Spanish series for children called *PIÑATA: Celebrating Literacy/Celebrando la Lectura*. We consider this celebration of Hispanic language(s), culture(s), and learning to be a small, yet important, contribution to our nation's children and teachers because of its authenticity, cultural relevancy, and its positive portrayal of Hispanic children. We are also very proud of our association with professionals like Barbara Flores, Elena Castro, and Eddie Hernandez. Their excitement for learning, their ability to listen to their students, and their skill in communicating this keen understanding to illustrators Mary and Michael Ramirez, made it possible to create "right-on" and truly authentic books. We urge more publishers to develop products that will help fill this gap in children's literature.

DDL Books believes that children, teachers, parents, and administrators must make important choices that allow our kids to realize their potential. Lupe Ramirez's story in the Reflection section of this issue should serve as motivation to all to "keep pushing" when confronted with hard realities. Literacy and biliteracy are the yardsticks used to measure success in our schools. By continuing to develop products that help provide authentic literacy experiences for our nation's Hispanic cultures, we hope to open an avenue to increased English language proficiency and literacy.

Good reading and good teaching!

Justo Rey

C.O.O., DDL
Books, Inc.

PrimaryVoices K-6

Volume 2 Number 2 • APRIL 1994

Inquiry-Based Evaluation

NATIONAL COUNCIL OF TEACHERS OF ENGLISH

CONTENTS

THANKS TO OUR 1993–94 SPONSORS

Heinemann Educational Books, Inc.   DDL Books, Inc.

Scholastic, Inc.   Richard C. Owen Publishers, Inc.

Primary Voices K–6 is published four times a year in January, April, August, and November by the National Council of Teachers of English, 1111 W. Kenyon Road, Urbana, Illinois 61801-1096. Annual subscription is $15. Single copy, $6.00 (member price $5.00). Add $3 per year for Canadian and all other international postage. Remittances should be made payable to NCTE by check, money order, or bank draft in United States currency.

Communications regarding orders, subscriptions, single copies, change of address, and permission to reprint should be addressed to *Primary Voices K–6*, NCTE, 1111 W. Kenyon Road, Urbana, Illinois 61801-1096. POSTMASTER: Send address changes to *Primary Voices K–6*, NCTE, 1111 W. Kenyon Road, Urbana, Illinois 61801-1096. Second-class postage paid at Urbana, Illinois, and at additional mailing offices.

It is the policy of NCTE in its journals and other publications to provide a forum for the open discussion of ideas concerning the content and the teaching of English and language arts. Publicity accorded to any particular point of view does not imply endorsement by the Executive Committee, the Board of Directors, or the membership at large, except in announcements of policy, where such endorsement is clearly specified.

Copyright 1994 by the National Council of Teachers of English. Printed in the United States of America. ISSN 1068-073X.

 Printed on recycled paper

A MESSAGE FROM THE EDITOR

The title of our original proposal to *Primary Voices K–6* was Authentic Assessment. From the start, we envisioned our collaboration as a wonderful opportunity to engage in an ongoing dialogue about the topic. We were determined to live the same reflective process that we wanted to discuss. Little did we know the depth of change that would occur in our thinking as, over many months, we read together, talked together, and reflected our way toward new understandings.

The current wording of this issue's theme, Inquiry-Based Evaluation, may begin to reveal to you the extent of our change in perspective. We entered into this experience believing that we had some solid ideas and experiences to share regarding assessment; we believed that through our writing we could help clarify some theoretical ambiguities and offer some practical support. Over time, both our beliefs and our language changed. We now understand that the term *assessment* has historically been used to depict an externally imposed set of measures, so we no longer believe the term is useful. From our current position, the term *evaluation,* specifically *inquiry-based evaluation,* better captures the essence of a process whose ultimate intent is self-knowledge and revaluing.

Obviously, our transformative process was not shared by you, our *Primary Voices* audience, so when we began to write, we were concerned that, potentially, you could leave this issue wondering if you had really read a journal on evaluation. Where are the forms? The structured procedures? The exact behaviors to be observed, evaluated, reported? Our inquiry efforts led us to understand that the real issues related to evaluation are neither procedural nor individual— they are dialogic and collaborative.

In this issue, we highlight our questions, inquiries, and conclusions so that you, too, can begin a critical examination of the issues related to one of the most discussed topics in contemporary education. To that end, we invite you to begin as our evaluation model does—with your own definitions, beliefs, and personal experiences. As you read, assume an inquiry stance and make reflection integral to your reading. In doing so, you will begin to create a personal inquiry cycle and, at the same time, eliminate the learning/evaluation boundaries that we believe have sorely constrained authentic perspectives on evaluation.

In the first article, you will see the theoretical model of evaluation that informs our pedagogical decisions. In the next article, Kathleen Visovatti describes how self-evaluation and reflective inquiry were components of her first-grade curriculum. The third piece, by Penny Silvers, argues that many educators of labeled students miss the critical everyday signs of learning that reveal these learners to be thoughtful creators and evaluators of their own work. The last classroom piece is by Roxanne Henkin. It chronicles her participation in a sixth-grade research discussion where she helps students take a reflective stance *during* the conversation so they can understand content, conflict, and each other better.

Writing "Reflections" provided an opportunity for us to stand back and look at our extended involvement in this project. By listening to our audiotapes and digging into our reflective journals, we tried to get underneath our learning process and to draw parallels between our own inquiry-based evaluation experiences and those discussed in the articles. We hope your engagement leaves you with new insights and future inquiries.

Linda K. Crafton

Inquiry-Based Evaluation: Teachers and Students Reflecting Together

Linda K. Crafton

Literacy
Consultant and
Adjunct Professor,
Northwestern
University

Carolyn Burke

Professor of
Language
Education,
Indiana University

I thought evaluation was something that only happened at the end—that someone else did it to you. For my middle ages research on tortures, I did the evaluating, I asked my own questions about what I wanted to do, asked myself and friends how it was going when I was doing it, wrote reflections almost every day in my research journal and then evaluated myself with my own criteria. Awesome.

Claudia, Grade 5

When Claudia engaged in this reflection, she had just completed four weeks of self-selected research. She was feeling proud of her independent inquiry and empowered by her critical stance in relation to her work. Claudia felt it was a job well done; her teacher, however, felt uncomfortable and worried that there was a crucial component missing.

Claudia and her fifth-grade classmates did, in fact, engage in an exciting learning experience: they generated many research questions, shared them with their peers, carefully selected the ones that would drive their inquiry, considered personal evaluation criteria, used multiple sources of information, shared their findings, and judged their inquiry process. This was a slice of curriculum worthy of examination and discussion. It was a strong example of a young, talented teacher taking the risk of moving her already effective teaching more toward inquiry-based instruction. This was an engagement informed by current assumptions about how language works and how knowledge is constructed. It was, however, also an engagement that did not go quite far enough. Through

conversations with us and others, the teacher, Laura Johnson, wondered why, despite the time spent on helping students to identify questions and construct their own research criteria, many students did not personally connect to their inquiry. More than that, she felt the reflective stance taken by the students in relation to their work was somehow limited, that their thoughtfulness was not deep enough and did not take them beyond the specific engagement. The evaluation helped them to think about their research but not about their values.

Claudia, for example, felt comfortable that she had answered her questions and now understood more about inquiry and "medieval tortures," but she had not considered the tortures of a modern-day Bosnia or thought about the more invisible but no less devastating impact of psychological abuse. She would have the luxury of taking her new knowledge and smugly storing it away, facts to be retrieved when her inquiry topic happened to present itself again. Laura wanted more than that for her students.

Inquiry-Based Curriculum

As holistic educators, we have recently turned to issues of curricula: We have explored the generation of knowledge through alternate sign systems (language, art, music, mathematics, dance), the impact of community and collaboration, and issues of authority and control over the learning process. We have come to see curriculum as the organizational frame that can empower or disempower learners, both students and teachers. Much of our work has been guided by the belief that the key source for curriculum is social learning theory (Short & Burke, 1991). We have begun to argue for classrooms in which learning is central, diversity is valued, and teachers and students collaborate in knowledge construction.

We contrast inquiry-based classrooms with those whose primary function is to transmit knowledge. In classrooms guided by transmission notions of learning, specific content is clearly designated, the delivery system is from expert to novice, and the goal is uniformity. Students are asked to compete, sometimes fiercely, to prove themselves to outside authorities. Even classroom reward systems as innocuous looking as stars, smiley faces, and charts end up managing and controlling both the learners and the learning. When we think of traditional curriculum, the term we keep coming back to is *external*. Grounded in a consensus view of human development, people outside the classroom have devised a massive system of content, goals, and objectives, a system external to the learners who are expected to pursue them wholeheartedly. Once achieved, it seems logical from this view to use testing for verification of just how well students have met others' expectations.

Inquiry-based classrooms operate on a different set of assumptions: knowledge is dynamic, not static, and it is socially constructed within collaborative groups. Classrooms are filled with ongoing opportunities for learners to identify questions and issues they feel passionate about. At the beginning of a school year, many teachers interested in inquiry curriculum begin, not by breaking out prepackaged programs, but by asking students what they want to know. From kindergarteners asking about aging and outer space to sixth graders curious about AIDS and Hillary Rodham Clinton, we have found there are no trivial concerns —and there are always questions. In these kinds of classrooms, genuine questions drive the learning process and reflective conversations pave the way for future action.

John Dewey (1963) talks about the differences between education and miseducation. Education begins with learners' passions and questions, growing from their current position in the world— what they believe and what they value. Then, the learning experience itself pushes them beyond that. Miseducation, on the other hand, does not extend beyond the current engagement. Learners do learn, but have no particular personal connection to the learning. If there are no deep-seated connections to the knowledge and the knowing, the potential for impacting future learning is limited.

We would argue that evaluation is the mechanism that can and should help learners move beyond the present. It provides an opportunity to interrogate existing values (Harste, 1993) and puts learners in a position to experience the world with a new sense of what we believe and a heightened understanding of who we are. This kind of evaluation is not used for external verification, it is used for internal exploration.

This kind of evaluation is not used for external verification, it is used for internal exploration.

Inquiry-Based Evaluation

Just as insights about language and learning have come from observations of learners in ecologically valid contexts, so too, do answers about the true function of evaluation. Successful learners do not wait until the end of a performance to think about its effectiveness, nor do they depend wholly on someone else to tell them how they did. They enter the engagement clear about what they value; they use themselves and others as monitors throughout the experience and exit with an altered sense of what to focus on in the future. Reflection and evaluation are ongoing parts of the larger learning cycle; they occur throughout. While effective learners do listen to others' opinions, the dominant voice is the learner's because it is the learner who acts on the evaluation in future performances.

If participants are allowed to complete the entire learning cycle—from initiation to evaluation—then learning is a self-adjusting process. Just as assessment is an integral part of good teaching, evaluation is an integral part of good learning. Indeed, we believe that first and foremost, the function of evaluation is to inquire more deeply into oneself. Evaluation criteria must be internally

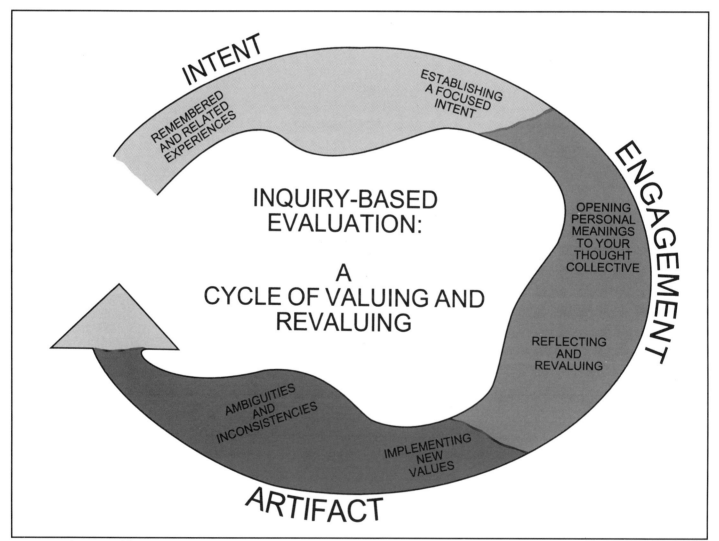

Figure 1. *Evaluation Model*

defined, tied to a specific social context, and constructed for specific learner purposes. From this perspective, evaluation, like the rest of the curriculum, is used to generate knowledge. From this perspective, evaluation continues the spirit of inquiry by providing one more chance to ask questions—and one more opportunity to learn. Evaluation occurs as learners take reflective stances in relation to their work and then invite others in to have conversations about it.

What we believe about language and learning, we also believe about evaluation:

1. Evaluation must be internal to the learner and internal to the learning process itself.

2. Evaluation should occur in supportive, social contexts in which learners have ongoing conversations about their learning.

3. Evaluation should support inquiry by providing systematic ways for learners to continuously question and consider the meaning of their work.

4. The primary function of evaluation is to interrogate individual values.

5. Evaluation should empower the learner.

Figure 1 displays an evaluation model in which valuing and revaluing are used as synonyms for evaluation. In this model, these processes occur throughout the learning/inquiry cycle. Learners begin the experience with personal connection through identification of existing values; they exit with new perspectives, altered values, and different questions by which to launch a fresh cycle of valuing and revaluing. Intent, Engagement, and Artifact (Short & Burke, 1991) describe different aspects of the learning experience that are considered during evaluation.

Remembered and Related Experiences

All learning starts with personal connections. Learners establish a relationship with their pasts so they draw on these experiences to help focus their futures. It is through this involvement with prior meaningful engagements that learners can begin to put an edge on their current learning by coming up with new inquiry questions. It is here that we, as teachers, must legitimize all experiences and all forms of knowing.

Traditionally, curriculum has been developed around assumptions about what kids *don't* know. When that happens, learners are not able to judge change; instead, the learning just begins, out there, somewhere, with someone else. If the engagement is to be more than an activity, learners must start with what is currently known and valued.

Establishing a Focused Intent

Learners always act with intention (Harste, Woodward, & Burke, 1984). *Focusing* the intent of inquiry can pay handsome dividends once the meaty part of the engagement begins. The issue learners must deal with is: Of all my potential questions, where is my focus and why did I choose it? Co-inquirers can help during this phase of inquiry. Conversations about why particular questions are important, and how they, in fact, even get selected, can make a significant difference.

If new inquiry begins with a grounding in the old, the learning takes on a personal significance that is critical for reflection and self-monitoring. It is here that the valuing process begins to get refined: As learners identify what it is they are curious about and get a sense of their intention for learning, they simultaneously take a position in relation to the

Learners establish a relationship with their pasts so they draw on these experiences to help focus their futures.

topic or situation. Knowledge is not neutral and our wonderings are tied directly to how we see different segments of the world, what's important to us and our perspective on it.

Opening Personal Meaning to Your Thought Collective

Fleck (1935) argues that engagements are best understood by examining their sociohistorical underpinnings, specifically within intellectual groups that share a history and common goals. These thought collectives function to provide learners with safe places in which they know it's ok to be vulnerable. They know that when they identify what they are learning and how they feel about that knowledge, it will be received in an open and validating way.

As meaning is constructed, it helps to open up our thinking to others. Organizational devices like Literature Circles and Author Circles give co-learners a chance to respond and potentially help shape the meanings being developed. Additionally, when learners move beyond one sign system (art, music, math, drama) and represent it in another, this transmediation (Eco, 1976) experience provides the potential to take even another perspective on meaning. Like sculpture, we should be able to walk completely around what we have generated so we can see and understand it from all sides.

Reflecting and Revaluing

Reflection encourages learners to ask themselves and each other: Did I fulfill my intent? What did I learn? How did I learn it? And, most important, how have my values and perspective on the world changed as a result of this experience?

This evaluation, as reflective inquiry, occurs through collaboration and conversation. Through interaction with others,

we can see the experience in a different way. The talk, the listening to other perspectives, gives us new choices and a fresh opportunity to position ourselves differently in the world. For what could the primary goal of reflection and self-evaluation be if not to understand ourselves better and to position ourselves more sensitively in relation to others?

New Implemented Values

It's one thing to think through a different perspective, but quite another to implement a newly held value. Real learning implies change and new contexts, challenging us to act.

Once a different perspective has been uncovered, it doesn't automatically mean direct implementation. Old ways of thinking have an annoying staying power that can make even the most tenacious learner shake her fist in frustration. Implementing new values often depends on seeing that they are socially rooted. It means tying them clearly to past experiences and future aspirations. To truly launch a fledgling understanding, learners must continue meaningful conversations about what they have learned and question if others have made similar connections.

Ambiguities and Inconsistencies

When reflection and revaluing assume their rightful place in the inquiry process, our way of looking at things changes. Our search for answers to questions we care about may have given us some solutions, but it also gives us a different set of problems. The trick in dealing with these problems is to develop a tolerance, an expectation, that "truth" is mutable—it has a personal history and we can position it both culturally and historically. As learners, we have to begin to accept that one predictable outcome of inquiry will be internal conflict—a new set of tensions

When reflection and revaluing assume their rightful place in the inquiry process, our way of looking at things changes.

that will help define our next set of questions. Our traditional tendency has been to achieve closure and to compartmentalize knowledge (the lesson is over, the unit complete, this is exactly what we've learned). But learners making a transition into new ways of knowing and alternate views of themselves and the world must learn to expect and to honor the natural ambiguities that come with the pursuit of interesting questions.

When evaluation is viewed as a learner's right and responsibility, we move language and learning to a whole different plane. When we help learners "... accept responsibility for evaluating and continually reevaluating their assumptions about knowledge, the attention and respect that they might once have awarded to the expert is transformed" (Belenky, et al., 1986, p. 139). Evaluation as inquiry supports diversity, not conformity, and in so doing sets the stage for a new vision of social relationships in the classroom and elevates the notion of learner empowerment to a new level. Evaluation as inquiry helps us understand that there are no simple answers and that consensus in education and assessment are old values that require major overhauling.

References

Belenky, M., Clinchy, B., Goldberger, N., & Tarule, J. (1986). *Women's ways of knowing.* New York: Basic Books.

Bintz, W., & Harste, J. (1991). A vision for the future of assessment in whole language classrooms. In B. Harp (Ed.), *Assessment & evaluation in whole language programs* (pp. 219–242). Norwood, MA: Christopher-Gordon.

Clay, M. (1990). Research currents: What is and what might be in evaluation. *Language Arts, 67*(3), 288–298.

Dewey, J. (1963). *Experience and education.* New York: Macmillan.

Eco, U. (1976). *A theory of semiotics.* Bloomington, IN: Indiana University Press.

Fleck, L. (1935). *Genesis and development of a scientific fact.* Chicago: University of Chicago Press.

Harste, J. (1993). Personal communication.

Harste, J., Woodward, V., & Burke, C. (1984). *Language stories and literacy lessons.* Portsmouth, NH: Heinemann.

Mischler, E. (1979). Meaning in context: Is there any other kind? *Harvard Educational Review, 49*(1), 1–19.

Short, K., & Burke, C. (1991). *Creating curriculum: Teachers and students as a community of learners.* Portsmouth, NH: Heinemann.

DEVELOPING PRIMARY VOICES

Kathleen Visovatti

Language Development Specialist, Des Plaines, Illinois Public Schools

After thirteen years as a middle school language arts teacher, I asked to be moved to the primary grades so that I could teach more holistically than forty-five-minute departmentalized periods permitted. After five exciting years in second grade where student inquiry led to day-long reading and writing workshops, I asked to go to first grade as a team leader to share my vision of natural language learning with beginning readers/writers, their parents, and my colleagues.

Establishing the Circumstances for Inquiry

On the first day, I asked my first graders to brainstorm possibilities for study during our year together. I had written a letter to each of them in early August, inviting them to think about what they wanted to learn and ways they could share that learning with others (Crafton, 1991). The children became, as Jerome Harste suggests, the curricular informants (Harste, Woodward, and Burke, 1984). We were creating the curriculum rather than covering it, or, as Dorothy Watson said (1993), the children would begin to uncover the curriculum through invitations to inquire.

I must admit, I held my breath as I gave them the control. I felt an enormous sense of responsibility about their learning to read. I sincerely believed that the majority would teach themselves, but what about those that would need my help? I have another admission: In all my years of teaching, I have never spent a more exhausting and yet rewarding time as the two years in first grade. I felt pulled in twenty-four directions at all times: if children could do something on their own, they wanted to show me they could; if children couldn't operate independently, they wanted help from me. Being in first grade was like witnessing time lapse photography—their gradual independence and blossoming of self-confidence were glorious to behold.

I started first grade as an inquiry teacher, but not a particularly reflective one, so my second year in first grade, with Linda Crafton as a collaborator in the classroom, I set two new goals for myself: first, to help children become self-evaluators by reflecting on and becoming more aware of their literacy processes, and second, to explore portfolio development as an instructional opportunity as well as an assessment tool.

Meanwhile, the children had established their goals:

- To Read and Write
- To Tell Time
- To Subtract
- To Use a Calculator
- To Add 3 and 4 Digit Numbers
- To Spell More Words
- To Color
- To Train Pets
- To Find Out if Grown-ups Are Bigger than Cacti

Reflecting on Ourselves as Readers/Writers

On the first day of school nearly every child expressed a desire to learn to read and write. So, on an Environmental Print Walk around school that day, I commented, "I bet you already can read some things around you." This was met with a chorus of response: "I can read stop signs." "I can read restaurant and grocery store signs." "I can read boxes in stores." "I write stories." "I can read my favorite bedtime story." "I can write my name."

My expectation was that all the children were or soon would be readers and writers. They followed my lead, looking at all the things they could read already. If they realized today that they were readers of environmental print, tomorrow they would see themselves as readers of stories.

These kinds of investigations occurred often in the first few days of school and allowed all of us to establish a baseline profile that we could use to measure future growth and change. Baseline information through testing is something imposed on children to find out what they do not know. In contrast, our baseline data helped us to understand what we each knew and felt about our literacy environment.

The expectation that children would be immersed in reading as a major form of instruction was explained to parents in the initial issue of our weekly class newspaper which went home the first week of school. Parents were asked to incorporate reading, writing, and math activities

into their child's daily routine. They were urged to let students choose their own read-aloud books, and to encourage questions and conversations about each page. Writing could take many forms, including a shopping list, a letter, or original prose. Parents were also reminded to allow their children to develop at their own pace, and to accept invented spellings as a normal step in literacy acquisition.

I asked the children how people learn to read and write. Some of the responses were: "From parents reading to me." "Older sisters and brothers playing school." "By sounding out words." I then introduced them to a text set on reading and writing which we added to all year and kept in a special place.

One student chose *I Can Read with My Eyes Shut* every day for Sustained Silent Reading (SSR) until he could! His mother sighed at the November conference, "He'll only read that one book and he isn't really reading it—he's memorized it."

At the January conference she said, "He's finally choosing a few other books, too. Do you know what he showed me? Some of the words in that first book are in the books he's looking at now. He recognized them. I am so proud. I think he's going to learn to read after all." I responded quietly, "I believe he already has."

During the April conference she confided, "I had misgivings when you said at the fall Open House that children learn to read by reading and being read to, and so both would go on throughout the

If they realized today that they were readers of environmental print, tomorrow they would see themselves as readers of stories.

school day and, hopefully, at home as well. But you were right. It worked. Look at him now." She pointed to Jay who was sorting through the reading section of his portfolio, looking at the photocopied covers of favorite books he had read (*I Can Read with My Eyes Shut* was on the top of the pile!), his response to literature journal, and his written thoughts about his reading. "Thank you," she said, "for giving him the time and the encouragement to teach himself to read."

Responding to children's avowed goal of learning to read and write in first grade led to a discussion of the routine we would follow every day. Thus the expectation was established right from the start that mornings and the first part of the afternoon would be devoted to reading and writing, reflecting, and sharing. Each child would have extended periods of time to read with others and to read alone. Support would always be available, but the reader would be encouraged to rely on her/himself by applying strategies. I made an observation at the first Sharing Time as the initial Reading Workshop came to an end, "I have been noticing how many books are being read in this classroom. You've brought favorites from home, know the ones from the text set about reading and writing, and have discovered others all over the room (e.g., books such as *The Art Lesson* and *Harold and the Purple Crayon* in the art corner, *As the Crow Flies* and *Folktales from Around the World* in the social studies corner, *Amazing Animal Facts* and *The Magic School Bus* series in the science corner, *The Doorbell Rang* and *How Much Is a Million?* in the math corner, *Pyramid* in the block area, *You Be Me and I'll Be You* and assorted plays in the dress-up area, and

Figure 1.

Raffi books and tapes and taped books [recorded by older students and volunteer parents] about starting school in the listening area). Can you read all the words in these books?"

Most responded, "No." There were a few yeses. "Well, what do you do," I asked, "when you don't know all the words?"

"Give up. Pick another book."

"Look at the pictures."

"Skip them."

"Go on."

I introduced the word *strategies* as "ways to solve problems," and asked if they'd heard of the word in connection with coaches or athletes who try to figure out ways to win. Then I asked if Linda and I could make bookmarks out of some of their suggestions (see Figure 1).

The next day each child received a brightly colored, laminated bookmark. "Let's focus on the strategy of picture clues for the next two weeks." Thus began the "Strategy of the Week" instructional procedure, suggested by Linda who visited the classroom regularly. We practiced reading pictures by looking at bookcovers and predicting what they would be about, then looked at the illustrations to predict the content, guess the endings, and imagine the book to be funny or serious, fantasy or reality. I asked if they thought they'd like to read the words as well as the pictures, and if so, they could keep the book for a while. This seemed like the right time to take from their backpacks the following supplies requested from home:

- a pocket folder
- a box of sealable plastic bags—one was kept in the folder for taking books home
- an audio tape—to periodically record fluency and strategy awareness
- a spiral notebook—to keep a record of books read and to respond to literature.

Figure 2. *"I know a lot about cheetahs. Here are some facts. . . ."*

"Sometimes I think better standing up."

I explained that I would meet with each of them once a week "so that you can talk about your reading and we can read together." There was much bustle as reading folders were begun that second day of school.

In the course of a week, I moved around the room during Independent Reading Time touching base with children, one on one. What had they learned about reading today? What would they do differently tomorrow? Would they like to read with or to me? What sort of entries had they made in their Writing about Reading Journal? These reflective questions set the tone for the whole year. The message was clear: You are in charge of your own learning. You can evaluate how it's going. You will always have choices and time. We will share responses as a group in order to support one another and to celebrate learning. I kept an alphabetical class list on a clipboard with me at all times so I could keep track of these conferences. I continued where I left off the next day. I kept anecdotal notes in a folder for each child. These proved an invaluable reference at future conferences. "I see in my notes that you've been reading the same book this week as last week. Would you like to take it home to finish it? Have you recorded anything about it in your journal this week? Last week you listed the title and author." This documentation was helpful at Parent-Teacher-Student conferences. I could support and extend

what the child shared.

A Reflection Table was introduced where the Strategy of the Week was named. Children were invited to share their strategy applications in one of three ways: writing in an open journal (called the Strategy Log), ringing a bell to make an announcement, or speaking privately into a hand-held tape recorder about what they had learned and how they learned it. This encouraged students to become more aware of their literary processes.

The most popular reflective technique by far was Pictured Reflections, an idea shared by Carolyn Burke at the Whole Language Umbrella in 1991. Students asked a classmate to take an instant photo at a moment of meaningful inquiry. The caption under the photo explained the process underway (see Figure 2).

Occasionally, the Strategy Log and, frequently, the photo album, dubbed "Catch Me Learning," were chosen as SSR selections by students. When the album sleeves were filled, the photos were put in students' portfolios and the album was returned to the Reflection Table to be used again. (The supply request list sent to parents in the summer included a double pack of instamatic film.) At the end of the year the photos went home.

As the months passed, one Strategy of the Week led to another. The strategy lesson was organized in the following way: demonstration, observation, conscious use, celebration, reflection, and action. The strategy sequence that evolved this particular year was:

- reading pictures
- making predictions
- confirming predictions
- rereading to make meaning
- substituting words that make sense
- using context clues
- using the first and last letter of a word to help sound it out
- scanning for important words
- looking it up

The order came about out of need (for example, scanning surfaced when children discovered the reference books in the room and began pouring through them, looking for key words) or what seemed logical to Linda or me (for example, following predictions with confirmation or rethinking). The growing list was posted above the Reflection Table (see Figure 3).

At first it was hard for five- and six-year-olds to express how they had processed their reading. Many were eager to share *what* they had read, but few were able to verbalize *how* they had done it. As their abilities to talk about their strategies developed, the process sharing grew beyond a mere parroting of, "I used the strategy of..." to reflections like this:

Figure 3.

Yea, yea, I get it. Oops. What does that mean? I'll go back and reread this sentence, maybe I'll get it on the second try. Nope, it still doesn't make sense. Well, I'll just go on. Maybe I'll understand it later on, hopefully, it won't matter. Argh! It does matter and I don't get it. Now what'll I do? What's messing me up? That one word. Have I ever seen it before? Don't think so. What would make sense there? I'll put a word in I do know, and get on with my reading. What would fit? Let's see, I'll try to pronounce the unknown word. Hmmm. It starts with an "e" and this whole thing is about elephants. Is the word *elephant*? No. That doesn't make sense. Could it be *enormous*? Does huge fit here? Yes! I think I've got it!'

Devoting as much time to process as to content during sharing times helped them become more reflective. The Reflection Table demonstrated abstract ideas concretely. The children decided to arrange books in crates on either side of the Reflection Table according to the strategies they highlighted (see Figure 4). This organizational system grew as the year progressed.

Once again, the children asked their own questions and found their own answers. This practice was true in the realm of evaluation as well as in curriculum planning and class management.

Ending and Beginning with the Learner's Voice

During the first month of school, Linda and I introduced the idea of portfolio building as an instructional tool. We suggested building time into the Friday schedule for reflection on the week's learning by organizing desks. The first Friday, the children arrayed desk contents in front of them on the floor. There were five folders. The reading folder has already been described. Other folders held writing and math investigations. I asked, "What are you putting into your reading folder?" The responses included:

"Books," "My 'Writing about Reading Journal,'" "Plastic bags," "Bookmarks."

When one child answered, "Me reading," there was much laughter and discussion that resulted in "Photographs of me reading," "Photographs of projects about books," "Photocopies of covers of books I've read," "An audio tape of me reading," "A videotape of me acting out a favorite book."

Linda and I set a positive we-know-you'll-think-of-things tone and offered suggestions for possible ways to document reading progress, but the final list posted as a result of brainstorming belonged to the children. They decided to call it, "Proof I'm a Reader." Someone said, "Now let's make one for writing and one for math." More charts went up, "Proof I'm a Writer" and "Proof I'm a Mathematician." Every Friday students sorted through their work of the week, checking the charts, adding more evidence of themselves as readers, writers, and mathematicians. After a few weeks, several students complained that their folders were too full and the contents were getting damaged. At first, they wanted to take their work home, but I reminded them that it was important to keep this evidence of their learning progress—for themselves and for parents and visitors.

It was at this time that Linda showed the class her artist friend's portfolio and I shared one I was creating of myself as a reflective reader and writer for a graduate class I was teaching. Mine was made from two pieces of tagboard and I just happened to have a drawer of tagboard in the art area. The rest of the morning was devoted to portfolio building, literally.

Some spent time deciding what should go in them, but most of the energy went into decorating them, which told a lot about their interests and how they viewed themselves as learners. We tried out a variety of names to distinguish their work-in-progress folders from the folders storing finished work. We settled on "Working Folders" for the reading and writing in progress that would stay in their desks. Every Friday desks were cleaned and completed pieces organized in the "Showcase Portfolios," which were kept in accessible cubbies. Children would often choose their portfolios as one reading choice during SSR, especially at Parent-Teacher-Student conference time. I observed them rehearsing what they would say when they presented their portfolios to their parents. This happened in the fall, winter, and spring.

Student-led conferences had been my practice for many years. This year, they were particularly effective because

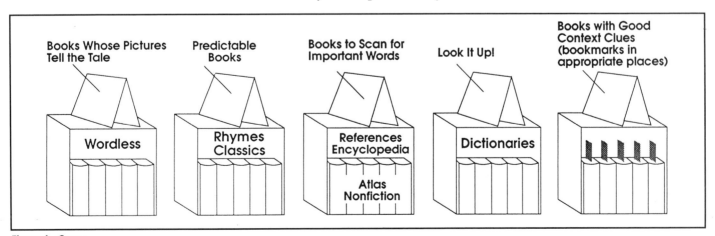

Figure 4. Crates

of the portfolios' concrete demonstration of growth. The child could say, "Look how my handwriting has changed. I'm not writing so big anymore," and, "Here are the books I have read so far this year. See, I really like Dr. Seuss. Let me read one to you," or "I used to get confused about what was adding and subtracting. Now I know this is adding (showing a photo combining sets of manipulatives). There are 15 here. And this is subtracting (pointing to a photo showing one set taken away). Now there are 10 here."

That the portfolios were instructional opportunities as well as reflective evaluation was demonstrated by comments to parents like these:

"Look at these journal entries. I have so many. Hmmm. Every page starts with I. That's kind of boring."

"I've read a lot of books. Most are real short. I might choose a chapter book someday."

"This photo shows my favorite manipulatives. These cubes are ones. This is a ten. That's the same as ten ones. Want to count tens with me?"

These moments of self-reflection were a pleasure to note and record, as were the smiles and winks of pride and appreciation the parents and I exchanged as children told us how they saw themselves as learners. Even more rewarding were the follow-through discussions at later conferences. At the end-of-the-year conference, Jeff responded to the query, "What changes do you notice about yourself as a reader and writer this year?"

I used to spend most of the Writing Workshop time drawing pictures. I got ideas from TV and computer games. I wanted to be an artist. Now I make up my own stories. I still draw pictures, but the words come first. It used to take me a long time to get an idea. Most of the Sustained Silent Writing (the first ten minutes of Writing Workshop) I'd doodle. Now I'm getting ideas all the time. I decide on the way in from recess what to write about.

Now all of the Writing Workshop is SSW for me. I groan when we have to quit for Sharing Time, but I always want to be one of the ones to share because I get ideas for how to continue from the kids. If they laugh at a part, I make it longer and do it again. Sometimes I work on the same story all week.

I used to be embarrassed when everyone was looking at me when I sat in the Sharing Chair (mini rocker on a rug). I'd mumble and everyone would say 'What? Speak Up!' Then I'd get even more embarrassed. Now I can hardly wait to share because I know they like my writing. Other kids get ideas from me. They'll come to my desk and ask me if they can write like me. That makes me feel good. I want to be a writer when I grow up.

One thing I've noticed. My stories are much longer than my journal entries. I write about myself in my journal. I've never written a story about me. I always write fantasies. Maybe I'll write about myself sometime, a chapter book, I think. I'll only write the good things, though.

At first, many students resisted analyzing why they had selected certain pieces. Jake, for instance, was unwilling to delve into the reasons for his choice. (See Figure 5.)

"Why do I have to tell you why? I already know this is good. That's why it's in my portfolio."
 "Why is it good?" I asked.
"Because."
"Because why?"
"Because I like it."
"Why do you like it?"
"Because it's good."
"What makes it good?"
"It's about my Mom."

As Donald Graves said (1993), children grow as evaluators of their work from naming it to comparing it.

"It's better."
"Better than what?"
"What I used to write. The kids didn't use to laugh before and now they do."

During one student-led parent conference, a father listened to all his daughter had to say, acknowledged the contents

Figure 5.

of her portfolio, and then turned to me and said, "Yes, but what does she need to work on?"

I looked him in the eye and replied, "Let's ask Rhonda what she needs." At that moment of turning the reflection over to the child, I thought, this is what inquiry-based evaluation is all about—children owning the process from beginning to end as they ask their own questions, think about their own answers, and plan their own futures—children in charge of their own learning. As Rhonda began to speak, I leaned forward to listen. So did her father.

Bibliography

Burke, C. (1991, August). *Curriculum as inquiry.* Presentation at the Whole Language Umbrella Conference, Phoenix, Arizona.

Crafton, L. (1991). *Whole language: Getting started . . . moving forward.* Katonah, NY: Richard C. Owen.

Graves, D. (1993, June). *Portfolio assessment.* Workshop given at the Walloon Institute, Petosky, Michigan.

Harste, J.C., Woodward, V.A., & Burke, C.L. (1984). *Language stories and literacy lessons.* Portsmouth, NH: Heinemann.

Watson, D., & Harste, J. (1993, February). *Moving into and moving with whole language.* Presentation during the Whole Language Umbrella Teleconference. Oklahoma State University Extension, Stillwater, OK.

Lingering Questions

1. How can students learn to really listen to one another and to give constructive feedback to others? Often they just wait, none too politely, for peers to finish so that they may begin sharing.

2. How can teachers help students express their metacognitive awareness so that students readily share the process as well as the content of what they are reading and writing?

3. How can teachers keep records that truly reflect children's growth over time so powerfully that parents and administrators will say, "This is enough. This says it all."?

4. Am I still seducing/programming others? When does my enthusiastic invitation leave off and their self-selected initiative take over?

5. How can I convince parents that children can be in charge of their own learning and evaluation?

Classroom Resources

Books around the Room

Asian Cultural Center for UNESCO. (1975–1977). *Folktales from Asia for children everywhere* (Vols. 1–6). New York: Weatherhill.

Cole, J. (1986–1992). *The magic school bus* series. New York: Scholastic.

De Paola, T. (1989). *The art lesson.* New York: Putnam.

Fortson, W. (1989). *Amazing animal facts.* Pittsburgh, PA: Fortson.

Hartman, G. (1991). *As the crow flies: A first book of maps.* New York: Macmillan/Bradbury Press.

Hutchins, P. (1989). *The doorbell rang.* New York: Morrow.

Johnson, C. (1958). *Harold and the purple crayon.* New York: HarperCollins Children's Books.

Kellog, S. (1987). *How much is a million?* New York: Scholastic.

Macaulay, D. (1975). *Pyramid.* New York: Houghton Mifflin.

Mandelbaum, P. (1990). *You be me and I'll be you.* Brooklyn: Kane/Miller.

Raffi. (1988–1992). *Raffi songs to read.* New York: Crown Books for Young Readers.

Books about School

Ashley, B. (1991). *Cleversticks.* New York: Crown.

Baehr, P. (1992). *School isn't fair.* New York: Macmillan/Aladdin Books.

Baer, E. (1990). *This is the way we go to school.* New York: Scholastic.

Cazet, D. (1992). *Are there any questions?* Chicago: Orchard Books.

Cazet, D. (1990). *Never spit on your shoes.* Chicago: Orchard Books.

Clements, A. (1992). *Billy and the bad teacher.* New York: Simon and Schuster/Picture Book Studio.

Cohen, M. (1972). *The new teacher.* New York: Harper Trophy.

Cowley, J. (1991). *Our teacher Miss Pool.* New York: Richard C. Owens.

Dakos, K. (1990). *If you're not here, please raise your hand.* New York: Macmillan.

Delton, J. (1993). *My mom made me go to school.* New York: Bantam.

Frandsen, K. (1984). *I started school today.* Chicago: Children's Press.

Gross, A. (1980). *What if the teacher calls on me.* Chicago: Children's Press.

Hallinan, P. (1987). *My first day of school.* Nashville: Ideals.

Harrison, D. (1993). *Somebody catch my homework.* Honesdale, PA: Word Song Boyds Mills.

Hennessy, B.G. (1990). *School days.* New York: Puffin Books.

Marshall, E. (1983). *Fox at school.* New York: Dial Books.

Moss, M. (1990). *Regina's big mistake.* New York: Houghton Mifflin.

Myers, B. (1990). *It happens to everyone.* New York: Trumpet Club.

Quackenbush, R. (1982). *First grade jitters.* New York: Harper College.

Thaler, M. (1989). *The teacher from the black lagoon.* New York: Scholastic.

Weiss, L. (1984). *My teacher sleeps in school.* New York: Puffin Books.

Wiseman, B. (1970). *Morris goes to school.* New York: Harper Trophy.

Books about Reading/Writing

Black, I.S. (1968). *The little old man who couldn't read.* Niles, IL: Whitman.

Bunting, E. (1990). *The Wednesday surprise.* New York: Houghton Mifflin/Clarion Books.

Collins, P.L. (1992). *I am an artist.* Brookfield, CT: Millbrook Press.

Cohen, M. (1977). *When will I read?* New York: Greenwillow Books.

Delessert, E. (1992). *I hate to read.* Mankato, MN: Creative Editions.

Dr. Seuss. (1978). *I can read with my eyes shut.* New York: Random Books for Young Readers.

Hessell, J. (1991). *Daniel.* Crystal Lake, IL: Rigby Literacy 2000.

Hilde, T.P., & Gilleland, J.H. (1990). *The day of Ahmed's secret.* New York: Lothrop, Lee, Shepard.

Hoban, T. (1983). *I read signs/I read symbols.* New York: Greenwillow Books.

Name:

Date:

Portfolio Evaluation: Reading

Have child select 2–6 favorite books from around the room.

1. What makes these books your favorites?

2. How did you choose them?

3. Do you have other ways of choosing books that work for you?

4. Is your way of choosing books different now than it was at the beginning of the year? (If yes, how?)

5. I see that your favorite books are (name them). Can you think of some others you also enjoyed?

6. Looking at these books you've chosen, choose one that reminds you of yourself. How is it like your life? In what ways?

7. Are there books you'd like to reread? Why?

8. Do you do most of your reading in school or at home?

9. Is there a book you were so excited about that you had to tell someone? Which one and why?

10. What books do you think you'll most remember even after first grade is over? Why?

11. What kind of reader were you at the beginning of first grade?

12. What kind of reader are you now?

13. How have you changed?

Summary/goal setting: Review the reflections, then say, "Now that we've talked about you as a reader, set one or two goals for yourself as a reader between now and the end of the year."

Name:

Date:

Strategies That Help Me Understand What I Read

When I come to an unknown word, I

_____ skip it and go on.

_____ substitute a word I do know that sounds like it and makes sense.

_____ use the context to figure out what it means.

_____ look it up.

_____ ask someone.

When I am reading and I don't understand what's happening, I

_____ use picture clues to help me figure out what's going on.

_____ re-read the confusing parts.

Before I start reading, I

_____ predict what it will be about.

During reading, I

_____ confirm my predictions.

_____ scan for the most important words.

After reading, I

_____ re-read the book.

_____ think about how my life is like the book.

_____ think about what I learned from the book.

EVERYDAY SIGNS OF LEARNING

Penny Silvers

Reading
Coordinator, K–3,
Pritchett School
Buffalo Grove,
Illinois

Dear Mom and Dad:

When you opin my portfolio you see that I ust to rit wrds ronge and now I now how to spele them betr. Now I no I can read and rite betr. I lrnd abawt dinasors and the envirmitt and I lrnd how to keep the evirmitt clean. I lik to shar my faks in class. I stil wnt to lrn abowt all kinds of things like dinasors and jagrs.

Love,
Jackie

Dear Mom and Dad:

I think that i have come a long way in reading and writing. In the begening, I only new how to spell words like hat and cat and other short words. In reding when I didn't now a werd I would only sond that werd owt or I wuould ask somebudy. Now I no how to skip the werd and keep on reding and it usuly makes sens - or I can go back and rede it agan. I think I relly impruvd. I didn't now I could write such good stories. I like to rede long books now. I like to rede about eksiting avnshurs.

Love,
Gene

For many years, I have tried to help labeled students, like Jackie and Gene, to understand and accept themselves as able learners. Their reflections and insights about their learning are the true markers of growth that too often go unnoticed. With nurturing, support, and demonstration of the reflective process by both their classroom teacher and me, we *all* began to notice and document the everyday signs of learning that occur in the rich context of the classroom throughout the school year.

As a reading coordinator and reading resource teacher, this process often has been as frustrating and complex for me as it has been for the students and teachers. Unfortunately, I still see many learner strengths go unrecognized or unacknowledged by teachers and administrators who focus on test scores and work products in isolation from classroom experiences. This often has a negative influence on parents, who take their cues from the school and begin to look at their child from a deficit perspective.

My assumptions about these learners differ significantly from more traditional ones. I assume that all students can learn and that the process is the same for everyone. As Frank Smith writes, "Learning is the brain's primary function, its constant concern, and we become restless and frustrated if there is no learning to be done." He suggests that to be alive is to learn, and that our brains are always making sense out of our world—we are learning constantly (Smith, 1986).

I assume that learning is social and collaborative. When choices are available and teachers and other students become literate models, children begin to take their cues from those around them as well as from the information they are sharing. When students are actively engaged in meaningful experiences, learning becomes constructive, rather than reductive, enabling them to take risks and approximate as they move toward literacy.

My vision for a classroom where this can happen is one in which all students create meaningful curriculum through inquiry, researching subjects they genuinely want to know more about, asking questions to frame their investigations, sharing the information with each other, reflecting on their learning, and generating new questions (Harste, 1992). The ownership that develops from this personally focused kind of learning becomes a powerful connecting link to self-evaluation as students begin to recognize their strengths and celebrate their accomplishments (Crafton, 1991b; Rhodes, 1993). I assume all students can reflect and, through that evaluative process, move their own learning forward.

This is a tall order for a typical resource pull-out program to accomplish in a few short periods a week. Over the years it has been frustrating to work within a model that isolates children from their homeroom classes, contradictory to the whole language principles of collaboration, learning as a social process, and the current thinking about inclusion. Gradually, I have begun to change the reading lab program into a literacy support service for children, working within their regular classrooms. By doing this, I am able to eliminate a fragmented curriculum and help my students begin to see that all their learning is connected, whether it is through thematically integrated experiences, the literature discussions we all have, or the special inquiry projects they choose to do. By participating with the students and their teachers in their classrooms, everyone continues to benefit from the diversity and social interactions provided by the whole class. It also provides opportunities for me to observe and document even more of the learning that is going on in a variety of contexts.

Valuing and Revaluing

Wendy Hood writes, "All children grow. That growth is documentable. And in their own good time, they all bloom. They are neither losers nor potential losers. They are learners." (Hood, 1989). The children I work with often feel defeated or defensive, keenly aware of not being able to measure up to grade level or curricular expectations. Even at five, six, and seven years of age, many already see themselves as failures. They often have massive anxiety about their worth and some become hostile and out of control. While it is considered my job to "teach" these children to read and write, I consider it my obligation to help them feel good about themselves as capable learners—only then can literate behavior take hold.

In the fall of second grade, one of my students, Haley, told me she hated school because she knew she "couldn't read or write as good as the other kids." Feeling inferior and inadequate, she was unwilling to take learning risks and was reluctant to write or read for fear of being wrong. Her early reflections focused on the mechanics of writing and other surface signs of learning, such as how many books she had read and stories she had written. By May of that year, Haley had learned some reading strategies and had published and shared research and stories she had written. She was reading and writing more confidently, reflecting not only on mechanics, but on her feelings, hopes, and needs. She was very aware of her accomplishments and clearly felt

I assume all students can reflect and, through that evaluative process, move their own learning forward.

much better about herself when she wrote, "I liked when I shared my writing with the class. I wasn't so embarrassed about my writing when I saw the kids like it. If I practice, I can read good to the class, too. It was great when they wanted me to teach them how I organized my portfolio and reflected on what I learned. Maybe I could be a teacher when I grow up."

Ken Goodman says that as students recognize their strengths and see that they can be successful in school, they will come to revalue themselves as able learners, rather than perceive themselves as learners in trouble (Goodman, 1991). The challenge is to help teachers, parents, and students understand that the learning process is the same for everyone regardless of individual differences and that all students are able to achieve goals. One way I can do this is by helping students reflect on their accomplishments, talking together about what was learned, recognizing how successful they were, and facilitating new experiences where they can apply their learning.

Edelsky et al. make a strong point regarding the need for education to focus on providing students with the resources that help them evaluate and revise their hypotheses about learning (Edelsky, Altwerger, and Flores, 1991). Through inquiry-based evaluation, students can do just that. They can see that they are learning and become articulate about what they are doing and why it is important to them.

When students know they can be successful, motivation is high and they feel good about themselves. Gradually, over time, revaluing occurs as personal feelings of inadequacy and anxiety begin to change to confidence and independence, and parents and teachers come to view them from a more positive perspective.

Literacy Profiles and the Teacher's Valuing Process

As a holistic educator, I look at all the things the students can do in a variety of contexts, at home as well as in school. To help me manage all this information, I keep a literacy profile for each child I work with, similar to the biographic literacy profile developed by Denny Taylor (Taylor, 1991). These profiles include extensive anecdotal observations, samples of student work over time, student reflections, teacher comments, a parent survey of goals and expectations for their child, and a variety of other data including miscue analysis, books read, published pieces, classroom work, project samples, and any other artifacts the child feels represent learning.

While this takes some time and organization, the information becomes the basis for documenting and reporting student learning to teachers and parents. Schools and teachers usually have a wealth of data representing students' deficits, but very little to highlight their strengths or show that learning is occurring. The literacy profiles become an important way to help focus attention on what the student can do, moving away from dependence upon deficit analysis, test scores, and report card grades. When used at conferences, staffings, and shared with parents and students, they help present a more balanced perspective of the student as an able learner.

One of my reading lab students, Leni, spent the first semester of first grade watching her classmates read and

Figure 1. Leni's Inquiry Questions about Jaguars. Translation: I want to learn about jaguars. 1) Where do they live? 2) What do they eat? 3) How fast can they run?

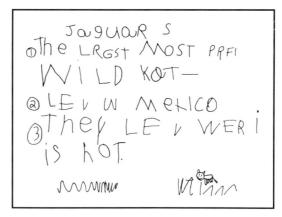

Figure 2. Leni's Information about Jaguars. Translation: Jaguars. 1) The largest most powerful wildcat. 2) Live in Mexico. 3) They live where it is hot.

write. Midyear, when I started to work with Leni in her classroom, she told me, "I can't read or write yet." However, I noticed that she had written an inquiry question about jaguars and knew some letters and sounds as she spelled GAKRS (jaguars) out loud (see Figure 1).

As we began to read together from a variety of resource books in the room, I noticed that she recognized the word *jaguar* every time I read it, picking it out of several paragraphs and picture captions. She decided to copy it out of the book onto her paper, softly saying all the letters as she wrote them. Then she compared the book spelling to the way she had originally spelled it. With some help from friends, she wrote a little more information about animals on her own (see Figure 2).

My anecdotal observations focus on a few key learning processes that I value and which I look for in a variety of class-

room contexts (Crafton, 1991). I have used a variety of forms and recording devices. However, noting the student's use of learning strategies, risk-taking, collaboration, inquiry, and reflection in various contexts on a simple grid, seems to work well for me (see Figure 3).

In my anecdotal observations for Leni, I indicated that in one-on-one and small group work, she used picture cues as a reading strategy; understood that reading was for finding information and had to be meaningful; used the context clues whenever possible; noticed the

Figure 3. Anecdotal Observations

Student		Grade		Date	
Learning Contexts	Strategies	Risk-Taking	Collaboration	Inquiry	Reflection
Whole Class	Shared personal experience	Shared draft		Asked a question	Shared how she felt about her research--"I love doing this!"
Small Group	Used picture clues Prior knowledge		Worked with M on project Shared information		Remembered and talked about strategy: "Skip a word and keep on reading."
Individual	Context clues	Wrote 2 sentences (research report) (will write more)		Wrote 3 questions about jaguars Found more pictures & facts	"I can read the word jaguar."
Other					

P
A
R
EVALUATION
N
T

I have three plusses and a
wish about my child's
learning experience in
school this year.

The plusses are. . . .

+ Develop her learning skills.

+ To be gentle and kind to others.

+ To experience learning and feel good
about herself—to be successful in
school and in life.

The wish is . . . .

Leni wants to start reading. However,
just like the time she started to ride
a bike, she told us when to take off the
training wheels—when she felt ready.

Figure 4. *Parent Evaluation*

word *jaguar* in various contexts; and was able to write information about what she had learned from reading, from the other children, and from her prior knowledge about animals. She was excited about learning, and willing to take a risk in asking a friend for help or sharing what she had learned with others.

My observations painted a different picture of Leni than we had from the special education testing. She didn't look so much like the student who had been described at staffings as a nonreader (not knowing any letters or sounds) who was unable to function successfully in the classroom. Although she was diagnosed as having a learning disability by the specialists who tested her, when she was engaged in inquiry learning and self-evaluation Leni didn't look much different from other children in her class. Her interest was high, and I could see that she felt good about herself as she excitedly ran to the library to get even more information and willingly showed her report to anyone who visited her room. She was sharing, collaborating, learning from her peers and teachers, and participating successfully in classroom life.

Her teacher and I felt Leni had a lot of learning strengths and we were able to show this by sharing a wide range of information from her literacy profile at the end-of-the-year staffing. We began to see a transformation in mother as well as daughter. The mother, who was so worried about Leni's slow beginning, began to feel that she wasn't to blame for her child's inability to read like the other children, and more hopeful that Leni was going to make it through school.

In a parent survey that I use to help me understand the student's background and parent expectations for the child, Leni's mother wrote three pluses and a wish for her daughter's success (Copenhaver, 1993). (See Figure 4.) Because the mother was more optimistic that Leni really could learn to read, she was much more willing to work with her at home. Through our conversations, she also became more knowledgeable about beginning reading and emergent literacy, understanding that the time it takes to learn is very individual.

There were a lot of visible signs of growth and learning for Leni beyond word recognition and naming letters and sounds, but until I could document what she was able to do in various contexts and share my information, it didn't get noticed. Like unmined gems or buried treasure, it was just there, waiting to be discovered. Comparing Leni with other children in the class only highlighted her deficiencies. Documenting the small signs of growth and learning from daily observations helped everyone—including Leni—see her strengths. (See Figures 5 and 6.) Not all students become "readers" by the end of first grade. However, like Leni, they can develop a strong sense of themselves as knowledgeable people and feel successful within the classroom community for whatever they have accomplished.

Leni's learning process really accelerated when she chose a topic to research that she was keenly interested in. She had some prior knowledge of animals and used this, along with the book information and facts from friends to develop her project. She had a definite intent. She wanted to share her project with the class and spent a lot of time talking to classmates about animals, making her project appealing, sharing information, and reading together with others. At the end of first grade, Leni wrote a final reflection in her portfolio:

I still can't read or write too good, yet. I really want to, but I'm learning a lot. I had fun doing our projects. I'm going to take paper home this summer and practice writing stories. I'm going to get some books from the library about dinosaurs and space so I know more when school starts next year.

Clearly, she felt more satisfied with herself and wanted to continue learning on her own over the summer. The literacy profile showed many signs of growth and helped key people begin to see Leni as a more successful learner. Best of all, while Leni was realistic about her development, she felt more positive about her ability to learn.

Portfolios and the Student's Valuing Process

It has taken time for me to realize that I am not the only one who needs to do the evaluating. The missing link in developing self-confidence and taking responsi-

---

Narrative about Leni

Leni has participated in the literacy support program provided by the reading lab since January when she was in the middle of first grade. When we began working together, she was extremely frustrated about her inability to read or write and her fear of being behind the other children academically. Although her anxiety was high, her desire to learn and her knowledge about the world have been strengths that have helped sustain her through frustrating and difficult learning experiences.

When I began to work with Leni, she was reluctant to write words she couldn't spell correctly and was uncomfortable taking learning risks or applying strategies to her reading other than phonics. However, I noticed that her miscues reflected a focus on meaning, and she used picture cues and predicting strategies to help her comprehend.

Special education testing showed some learning disabilities, but Leni has been able to participate successfully in class projects and literature discussions. Although she still becomes frustrated easily when she perceives the work is too difficult, she has learned to use a wider range of strategies such as skipping a word to keep on reading, using prior knowledge and using context clues to help with meaning. These are strategies of a reader moving toward proficiency. Her writing is more readable and she is also beginning to use more conventional spelling.

Leni enjoys researching topics of her choice, collaborating with other students, learning from their discussions, and incorporating this information into her own pictures and stories. She knows how to ask and find answers to her inquiry questions and is gaining confidence in herself as a learner. When she forgets her anxiety about reading and becomes engaged in studying or reading something of interest to her, she feels successful and capable, just like all the other children.

Leni's parents have expressed concern about how slowly her reading is developing, and have been very anxious about her ability to learn and to be successful in school. They are hopeful that she will soon begin to feel more comfortable as a reader and writer. I've enjoyed working with Leni and look forward to continuing to support her literacy development. Attached is a list of what Leni can do as a reader and writer at this time.

Sincerely,

Penny Silvers
Reading Coordinator

Figure 6.

What Leni Can Do as a Reader and Writer

Reading

Predict from pictures and when listening to a story
Retell a story she's heard
Discuss story characters
Notice similarities and differences in words
Recognize words from environmental print
Reread a story she's heard read to her
Recognize some letters and sounds
Use picture cues for meaning
Understand that reading has to be meaningful
Use context clues whenever possible
Share stories with other children
Use her prior knowledge to comprehend a story

Writing

Express an idea in writing
Use invented spelling that approximates sounds and letters that she pronounces
Conference with others about her writing
Publish research reports and stories
Write an inquiry question and answer it
Write information about what has been learned in social studies and science
Get information from other children and use it for her reports
Share her writing with other children

Figure 5.

---

bility for their own learning lies with the students. They need to begin to take a more active role in reflecting and evaluating their learning by themselves. One way they can begin to do this is through portfolios.

To me, portfolios are first and foremost a strategy for student learning and self-awareness (Crafton, 1991). To be an effective learning tool, the students need to have ownership of the contents, the selection process, and the interpretation of the learning that portfolios represent. The caution here is that if the focus veers toward assessment and away from an opportunity for learner self-knowledge, portfolios become just another management tool rather than an extension of the learning process.

As my district has begun to implement portfolios, I've observed that students are keeping all sorts of work but their collections are random and their reflections often remain at the surface level. Just keeping portfolios and collecting work hasn't been enough to move students beyond the first level of reflection—noticing the mechanics of writing, the length of a story, the number of books read, and the papers they feel are their best work.

Kathy Short and Carolyn Burke (1991) talk about two dimensions of learning: process and perspective. They say that learners need to consider why they do something (intent), to experience doing something (engagement), and to produce a result at the end of the process (artifact). The evaluation process includes looking at learning from the perspective of the self, collaborative others (peers and colleagues with whom one can talk and get feedback), and society (institutional measures, like report cards and tests). The shift is in helping students to look more at what and how they learned (process) based on their personal needs and inquiry, rather than only examining the products and fulfilling the teacher's expectations.

Portfolios become more than just an assessment tool when we help students become more thoughtful about the pieces they select so that they represent work that is personally significant and important to them. Time devoted to conferencing with students and talking about the portfolio contents will deepen the student's and teacher's understanding of the learning that is revealed. These conversations, focused around questions that help students move their reflections beyond "noticing," will help them recognize that portfolios represent more than just collections of work. Often, these questions come at the end of the selection process, as work is being sorted and compared. However, it is important to help students learn to ask thoughtful questions of themselves throughout all phases of their learning experiences, from initiation to completion, so that self-reflection and evaluation are an integral part and not just something that is done at the end. Figure 7 suggests some reflective questions that span the entire inquiry process.

Just as extensive and intensive discussions occur in literature groups, students need to look through their portfolio collections over and over again, first taking a broad overview, and then focusing more deeply on the individual contents. Meaningful reflections take time, and one cursory look is not enough to really uncover the personal significance of the portfolio. Portfolios need to be shared with peers, teachers, and parents as they are revisited over a period of days. It's like solving a mystery, peeling away layers of information to get to the heart of the learning. It takes time to practice looking for "clues" and a lot of talk between students and teacher to notice what is really meaningful and significant.

Self-reflection and personal awareness don't happen quickly or easily for anyone. They certainly don't happen

---

Reflective Questions That Span the Inquiry Process

Intent:
　What's my intent?
　What's important about this to me?
　What am I trying to do?
　How can I keep track of my learning and
　　thinking?
Engagement:
　How is my learning going?
　What—if any—adjustments do I need to make?
　What new strategies am I using?
　What risks am I taking?
Artifact:
　What growth and change can I see in myself?
　What have I learned about myself from this
　　experience?
　How am I different now than I was before?
　What do I know now that I didn't know before:
　　About writing, and about myself as a writer?
　　About reading, and about myself as a reader?
　　About learning, and about myself as a learner?

Figure 7.

when kids are asked to reflect on their learning only at the end of a marking period or at the end of the year rather than as an ongoing integral part of the learning. Through interactions with students as they explore their portfolios, I've learned more about the reflective process and begun to notice things I might have missed before. I have also seen student responses move away from those that say, "I chose this because it was my best story," or, "I want this in my portfolio because I learned a lot about dinosaurs." Now I am seeing more thoughtful reflections such as this excerpt from one boy's comments: "I found information from books and each other. I learned to share. We got to be friends. What a good time."

Portfolios can tell a story about learning and understanding. By sharing those stories with peers, teachers, and parents, students can expand their personal knowledge about themselves as learners. Through this sharing, they can begin to reflect on their accomplishments and revalue themselves in light of the new knowledge and new insights, inquiring and connecting learning and personal awareness as this cycle continues.

Tom Moves beyond Remembering

Tom stood in the middle of the sharing circle, proudly reading the first book he ever published. I was close by, ready to help at any time. But he came through like a trooper, reading about how his dog, Spice, had bitten his brother, and embellishing all the action with vivid extemporaneous descriptions. This reading/writing celebration came late in first grade. His teacher and parents had been concerned about his slow development, coupled with what seemed to be hyperactivity and an inability to get organized and focused. Staffings with the special education team had pointed strongly to intensive learning disabilities intervention, or perhaps a self-contained special education placement.

The writing and sharing of his book was a major breakthrough for Tom. It was the beginning of his belief that he could read and write, and he shared his story over and over with anyone who would listen. He also began to participate in paired and shared reading, and used holistic remembering to read favorite stories to kids in his class. He ventured further into literacy with a note to the publishing center volunteer asking when his book would be ready, and a reminder to me to make copies of his book to take home and share with his family. In his journal, he began to write more rather than just draw pictures. He started to write about skateboarding, his brother, and moving to a new house.

At the end of the school year, Tom's class was asked to select some work that "showed real learning," for their end-of-the-year portfolio that would go with them to the next grade. The class brainstormed a wide variety of things that they remembered learning throughout the year, and discussed ideas for setting future learning goals. However, many of the children, including Tom, merely copied these ideas from the class list, or gave meaningless comments they had heard mentioned in class, like "I learned to read better," or, "I can write longer stories." I wasn't willing to let Tom stop there, because I knew that dialogue and extended opportunities to reflect could lead to deeper understanding of what he had really learned. For any significant revaluing to occur and any real change in Tom's thinking about himself, he had to recognize his accomplishments and be aware of his more positive attitude toward school and learning.

Tom and I started to look at all the papers scrunched up in his folders, his desk, and in his work portfolio. I asked him what he noticed about his writing this year—what he could do now that he couldn't do before. He said he could use

Portfolios can tell a story about learning and understanding.

periods, make longer sentences, and write longer stories. My question seemed only to focus his thinking on the conventions and mechanics of writing rather than what he had learned about himself as a writer.

I rephrased my question, hoping that it would move him beyond the surface features of his writing to become more reflective about changes in his thinking process. This time, I asked him what he learned about himself as a writer. He thought for a while, then seemed confused and became disinterested. We just sat together and continued to look through his work. I thought that sharing my thinking about his work might help and I began to reflect on what I noticed he had started to do as a writer. I commented about how his descriptions of his dog made me see him in my mind so clearly, and how pleased his brother would be to see that Tom had written a story all about him. I mentioned that a reader would really enjoy his stories because they had so much more information in them now than they did before.

That first day, we just sat together and talked. A few days later, Tom asked me to help him look through his portfolio again. I was surprised that he wanted to do this again and that he initiated the interaction with me. I hadn't thought about returning to the portfolio for a second look, and his request helped me see that our talking together had been more meaningful to him than I had realized. This time, as we started turning the pages, he began to reflect, "I can think in my head now." I asked, "What do you mean?" Tom said, "I can write what I know and what I remember—like my story about Spice. My brother will love this story. My mom will laugh when she reads it, too. She'll really like it. I think it's my best story." Tom was truly engaged in thinking that represented inquiry-based evaluation. He was beginning to answer the questions,

"What can I do now that I couldn't do before?" and "What do I know now that I didn't know before, about writing, and about myself as a writer?"

This was the first time I noticed Tom being thoughtful about his work in a genuinely evaluative way that acknowledged how he had grown and changed. Our discussion and my reflections about Tom's portfolio contents helped him view himself more positively, giving him a strategy for thinking about his work from a different perspective. Also, it helped me rethink and understand the evaluative process in a different way and validated for me the need to have multiple reflective experiences over time for deeper, more meaningful insights. If I had stopped with my first questions at that initial session, superficial reflections would have been the end of Tom's experience. My first questions weren't adequate and I had to talk with him, demonstrate reflecting, and restate the questions to support the beginning of his inquiry-based evaluation. My reflections about this experience with Tom helped me see that while it's important to ask thoughtful questions, time, demonstration, and personal significance are critical components for the learner (Crafton, 1991a).

Once we started to really move beneath the surface of Tom's stories, he began to remember and relate important life experiences and become motivated, establishing a strong intent (to write for his brother and mother). He expanded his thinking about what he had done through lots of talk about his writing, and reflected deeply about his accomplishments and his ability to continue writing in a way that would please his audience.

In his classroom, Tom was comfortable with inquiry-based learning and was used to making decisions and choices about what to research. Now, by himself, he was asking questions about his thinking and noticing real learning. The ownership of his learning, the confidence in his statements about himself, his awareness of audience and his ability to write for them, revealed a capable, thoughtful, fully functioning student who was actually thinking at a higher level than many of the other children in his classroom.

At the end of the first grade, Tom's positive feelings about himself and his accomplishments came through strongly as he wrote in his journal: "I want to get lots of books and keep reading. Even though I'm going to a new school, I want to write to you. I'll write to the kids, too. They like my writing. Maybe they will write back to me, too."

In the past, I might have missed the change in Tom's thinking and his reflections would have been lost because I didn't recognize what was going on. Revisiting his work over time, and talking and thinking out loud, helped him take some learning risks and really grow. Paying attention to the questions that help connect to process, observing his responses, and taking the time to listen, helped me grow. This ownership of the learning can happen in classrooms where inquiry and self-knowledge are the expectations for all learners—teachers and students alike. Portfolios provide a window which allows us to view thinking and understand the learning process more deeply. Through portfolios "we know the direction we are going and have the strategies we need to get there. We are authors of our own lives" (Short and Burke, 1991).

Bibliography

Copenhaver, J. (1992). Instances of inquiry. *Primary Voices K–6*, Premier Issue, 6–14.

Crafton, L. (1991a, August). Slowing down in an effort to move forward: The role of reflection in learning. Paper presented at the Whole Language Umbrella Conference, Phoenix.

Crafton, L. (1991b). *Whole language: Getting started . . . moving forward.* Katonah, NY: Richard C. Owen.

Edelsky, C., Altwerger, B., & Flores, B. (1991). *Whole language: What's the difference?* Portsmouth, NH: Heinemann.

Goodman, K. (1991). Revaluing readers and reading. In S. Stires (Ed.), *With promise* (pp. 127–133). Portsmouth, NH: Heinemann.

Harste, J. C. (1992). Inquiry-based instruction. *Primary Voices K–6*, Premier Issue, 2–5.

Hood, W. (1989). If the teacher comes over, pretend it's a telescope. In K. Goodman, Y. Goodman, & W. Hood (Eds.), *The whole language evaluation book* (pp. 27–43). Portsmouth, NH: Heinemann.

Rhodes, L., & Shanklin, N. (1993). *Windows into literacy.* Portsmouth, NH: Heinemann.

Short, K., & Burke, C. (1991). *Creating curriculum.* Portsmouth, NH: Heinemann.

Smith, F. (1986). *Insult to intelligence.* Portsmouth, NH: Heinemann.

Taylor, D. (1991). *Learning denied.* Portsmouth, NH: Heinemann.

Lingering Questions

1. How can we help students confer together in a way that supports deeper reflection about their learning processes?

2. What kinds of teacher demonstrations have the greatest impact on student thinking?

3. How can reflection become a more natural, integral part of the daily classroom life?

4. How can inquiry-based evaluation be managed for a whole classroom?

5. How can a teacher find the time to talk with all the students about their portfolios in a classroom of 25–30 children?

6. How can parents become an integral part of the total evaluation process?

7. How do you set aside the time and provide opportunities for multiple revisits of students' portfolios?

8. What are the long-range implications for curriculum and instruction that result from reflective evaluation?

ANECDOTAL OBSERVATIONS

Student _____ Grade _____ Date _____

Learning Contexts	Strategies	Risk-Taking	Collaboration	Inquiry	Reflection
Whole Class					
Small Group					
Individual					
Other					

LEARNING TO HEAR EACH OTHER

Roxanne Henkin

Teacher Educator,
National-Louis
University,
Evanston, IL

Sarah: This has been the best year of my life because I've had the best teachers.

Roxanne: What do you mean?

Sarah: This year we learned in a different way than all the other years. We do a lot more group things. Like last year, we sat in a group, and once in a while we might compare answers on a math page or something. This year we *really* work in groups, instead of just sitting in a group. Our teachers work together and they show us how to do that. They're members of the group and to each other.

Sarah is talking about her sixth-grade teachers, Arlene Langley and Lisa Forsythe. Arlene and Lisa have worked together in Downers Grove, a suburb west of Chicago, for the last four years. They have removed the wall between their adjacent classrooms so that they can teach the 50 students cooperatively as one unit.

Arlene and Lisa share a common belief system. They agree that school should be meaningful and purposeful, and that students should have choices in their learning. They believe in collaboration both for their students and themselves. The students in their classroom work together throughout the day. The teachers' collaboration is central to their teaching.

The students' relationships with these teachers develop and deepen with time as students get used to them and come to understand their teachers' belief systems. Arlene and Lisa are sensitive to their students and get involved in their lives. Relationships are important,

and both teachers take the time to understand students and work with them individually.

All fifty students are taught by both Arlene and Lisa. Both teachers are involved in every project that occurs throughout the school day. One teacher begins a sentence, and the other ends it. One teacher starts a mini-lesson, and then stops and helps an individual. The other teacher then continues the mini-lesson. Arlene and Lisa negotiate this change in front of their students. Their students learn to collaborate by participating in classroom life.

It's often hard to locate Arlene or Lisa in the classroom. They blend in because of the learner's role they assume. They may join literature circles as participants, or help individual students through writing conferences. They work with students continuously throughout the school day, sharing their questions with their students and serving as co-learners in the classroom. Math, science, and social studies are often integrated through inquiry projects and focused study groups. Students can be observed working on computers and conferring with their teachers before school, at lunch and recess, and after school.

I had worked with both teachers before this six-week study began, and was working with them again as a participant observer who hoped to study students' evaluation of their learning. I was interested in the range of learning that took place throughout the day. I observed and interviewed children during writing workshop and a variety of inquiry projects. I participated in literature circles and focused study groups. I also talked with children during math and art and science. Although self-evaluation was present in the classroom, we became increasingly aware of just how often, and how much earlier in the process, it really occurs. We also came to understand its power to complete the learning cycle.

Forming a Thought Collective

Forming thought collectives is a shared goal in this classroom. Students work across the curriculum on many projects in groups, but cooperation is only the first step. Collaboration is necessary for thought collectives to develop. Students learn to collaborate by sharing a commitment to their joint goals, by valuing diversity, and by supporting risk taking (Short & Burke, 1991). In thought collectives, perspectives are established in relationship to others. Students move beyond individual reflections to joint insights and understandings. In order for thought collectives to grow, the group needs to establish a focused intent. Members share perspectives, which are listened to and incorporated into the group's joint understanding. Reflecting and revaluing are necessary for new values to be implemented.

Sarah, for example, was an enthusiastic student, eager to share her insights with me. In Sarah's life as a student, she demonstrated the kind of reflective learner that Crafton (1991) describes, in that she:

1. self-initiates

2. problem-solves

3. reflectively evaluates her learning

4. collaborates and shows concern for others

5. engages in complex thinking strategies.

It's significant that when Sarah assessed her learning, she discussed collaboration.

Roxanne: What have you learned this year about yourself as a learner?

Sarah: Well, I can work individually or in a group. It depends on what I'm doing. Like in math. I prefer to work individually because I'm quick in math. I can do the things quickly. But then in something like social studies, it's fun to get different opinions, like kind of a debate to decide, not really who's right, but just to compare thinking. So it's fun to do that.

Conflict, Reflection, and Inquiry

During my participation in this classroom, I was especially interested in the evaluation that occurred earlier in the students' inquiry projects. Sarah, Areila, and Sue were participating in a focused study group. They had formed this group based on their shared interest in the role of religion in the Middle Ages. Sarah was a confident learner, as her previous reflections reveal. Areila often agreed with Sarah and followed her lead. Sarah and Areila sat near each other. Sue sat farther away, alone and somber. The girls were deciding how to present their project to the class. When I joined the triangle, they were in the middle of an argument:

Sarah: We took a majority vote and, Sue, you lost.

Sue: Well, obviously you guys don't want to do it. So it's the easiest way to get out of it.

Areila: Well, we're not obligated to tell everything about that. All we need to do is…

Sarah: I think we need to, that's not the most important thing, we have to talk about the most important thing.

Sue: Well, I'm talking about how they would steal and everything like that. You would think, oh well, the church people wouldn't steal or do bad things like that.

Sarah: Well, I think we would tell how the church was so important to them and they did have the ten commandments to not steal.

Sue: But they did!

Sarah: Excuse me, excuse me, excuse me. That would, should show…

Areila: I don't care what the church says.

Sarah: But really the church was so important in their lives.

Sue: The church was doing it.

At this point, I didn't understand the problem of the group. Sue was emotional, her voice rising and falling. The other two girls were calm and seemingly rational. I wondered what Sue's problem was. There was a long silence and then all three girls began talking at once.

Sue: You guys aren't understanding.

Sarah: Churches don't steal.

Sue: On the way there, they stole food and stuff!

Areila: On the way there they stole food?

Sue: (Emphatically) People of the church!

I began to understand the issue they were discussing. Sue's research had led her to the discovery that the Crusaders stole and raided. Sarah's and Areila's research had focused on the ethical underpinnings of the Crusader's religion. People should not steal. Yet Sue was saying they did. Could Sue make her point and would Sarah and Areila be able to hear it?

Sue: You don't have to go making jokes about it. Every idea that I have, you guys won't do it.

Sarah: That's not true. We have used some of your ideas.

Sue: Which ideas?

Sarah: The one about speaking.

Sue: This is not about…

Areila: How can we put that in and make it fun?

Areila seemed especially concerned that the presentation of the project be something fun. This was a cause for concern because their topic under discussion was anything but fun. It was serious and difficult to grasp. Sue, feeling frustrated, continued to raise her voice, accentuate her words, and to accuse the others of not listening to her.

Sue: You're just talking everything down.

Sarah: We need help. We're a group, but we have to work as a group.

Sue: Every time I say something, you guys don't listen!

At this point the group looked at me with frustration. I suggested that we step back and reflect on the process and the progress of the group. I asked them to describe the conflict.

Sarah: I think Sue is asking us to put in how they got to Jerusalem, how they stole, and we don't want to put that in, because we interpreted it differently than Sue did, and we decided they stole once they were there, rather than on the way there.

Areila: We're trying to get the main idea here, and Sue is putting in the minor details which aren't too important.

Sue: This is what I would do. On the way there they, the people, would steal or anything that they did, the church people, the popes, everyone, they stole on the way there.

I wasn't sure how to help them. Before I could ask them to evaluate their group process, I wanted to make sure

I suggested that we step back and reflect on the process and the progress of the group.

that we were in agreement about the area of conflict. So I acted as an observer, trying to summarize and restate the issue.

Roxanne: So we have a real ethical problem here. Sue thinks it's very important to tell the truth about the whole thing, and she thinks that if you tell about the stealing when they are in Jerusalem, you're leaving out a major part of the story. What I'm hearing is, that you don't want to put in the stealing part, you're just going to talk about it when they get there. So you're going to talk about the stealing, but you're not going to tell the whole story about how they stole and took all those things on the way.

The girls nodded their heads in agreement. I felt that we could begin the process of reflection.

Roxanne: I want to stop us now and take time to reflect on this. There's a real conflict that's unsolved. The first thing I want to ask is how you think this work is going.

Sarah: I think it's not going too well.

Roxanne: Why is it not going too well?

Areila: We have different ideas about this and we're having a relative hard time agreeing with each other. We have different opinions and we're not trying to understand each other that well.

Roxanne: Sue, what do you think? How do you think this group is going?

Sue: It was going pretty good, up until today.

Roxanne: How was it going good, up until today?

Sue: We were all working together.

Roxanne: What's the problem with today?

Sue: Well, probably my ideas, it's not what they want to do. They're not listening to what I had in my notes, and then throwing it out.

Areila's conciliatory statement seemed to affect the mood of the group. Sue was willing to concede that the group had worked well together, and was less emotional when explaining her position.

I wanted the girls to realize the importance of evaluating their progress, or lack of it, while they were still working together and could have the opportunity and the time to change. Here was an opportunity to move them beyond simple remembering.

Roxanne: How can thinking about how the group is going make it better?

Sarah: Right now, it's not going too good, and we can, like, listen to each other more carefully which is, I think, what our problem is, kinda. Also, we can be more flexible.

Sarah and Areila were so uncomfortable with Sue's information that they chose to reject it, believing that she was wrong. I wanted to nudge them toward a recognition of their discomfort (inconsistencies) with the conflicting information and toward revaluing this data. I wanted to show them that inclusion of alternate perspectives was key to collaborative group work.

Roxanne: So you think that by listening to each other more carefully, and by being more flexible (considering other perspectives), you can resolve this and eliminate further conflicts.

Areila: I know that you think the part about stealing on the way is important, and we can include it, we just didn't understand how important it was.

Sarah: Maybe what we could do to put it in, we could say, it took over a hundred years for the Crusaders to reach Jerusalem. As they went there, they demolished cities and towns, and…I don't know what else.

Sue: That was what I was trying to say before. That was my idea before, but you weren't listening to it carefully.

Now that Sarah and Areila had conceded, they expected Sue to understand their viewpoint.

Sarah: Don't take this as an insult. Wait. When you talk, I think maybe, to help us understand you better, you should state your ideas more clearly, because…

I wanted the girls to realize the importance of evaluating their progress, or lack of it, while they were still working together and could have the opportunity and the time to change.

Sue: Well, you didn't…

Sarah: And another thing we can do is to stop interrupting each other, 'cause that's a big thing, we keep interrupting each other and getting in fights and stuff.

The girls had returned to their verbal sparring. However, they realized it quickly, and continued to reflect on their interactions. Sarah noticed, pointed out, and suggested that they stop interrupting each other. I wanted them to deepen their evaluation.

Roxanne: What made you decide to include the raiding along the way?

Sarah: Because we were being more flexible.

Roxanne: Do you think if I weren't here you would have decided this?

Sarah: Probably not.

Roxanne: So how did my role change what happened here?

Sarah: You asked us to reflect on what we were saying.

Roxanne: Why is it important to evaluate what you're doing while you're doing it?

Sue: Maybe sometimes you just have to compare before people can see, so when you reflect, then you can kind of compare it.

Sarah: I think it's important to reflect, because in this situation, Areila and I didn't realize what we were doing. We didn't realize what Sue was saying. So since we thought about it more, we didn't end up saying no, we don't like that. And we decided that it was a good idea, and we did need to say it.

Areila: I think I agree with Sarah. At first we didn't know how important it was. We realized that we were wrong and we gave it some thought.

Roxanne: What have you learned from this, that because of it, you'll do differently next time?

Areila: I think I will try and put myself in kids' places and think how I would feel if there was something I knew that had to be in there.

Sarah: If we didn't understand what someone is saying, we could stop them and have them repeat the idea. And we could reflect, too.

Evaluation is important throughout the learning process, not just at the end. Reflection leads to action.

Underlying Processes in This Classroom

Reflection, collaboration, and inquiry-based evaluation were supported by the underlying process in this classroom. *Learning to hear each other was central to the process.* This was not an easy task for any of the girls. *Next, we needed to move beyond memory to reflection. Third, evaluation was internal to the learning process.* Through evaluation, the group moved to a deeper level as a thought collective. *Fourth, the individuals were operating within the confines of a thought collective.* The shared perspective was formed by the research of each group member.

As I interacted with the sixth-grade students, I realized that there were at least four crucial aspects of evaluation that occurred in this classroom:

1. *Discussion.* The role of discussion was honored and valued. Evaluation wasn't just elicited through writing in learning logs and journals. Much of the evaluation from both the students and the teachers was done orally. To study this, we used tape recorders; transcripts of the discussions provide the central focus of this article.

2. *Cooperation.* Collaborative problem-solving was highly valued in this classroom. Therefore, evaluation often highlighted aspects of group work, and how groups might function better. Students were evaluated as a group, not just individually.

3. *Teacher facilitation.* I found my role as another cooperative teacher in the classroom quite different and more important than I first imagined. The teacher, as facilitator, helped the group move ahead when communication broke down. There were times during group work when students were unable to resolve their differences. I acted as a facilitator and helped students to evaluate the process and

progress of the group. It was important for some member of the group to assume this function—to move beyond remembering to true reflection.

4. *Continual implementation.* Evaluation is an ongoing process. Not only do we remember and reflect on our learning, but we use this information to make change. Therefore, evaluation is important throughout the learning process, *not just at the end.* Reflection leads to action.

Forming Potential Thought Collectives

In thought collectives, members progress as thought is made available to the group. The perspective has to be established in *relationship* to others. Pragmatic circumstances, shared life experiences, and significant interests are recognized and matter to the collective. Evaluation helps make change possible and moves thinking forward. Reflection and revaluing are necessary before conflicting data can be examined and new perspectives integrated.

Students need to examine information. There are multiple perspectives on all knowledge. I missed an important opportunity to help the girls move beyond their evaluation of their social awareness to an examination of why it was so difficult for them to accept conflicting research. We might have begun to understand and explore the idea that there are alternate perspectives on all knowledge. This may have led to new implemented values, and to further study. We also could have shared our inquiry with the classroom, inviting others to reflect with us. I hope that next time I will be able to nudge students further. Thought collectives offer all of us rich opportunities to grow.

References

Crafton, L. (1991). *Whole language: Getting started ...moving forward.* Katonah, NY: Richard C. Owen.

Short, K., & Burke, C. (1991). *Creating curriculum: Teachers and students as a community of learners.* Portsmouth, NH: Heinemann.

Lingering Questions

1. How can I help students reflect on and integrate multiple and conflicting perspectives of knowledge?

2. How do I know which questions encourage deep reflections? How do I recognize important moments in students' reflections and evaluations?

3. How can I get past this feeling of wanting to rush the process? Of worrying about time?

4. How can I stop myself from talking too much? Of doing the actual reflection for the students, rather than allowing students to experience the process for themselves?

5. How do I evaluate my own teaching if I teach alone? How can I deepen this experience for myself?

Examples of Children's Self-Evaluation

Lindsay

+ + + and a Wish

1. One thing I did well on my research report was that I changed the format from journal form to report form. I had realized that I was not able to put the support in that I needed.

2. Another thing I did well was that my final draft was very organized with subtitles and paragraphs.

3. The last thing I did well was that I had my mom and dad look over my final copy because sometimes I over look my mistakes.

Wish: I wish I would have interviewed my grandma to get her opinion on cancer treatment because my grandma had to go (and be with my grandpa (who had cancer) through every step of treating cancer.

Amy
5-13-93

Q.1. What did you learn about doing research?

A: I agree with Steve that it was "fun and hard." I thought it was fun because we chose our topics. Last year I was hardly excited about my report because I wasn't interested in the topic. This year it was fun because I had always wondered about my topic, prohibition in Chicago in the 1920's. But I also learned that it takes hard work & mainly persistance.

Q.2 _____

A: _____

Q.3 _____

A: _____

6-13-93

Heather

1. Why is it important to think about learning?

Because most things we lean well happen in real life. If we did not look back then how well we rember to do it right. If we did not think about what we lean then how would we understand. We mitt have more qustions that we did not think about right then and their.

2. _____
   _____?
   _____
   _____

3. What will you do differently next time.

I would sudy more about it. I woud also take more time on the first draft. I would try to make the due dates. I would not forget it at my baby sitters. I would sudy on ghost storys and meny meny more topyics than just ghost. I would also get more ornized than I was.

4. _____
   _____

Q.4. What have you learned about how you learn?

A: I have learned that I don't just learn from books. In my research I consulted my grandpa and great Uncle George and they told me some facts that I would have never have been in books. Like that it was legal to brew your own beer but not sell it, and that its a well known fact how to brew beer. Also that they sold wine bricks! They looked like bricks but when you bailed them you had a pot of wine.

Q.5 _____

A: _____

Our group began our work not only with questions about assessment and evaluation but with the comfort that comes from long-term relationships. There was the expectation that, while we would have lively discussions, a common belief system would move us smoothly forward: we would remind ourselves of what we knew, strengthen it a bit through conversation, and then write it up. Our inquiry process would be "nice." Somewhere along the way we rediscovered what was, for most of us, an old truth: The true function of collaboration is not to establish a forum for happy, easy learning. Its function is to create tension. Its reason for being is to shake things up.

The more we talked, the more we questioned our extant beliefs about assessment and evaluation. At one meeting, Carolyn talked about the growth that comes from discomfort. As our inquiry became more intense, we projected, then, that since we were becoming extremely uncomfortable, we certainly should learn a lot from our months of working together. All of us were willing to tolerate the discomfort—unanswered questions, the tension of not knowing—because we felt passionate about the topic and committed to the project and each other. The topic, the commitment, working in a collaborative, accepting the inevitable tension—it all made an evaluative difference.

When learners come together to explore, there is an ever-present danger of becoming too comfortable too quickly. Already established relationships, belief systems, and/or common goals make this an easy possibility for any collaborative. As editor, I came into the *Primary Voices* process with assumptions about shared values within the group. Some of those values were implemented immediately. We wore our social views of learning on our sleeves as we all committed to time

for purposeful conversations about the topic. We all felt relatively clear on the relationship between action and reflection and so vowed to implement reflective strategies throughout our extended project. Other values and perspectives were not so clear. These were the ones that were created and recreated through our experiences with one another. These were the ones that caused us tension and, eventually, allowed us to reach new levels of understanding and our own new implemented values.

In the Beginning, our first sessions were spent discussing assessment and evaluation in general, sharing stories, making personal connections, and fleshing out our beliefs:

I was excited by our joint desire to live the process, to experience any and/or all of the strategies that we might hope to see in classrooms. I also felt a commitment to push our thinking forward, past where any of us may presently be at the moment. Linda asked what assessment might mean to each of us. We kept talking about the learner's sense of purpose and I suddenly made the connection to Women Who Run with the Wolves *(Estes, 1992). As we assess ourselves and our lives, we seek the place where we belong, our people, our pack. We made the connection that perhaps we were our own "pack"—like-minded, fellow learners, with similar questions. Our own community.*

Roxanne
February 1993

Focusing Our Work

There were few points of contention during our initial meetings and, because several of us had been involved together in presenting workshops on authentic assessment, we initially focused our work more quickly than we might have otherwise. I suggested that we consider the same guiding principles that I had been

Linda K. Crafton

using in my thinking and presenting about assessment and evaluation:

evaluation as an integral part of a larger learning cycle (evaluation should be one more opportunity to learn)

evaluation as inquiry (evaluation should continue learners' inquiry by encouraging them to ask questions about the meaning of their work)

evaluation as internal to the learner (evaluation should encourage learners to turn inward and think about what they have learned, how they have learned it, and what they want to do next)

Conversation did not surface as a major perspective until well into our process—until we had had our own conversations. Because we were engaged in reflective work throughout the project, it was natural that we would, at some point, begin to think more deeply about our exchanges with each other. It was through these reflective acts that we began to think of *conversation* as a key process in evaluation. As we peeled back the layers of discussion, we could see that our group exchanges served at once a social and cognitive function:

In this group, unlike others, I felt safe enough to ask what I thought might be an insignificant (silly) question and was surprised that it was actually a key question for the group: When does reflection become evaluation?

Penny

It was frustrating to meet only occasionally, on school nights. I just wanted to go away for a long weekend so our conversations would not be interrupted, so we could maintain the thinking and the feeling. That frustration actually helped me to see even more the importance of connected time blocks for kids, knowing they can count on continuing their reading and writing and reflecting together every day. But, when we did meet, listening

> **As we peeled back the layers of discussion, we could see that our group exchanges served at once a social and cognitive function.**

to everyone talk and then share their writing would remind me of what was important to include in my own writing. Opening up to each other added new dimensions, new perspectives.

Kathleen

It seems to me essential that we continue to push our thinking forward by pushing each other to reflect on assessment in terms of enriching our lives and the lives of our students. I find myself collecting articles and artifacts to share with the group. I've copied my portfolio article that describes my work with other teachers. I find I'm hungry for discussion with this group.

Roxanne

Conversation and Reflexivity

Our dialogue was continual and our stance in relation to our inquiry was always reflective. With conversation and reflexivity as key dimensions of our inquiry, we started moving in a different direction. The central issue, valuing and revaluing, emerged as we struggled with questions related to terminology (e.g., why might evaluation be preferable to assessment, what is the history behind each, what particular meanings do they carry in the profession?) and, with a tentative theoretical model sketched out, we could see more clearly that our ongoing reflection and evaluation of our own work was resulting in a new position. Conversation and reflexivity allowed us to reshuffle our existing schema:

When I shared my second or third draft, I felt discouraged, since I had been pressed for time. The responses were still positive, but I felt bogged down and my thinking felt stagnant and somewhat muddled. Things began to gel for me when Linda shared her discussion with Carolyn about reflective and inquiry-based evaluation. After we talked, I began to rethink what I believe and what I want to change as I work with kids. My article suddenly needed more—and I had to dig even deeper and rethink even more. Our collective pieces, discussions, and my personal reflections helped my writing take on a new life—and a new focus.

Penny

Evaluation and Voice

Currently, our profession is caught up in a debate about new standards. The operational assumption is that if we develop a clear set of standards that come close to our present understandings of language and learning, then our curricula will undergo a major qualitative transformation. While the function of evaluation has been part of many of the standards conversations, the product of this work will be a focus on content standards, documents that outline what is externally valued and expected. We have no doubt that our profession can create a better set of standards than the ones we have now (whether explicitly stated or intuitively implemented), but this focus on standards external to the learner perpetuates an old model of evaluation and encourages a continuation of the self-evaluation tokenism that we see in so many classrooms now: students dutifully completing self-evaluation worksheets once a week with the broad contexts to be judged and the qualifiers for each clearly laid out, the same for everyone. We have to be willing to alter who is genuinely in control of evaluation.

Grant Wiggins calls self-evaluation the most undervalued ability in American schools. We wonder about an education system situated in a democracy that would not encourage learners to continually discuss their work with themselves and with each other. Our interest in inquiry-based evaluation is a logical extension of our interest in voice and democratic values. Continuous dialogue

and reflection about our own and others' work can only elevate the idea of schooling for an egalitarian society to new heights. If evaluation does not become an embedded enterprise done by the learner and for the learner, schools and society will remain disparate institutions.

> ## Our interest in inquiry-based evaluation is a logical extension of our interest in voice and democratic values.

All of this calls to mind Sue's plea to her group (in Roxanne's article): "You aren't listening to me!" Because so many traditional evaluation procedures are imposed and definitive, they tragically result in learners who are dependent and silent—waiting to hear from someone else about the most critical aspect of their learning—how did I do? Inquiry-based evaluation encourages learners to define what they value, and, in the process, to discover who they are. Changing the face of evaluation in this society looks like a daunting proposition. But, as with all change, those most intimately involved, those who have the most at stake, must take responsibility and, as we have with the rest of curriculum, move it positively and firmly forward, maintaining a steady focus on the learner.

As a profession, our vision of evaluation has lagged behind our understandings of learning and literacy, partially because we have continued to view it as an issue of methodology. The beliefs that guide our collaborative work with students as we create curriculum together must be the same beliefs that guide our implementation of evaluation in the classroom. Imagine a classroom in which these beliefs are realized; imagine the nature of the relationships in a classroom that puts all learning, including evaluation, at its center. Inquiry-based evaluation calls for a revaluing of learners' inherent ability to identify their own questions and then to step back from their work in progress, to think, talk, and ask questions about it, and then to proceed with an altered sense of direction. It calls for a deeper understanding of learning-focused curriculum and asks that teachers consider the transformative potential of classrooms that encourage students to constantly take a critical stance in relation to their learning.

Throughout our collaborative writing and evaluation experience, we found these processes invaluable in moving our thinking forward:

- Conversation

- Tension

- Reflexivity

- Revaluing

These processes helped us to see again why we are so committed to collaborative thinking and the clear difference between cooperating toward a common goal and collaborating toward changing ourselves.

We leave our current collaboration knowing that its publication will launch us into a whole new cycle of valuing and revaluing. Our voices have dominated the conversation so far but, now, as we receive responses to our work, the dialogue becomes wider, richer, one filled with new inquiries and different tensions. Kathleen has left behind the classroom she describes in her article for a coordinator's position in a different district. Her final reflection echoes a feeling we all share—wondering about alternative ways to implement our newfound values:

When I finished my final draft and realized how much I had learned, I wanted to teach again—I wanted to do it better. I am a different teacher now than the one described in the article. I can still see places where I directed too much, where I did the evaluating when they could have—no, should have. Maybe no one else can see it, but I can. That's my tension, my discomfort, my ambiguity.

Kathleen
October 1993

Bibliography

Anthony, R., Johnson, T., Mickelson, N., & Preece, A. (1991). *Evaluating literacy.* Portsmouth, NH: Heinemann.

Barrs, M. (1990). The primary language record: Reflection of issues in evaluation. *Language Arts, 67*(3), 244–253.

Baskwill, J., & Whitman, P. (1988). *Evaluation: Whole language, whole child.* New York: Scholastic.

Brown, R. (1987). Thoughtfulness. *Phi Delta Kappan, 69*(1), 49–52.

Dietz, C. (1988). Good question, Susan. *Language Arts, 64*(3), 285–288.

Five, C. (1992). *Special voices.* Portsmouth, NH: Heinemann.

Gardner, H. (1990). Assessment in context: The alternative to standardized testing. In B. Gifford & M.C. O'Connor (Eds.), *Future assessments: Changing views of aptitude, achievement, and instruction* (pp. 77–119). Boston: Kluwer Publisher.

Goodman, K., Goodman, Y., & Hood, W. (Eds.). (1989). *The whole language evaluation book.* Portsmouth, NH: Heinemann.

Goodman, Y. (1991). *Education as inquiry* [Videotape]. In J.C. Harste & E. Jurewicz (Eds.), *Visions of literacy* [Videotape series]. Portsmouth, NH: Heinemann.

Gould, S.J. (1981). *The mismeasure of man.* New York: W.W. Norton.

Guba, E., & Lincoln, Y. (1981). *Effective evaluation.* Beverly Hills: Sage.

Harp, B. (Ed.). (1991). *Assessment and evaluation in whole language programs.* Norwood, MA: Christopher-Gordon.

Harste, J. (1989). *New policy guidelines for reading: Connecting research and practice.* Urbana, IL: National Council of Teachers of English.

Johnson, P. (1987). Teachers as evaluation experts. *The Reading Teacher, 40*(8), 744–748.

Levy, J., & Moore, R. (1990). Beyond labels: Toward a reading program for all students. In N. Atwell (Ed.), *Workshop 2* (pp. 118–124). Portsmouth, NH: Heinemann.

Matthews, C. (1992). An alternative portfolio: Gathering one child's literacies. In D. Graves & B. Sunstein (Eds.), *Portfolio portraits* (pp. 158–170). Portsmouth, NH: Heinemann.

Rhodes, L., & Dudley-Marling, C. (1988). *Readers and writers with a difference.* Portsmouth, NH: Heinemann.

Rhodes, L., & Shanklin, N. (1993). *Windows into literacy.* Portsmouth, NH: Heinemann.

Stires, S. (Ed.). (1991). *With promise.* Portsmouth, NH: Heinemann.

Sumner, H., (1991). Whole language assessment and evaluation in special education classrooms. In B. Harp (Ed.), *Assessment and evaluation in whole language programs* (pp. 137–157). Norwood, MA: Christopher-Gordon.

Tierney, R.J., Carter, M.A., & Desai, L.E. (1991). *Portfolio assessment in the reading-writing classroom.* Norwood, MA: Christopher-Gordon.

Wolf, D. (1987). Opening up assessment. *Educational Leadership, 45*(4), 24–29.

RICHARD C. OWEN PUBLISHERS, INC.

If we want children to view themselves as learners, then teachers have to see themselves as learners and principals have to see themselves as learners and authors have to see themselves as learners and publishers have to see themselves as learners.

Mission Statement
Richard C. Owen Publishers, Inc.

A recent comment by Margaret Early echoes in my head. In her article, "What ever happened to…?" (1992–1993. *The Reading Teacher, 46*(4), 302–308), she notes that articles in that journal over the last forty years reflect far greater change than what she has seen in the classroom. The more things change, the more they remain the same.

Does that bother you? It does me. Margaret Early's observation raises questions in my mind about how scholars define knowledge, it raises questions about teachers, and it raises questions about the avenues that connect the two: colleges, school administrators, and publishers.

I fall into the last group: I have been involved with educational publishing since 1967. For the first fourteen years of my career, I was with Holt, Rinehart and Winston. Since 1982, I have worked for Richard C. Owen Publishers, which was established to publish college and professional books on reading and writing.

During the last decade, we have tried to make sense of literacy. Early in the existence of the company, Yetta Goodman urged me to become a whole language publisher. I'm not sure we qualify, but we have focused our efforts at that end of the spectrum—what I like to describe as the side of the angels.

We are honored to be the publisher of *Whole Language: Getting Started…Moving Forward* written by Linda Crafton with contributions from Penny Silvers, Kathleen Visovatti, and several other teachers. Thoughtful expression of ideas, as in Linda's book, broadens a teacher's thinking. Teachers need to read professional books. The best books should be read again and again. It is amazing what new understandings emerge from a second and third reading of some books.

But is reading good books sufficient for the growth that teachers need? No. If all it took was reading, then I believe Margaret Early would have seen greater overlap between the articles in *The Reading Teacher* and the events of the classroom. Something is missing. There is still a gap between theory and practice.

All of us involved with children and learning have to look carefully at *real change*—at digging beneath the surface of ideas. We cannot afford to be dilettantes, dancing around the issues in an undisciplined way. Without real change, the muddle that exists in so many of our schools will only get worse.

I see real change as shifts in core beliefs and values. They are reflected in the most deeply embedded routines that we turn to when confronted by challenge. A New Zealand colleague, Peter Duncan, has become quite good at driving on the right side of American roads. But when he was distracted by a median barrier on entering a street in Omaha last summer, he followed a natural tendency to pull to the left and was faced with oncoming traffic. Deeply embedded routines do not change easily or quickly.

Real change will come from teacher development. Teacher development will occur when administrators no longer see the staff development budget line as expendable, and when they stop relying on occasional visits from outsiders—what Canadian educator Lorri Neilsen refers to as the parachuting expert.

These simple ideas seem self-evident. But the reality is that too few schools yet invest in teacher development in a serious way. In the annual spring rite of preparing the school budget, staff development funds get slashed before almost any other item. Such acts say much about how little value is placed on the professional development of teachers.

Our growing awareness of means other than books for bringing about real change has led RCO to nonprint work. Almost 10,000 teachers have taken our summer institute, **Literacy Learning in the Classroom,** and now we have designed an ongoing teacher development program called **The Learning Network,** which is currently being implemented in schools in Massachusetts, Vermont, New York, North Carolina, and Texas. **The Learning Network** relies on the active support of an administration eager for school-wide exploration of a meaningful instructional model. **The Network** strives to maintain consistency and quality. It combines interaction between teachers with frequent opportunity to implement theory and ideas in the classroom and with careful reading of meaningful professional books.

Effective teacher development is an investment in the future of our children. If you want to know more about our publishing program or our teacher development work, I encourage you to call 1-800-262-0787 or write to us at P.O. Box 585, Katonah, NY 10536. We look forward to hearing from you.

Richard C. Owen

President and Publisher, Richard C. Owen Publishers, Inc.

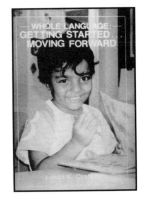